D1601527

China's Unequal Treaties

ASIAWORLD
Series Editor: Mark Selden

This series charts the frontiers of Asia in global perspective. Central to its concerns are Asian interactions—political, economic, social, cultural, and historical—that are transnational and global, that cross and redefine borders and networks, including those of nation, region, ethnicity, gender, technology, and demography. It looks to multiple methodologies to chart the dynamics of a region that has been the home to major civilizations and is central to global processes of war, peace, and development in the new millennium.

Titles in the Series

China's Unequal Treaties

Narrating National History

Dong Wang

LEXINGTON BOOKS
A Division of
ROWMAN & LITTLEFIELD PUBLISHERS, INC.
Lanham • Boulder • New York • Toronto • Oxford

LEXINGTON BOOKS

A division of Rowman & Littlefield Publishers, Inc.
A wholly owned subsidary of The Rowman & Littlefield Publishing Group, Inc.
4501 Forbes Boulevard, Suite 200
Lanham, MD 20706

PO Box 317
Oxford
OX2 9RU, UK

British Library Cataloguing in Publication Information Available

Library of Congress Cataloging-in-Publication Data

Wang, Dong, 1967–
  China's unequal treaties : narrating national history / Dong Wang.
     p. cm. — (AsiaWorld)
  Includes bibliographical references and index.
  ISBN 0-7391-1208-2 (hardcover : alk. paper)
  1. China—Politics and government—1912–1949. 2. China—Foreign relations—
1644–1912—Treaties. 3. China—Foreign relations—1912–1949—Treaties. I. Title.
II. Series.
DS775.7.W336 2005
320.951—dc22   2005012495

Printed in the United States of America

♾™ The paper used in this publication meets the minimum requirements of
American National Standard for Information Sciences—Permanence of Paper for
Printed Library Materials, ANSI/NISO Z39.48–1992.

To my parents

Contents

Acknowledgments

The making of this monograph dates back to 1991 when my late mentor, Ding Mingnan of the Modern History Institute at the Chinese Academy of Social Sciences (CASS), handed me the then-unpublished Chinese Maritime Customs archives on the 1902–1907 negotiations of the New Commercial Treaties between China and Britain, the United States, Japan, Portugal, Germany, and Italy, respectively. It is with profound sadness that I acknowledge my intellectual debt to Ding Mingnan, who cannot see this work in which he kindled my initial interest. My years at CASS also brought me—as one of the very few female Ph.D. candidates then in China—into contact with a host of scholars such as Dai Yi, Li Wenhai, Zheng Zhenkun, Tao Wenzhao, and Wang Jianlang, who have inspired me to pursue diplomatic history and United States–China relations. Lu Yao, my mentor at Shandong University, guided me through the early years of my study of modern China, which ultimately imbued me with the passion for historical research.

On the American side, my deep gratitude is, first and foremost, due to Daniel H. Bays, my dear mentor and friend, who brought me to the United States as part of the Pew Charitable Trusts grant on Christianity in modern China. Dan's distinguished intellect and admirable knowledge of China and the China field enabled me further to pursue the topic of the treaties. Over the years, I also received unstinting counsel on various matters from a long-time friend and mentor, Paul A. Cohen. I am grateful to Paul for going through the manuscript in its various phases and always giving me constructive feedback. The shift in the book's nature—from an empirical diplomatic study of the negotiations of the treaties to an analysis of the narratives constructed by the Chinese of their nation's encounter with the outside world since the 1840s—must be ascribed to Paul's brilliant scholarship on modern China.

This volume would have been impossible without Mark Selden. I wish to thank Mark for his advice (which I always followed!) and his time in helping me to reconceptualize and complete the book. Thanks go also to Paul Sorrell, who offered crucial editorial assistance. Other scholars who have provided help of all sorts during the fourteen years of research that went into the making of this study are Stein Haugom Olsen, Michael Schoenhals, Akira Iriye, Timothy Cheek, Jessie Lutz, John Fitzgerald, James Hevia, Wang Gungwu, Peter Zarrow, Christopher A. Reed, Ann Collinson, Richard Pierard, John Dardess, William Tsutsui, Terry Weidner, Joseph Esherick, David Buck, Liu Tianlu, Tao Feiya, Shen Xiaoyun, Jin Guangyao, and Cai Jiahe.

The East-West Institute of Gordon College, my home base, has given me generous funding for my research. At Gordon, I would like to express my gratitude to Tomas Askew for his unfailing moral support, Shirley Houtson for administrative assistance, Martha Crane and Alec Li for securing certain library materials for me, and my history colleagues for sharing with me their deep knowledge of history.

A few words of acknowledgment are also due to the Harvard-Yenching Library, the Widener Library at Harvard, and the No. 2 Chinese Historical Archives, for allowing me to make use of their extensive collections. I want to single out the librarians at the Harvard-Yenching Library, including Chia-yaung Daisy Hu, Ma Xiaohe, and Ellen McGill, for their help in locating some difficult-to-find references and biographical information for me.

Indispensable assistance from editors at Rowman & Littlefield Publishers, Inc., including Rebekka Brooks Istrail, Erin Hill-Parks, MacDuff Stewart, and proofreader Gail Fay, allayed my anxiety about production and made the book a reality. Needless to say, all errors are solely my responsibility.

Chapters 3 and 4, and parts of the introduction and the conclusion, have been published in article form as the following: "The Discourse of Unequal Treaties in Modern China," *Pacific Affairs* 76, no. 3 (November 2003); and "Redeeming 'A Century of National Ignominy': Nationalism and Party Rivalry over the Unequal Treaties, 1928–1947," *Twentieth-Century China* 30, no. 2 (April 2005). Permissions to reprint from *Pacific Affairs* and *Twentieth-Century China* are hereby gratefully acknowledged.

Finally, the book is dedicated to my parents, who are always there for me. They, together with my siblings, Peng and Jing, are my sources of strength. Rose, the first-grader, takes pleasure in creeping into my War Room, climbing over my chair, watching over my shoulders, and reading aloud what her mother writes on the computer. I thank Rose for her love, for making my life so meaningful!

Introduction

Bupingdeng tiaoyue (the Unequal Treaties) has occupied a central position in the Chinese collective memory of the nation's humiliating experience —known as *guochi*—in the one hundred years from 1842 to 1943, which was characterized by John K. Fairbank as the "treaty century."[1] The strongly charged meanings behind the endless repetitions of the phrase and the constant agitation over the Unequal Treaties show no signs of fading more than half a century after the end of that epoch. The sensitivity of the issue for Chinese nationalists, including both the Communist Party (CCP) and the Nationalist Party (Guomindang, GMD) in their competitive efforts to define *China* and *national crises*, and to establish party authority, makes clear that nationalism remains central to Chinese politics. Surprisingly, the actual use of the expression itself remains little studied, despite its frequent occurrence in both Chinese and English language historiographies.[2]

This book offers an account, based on a thorough study of the primary sources, of the linguistic development and the polemical uses of the expression *Unequal Treaties*, and shows how the phrase became the focus of a sustained effort to establish party authority and legitimacy, as well as to attain and preserve Chinese national independence, unity, and identity in a variety of contexts. The "discourse of the Unequal Treaties" is examined as a distinctive form of diplomatic, legal, political, and cultural nationalism that yields manifold regional and global meanings.

The expression *Unequal Treaties* has a long history, as well as a significant prehistory. Throughout the nineteenth century, the term itself was apparently not used by the Chinese, nor did the expression *Unequal Treaties* figure in Western discourse. The phrase did not in fact come into use until the early 1920s. There are, moreover, problems with the concept of the Unequal

1

Treaties as it is commonly employed. While the phrase has long been widely used, it nevertheless lacks a clear and unambiguous meaning. Furthermore, there is no agreement about the actual number of treaties signed between China and foreign countries that should be counted as "unequal." Some claim that there were over 1,000 treaties, agreements, and conventions that fall into this category.[3] Others put the figure at 745,[4] while others again put it at 500.[5] In a world of power politics, many treaties contain unequal provisions. The question is why, in spite of this basic disagreement about what the phrase should designate, it became, and remains, a—perhaps *the*—rallying cry for Chinese patriots of different political and social allegiance.

This book also attempts to understand the various interpretations of the period of Chinese history from 1840 to 1943, offered by competing forces within China. The narration of the one-hundred-year national history became a contest about how the party played a decisive role in creating a strong "New China," which would stand up as an equal or even a superior in the world community. Changing memories and judgments about the treaties functioned as a vital resource for both the GMD and CCP in developing their grand strategies for winning China. Therefore, the power struggle involved in nation-building led to a high degree of subjectivity in the interpretation of these treaties. Claims for legitimacy and authority were asserted and reasserted through the repeated labeling and relabeling of the Unequal Treaties in party- and state-influenced historiographies.

NARRATIVE, RHETORIC, AND NATIONALISM

Before the topic of the Unequal Treaties can be treated in any depth, a number of issues central to the historiography of modern China in both English and Chinese need to be discussed more generally.

First, there is the unsolved problem of defining nationalism, whether in the age of imperialism, postimperialism, or in the era of nationalist movements. Focusing on a topic that ostensibly belongs to diplomatic history, this study puts to the test some core concepts of nationalism, whether defined by ethno-symbolist scholars such as Anthony D. Smith and John Hutchinson or modernists/constructivists such as Benedict Anderson and Eric Hobsbawm.[6] In contrast to constructivist views that emphasize discontinuity and epochs rather than continuity in history, Smith and Hutchinson insist on the importance of the reinvention and re-presentation of long-established ethnic and cultural ties, symbols, and myths, as well as memories, in the process of identity formation.

The point I want to make by discussing the various narratives of the Unequal Treaties is that partisan strife within certain ethnic and cultural parameters should not be ignored as a factor when charting the development of Chinese nationalism in the twentieth century. The republican Beijing state (1912–1928) failed to provide a national purpose for its subject populations, and to exercise authority effectively over them. On the other hand, the rival forces of the Guomindang, the Chinese Communist Party, and other nationalists succeeded in molding popular conceptions of political grouping—for example, warlords, imperialists, patriots, and traitors—and reinterpreting China's encounter with the West within the Chinese cultural context. Chinese nationalism is reflected in the various representations of the Unequal Treaties that display a triple concern for the linked themes of internal unification, international position, and a common Chinese culture. These components have survived to this day in popular consciousness in mainland China, Taiwan, Hong Kong, and among overseas Chinese, often transcending differences in party and political affiliation.

Second, this book deals with the constantly changing nature of Chinese nationalism in the age of globalization. This is what Prasenjit Duara has defined as "relational nationalism," by which he means "the multiplicity of nation-views and the idea that political identity is not fixed but shifts between different loci."[7] Globalization paradoxically complicates the awareness of national and ethnic identities. Anthony D. Smith has argued that "far from diminishing the influence of nationalism or dissolving the fabric of nations, processes of globalization actually disseminate that influence and encourage nations to become more participant and distinctive."[8] While I have some reservations about the general validity of this view, it has some relevance in the case of the Chinese.

Third, this study offers an analysis of different historical understandings of the Unequal Treaties through the widely varying rhetorical and polemical strategies adopted by their proponents. Three types of understanding constituted through three different kinds of interpretation—moral, legal, and rhetorical—are distinguished. The moral interpretation embodies the construal of the establishment of the treaty system by late Qing literati. The discourse that embodied this kind of interpretation was aimed at moral persuasion, an appeal to the foreign powers in China to recognize the unfairness of the treaties. The vocabulary employed in this mode of discourse, which consisted of classical Chinese terms, reflected a lack of conscious effort to communicate the issues involved to the general public. Likewise, the legal discourse employed by the diplomats of the Beijing government (1912–1928) was not oriented towards encouraging the participation of ordinary Chinese in the debate. Unlike the moral discourse, however, this approach stressed the legal invalidity of imposed treaties. In stark contrast to both, the rhetorical discourses adopted by both the GMD and the CCP in connection with the Unequal Treaties used vernacular Chinese, which carried a powerful emotive charge and was intelligible to a broad audience. The rhetorical mode of discourse also involved a dual process characterized as "dulling" and "awakening," a form of consciousness-raising controlled and manipulated by the party through repetitions of certain slogans.

This constant redefinition of the past to serve the political needs of the present would in some recent theories of discourse be taken to support the view that narratives about the past are ultimately imaginative fictions[9] constituted through the linguistic devices available to the writer. There is nothing in the present study that would support this view. The analysis offered here of the rhetoric and polemic focused on the Unequal Treaties rests squarely on the distinction between discourse and reality. What gives particular point to this study is exactly that the different kinds of discourse constitute different interpretations of the *same* reality: the texts of the Unequal Treaties.

FRAMEWORK

Chapter 1 traces the development in the late Qing (1840–1912) of the concepts that were later to be embodied in the debates surrounding the Unequal Treaties. The primary purpose of this chapter is to explore the legal origins of the texts of the treaties. My major departure from existing English and Chinese historiography[10] is to place the establishment of the treaty system against the backdrop of the ongoing rhetoricalization and politicalization of the phrase *Unequal Treaties*. To this end, the emergence of concepts that have a clear relation to the concept of the Unequal Treaties is traced. The earliest occurrence of an expression close to the term *Unequal Treaties* I have found is *bupingdeng zhi tiaoyue* (treaty of inequity) in 1908.[11]

In chapter 1, three sets of treaties with far-reaching implications are examined—the Treaty of Nanjing of 1842 (with its two significant annexes, the General Regulations for Trade and Tariff and the Supplementary Treaty), the Sino-British Treaty of Tianjin of 1858, and the New Commercial Treaty of 1902 between Britain and China (the Mackay Treaty). The negotiations surrounding these three sets of treaties illustrate how the Chinese attitude changed from a total lack of understanding of the significance and consequences of signing written treaties with binding force, to an unquestioning faith in the established treaty scheme.

Notwithstanding the absence of the term *Unequal Treaties* throughout the nineteenth century and the 1900s, related concepts such as *gongping* (fairness), *bugong* (unfairness), *ziding guanshui* (tariff autonomy), *shibao* (reciprocity), *xilü* (Western law), *ding zeli* (legal reform), *zhuquan* (sovereignty), *zhiwai faquan* (extraterritoriality), *zuihuiguo tiaokuan* (the most-favored-nation clause), *buduideng zhi tiaoyue* (nonreciprocal treaty), *jiu tiaoyue* (old treaties), *gaizheng tiaoyue* (treaty revision), *gaiding tongshang tiaoyue* (revision of commercial treaties), and *bupingdeng zhi tiaoyue* (treaty of inequity) recurred in both the official and unofficial remonstrances of the Qing literati. The use of such concepts indicates a determination among the Chinese elite at the turn of the twentieth century to revise or remove certain treaty provisions, but without any intention to demolish the entire edifice of the treaty system.

Chapter 2 throws light on a new phase in the Chinese understanding of the Unequal Treaties in the first quarter of the twentieth century by considering not only state-to-state diplomacy but also the management of treaty rights and obligations at the local level. Centrally important in this period (1912–1928) is the fact that the management of foreign relations in the Beijing government was taken over by a foreign-trained elite, a striking contrast to the inadequate diplomatic leadership under the imperial Qing.

In contrast to other works on the treaty revisions conducted by the Foreign Ministry of the Beijing government,[12] this chapter discusses China's effort to annul treaties signed under duress through contesting their legal basis, at the same time as China took pains to implement its international treaty obligations. In international law, the meaning of the term *Unequal Treaties*, as well as its scope, remain imprecise. What is an unequal treaty? Are treaties signed under duress void in international law? What constitutes inequality in treaties where the stronger contracting power has forced or induced the weaker party to bind itself against its will and to the detriment of its own interests, and what are the grounds for invalidity in the case of such treaties? Are all treaties between powers of unequal strength—that is, virtually all international treaties—unequal treaties? Finally, how is one to define the use or threat of force? As Fariborz Nozari has put it, the problem is "the recognition in international law of the legal consequences of unequal treaties and the codification of the rules admitting nullity or modification of such treaties."[13] Despite the rulings on the invalidity of treaties, signed after 1980 and under duress, in the 1969 Vienna Convention on the Law of Treaties, answers to these questions still lack consensus and this often causes confusion when a situation arises involving an unequal treaty.[14]

Chapter 3 centers on the polemical discourse on the Unequal Treaties employed by the two major political parties in the republican experiment, the GMD and the CCP, a discourse that shaped the political landscape of China throughout most of the twentieth century. This chapter provides insight into the strained and precarious relationship between the GMD and the CCP from 1923 to 1927, the period of their first united front, by focusing on their approaches to the treaties. Both parties were vocal in airing their strategies for bringing down their common enemies—imperialism and warlordism—and their emphatic presentation of China's humiliating recent past added a new political lexicon to the Chinese language. However, despite efforts to maintain an appearance of unity, the discourses, employed by the GMD and CCP in the period leading up to April 1927, were characterized more by conflict than harmony. An analysis of this relationship, and the discourse on the Unequal Treaties that the two parties ostensibly shared, necessitates an inquiry into Chinese nationalism, including tangled party differences and their implications. In the course of the twentieth century, however, the arguments, style, and rhetoric of the discourse on the Unequal Treaties became an integral part of the common inheritance of Chinese-ness.

Chapter 4 argues that an analysis of party pronouncements on the Unequal Treaties in the 1930s and 1940s allows us to approach the CCP's 1949 victory from a new angle. Although the GMD and the CCP stood together in condemning the treaties as an unequivocal emblem of Western aggression, their consensus broke down over the question of who should be regarded as the legitimate patriot and redeemer of the Chinese nation, and the appropriate course for achieving that goal. Over the years, the two rivals argued over three sets of treaties—the 1943 Sino-American, Sino-British new treaties, the 1945 Treaty of Friendship and Alliance between the Republic of China and the U.S.S.R., and the 1946 Sino-American Treaty of Friendship, Commerce, and Navigation—as a way of reasserting their political legitimacy and leadership. Over the twenty years from 1928 to 1947, the two parties molded memories of the Unequal Treaties in a variety of ways, reflecting attempts to connect support for party and state with broader issues of national unification and independence.[15]

Chapter 5 turns attention to the features that have shaped the dissemination of international law in China from the nineteenth century onward. In contrast to existing literature that by and large deals with the nineteenth century,[16] I focus on several less studied but important patterns of information flow within a much broader time frame, that is, from the nineteenth century to the present. First, shifting from the focus on language and translation as a tool of cultural transmission—so popular in studies of modern and contemporary Chinese culture and literature—I argue that the diffusion of international law in China was to a great extent motivated by what the Chinese learned from their efforts to revise and annul the Unequal Treaties. Second, chapter 5 argues that the equality/inequality issue presented a paradox that came to influence the Chinese understanding and use of international law. Third, I take a closer look at the indigenization of international law in China and its concomitant political, diplomatic, and cultural consequences. Fourth, I show that China's experience with the Unequal Treaties determined the nature of the challenges posed and contributions made by Chinese to the theory and practice of international law in the twentieth century. And this points to the conclusion that the spread of international law can take place only in the context of a given nation's culture and history at a specific historical moment.[17]

NOTES

1. John King Fairbank and Merle Goldman, *China: A New History*, enlarged ed. (Cambridge, Mass.: Harvard University Press, 1999), 201–5.

2. Recent scholarly discussions on H-Asia have also remarked on such a pattern in Chinese historiography, i.e., "endless repetition of slogans such as 'gundipl' [Gunboat diplomacy] or 'uneqtreaties' [Unequal Treaties], etc., but equally the paucity of the information upon which these slogans rest." Ian Welch, "Gunboat diplomacy in China (Response)," http://www

.h-net.msu.edu/~asia (posted January 15, 2005). Standard works in English on modern China and Chinese foreign relations have paid scant attention to the rhetoricalization and politicalization of the expression *Unequal Treaties* in the rise of Chinese nationalism. Some examples are the following: Jonathan Spence, *The Search for Modern China*, 2nd ed. (New York: W. W. Norton & Company, 1999); Fairbank and Goldman, *China: A New History*; Patricia Buckley Ebrey, *The Cambridge Illustrated History of China*, reprint ed. (Cambridge: Cambridge University Press, 2003); Warren I. Cohen, *America's Response to China: A History of Sino-American Relations*, 4th ed. (New York: Columbia University Press, 2000); Robert E. Gamer, ed., *Understanding Contemporary China*, 2nd ed. (Boulder, Colo.: Lynne Rienner Publishers, 2003); Gungwu Wang, *Anglo-Chinese Encounters since 1800: War, Trade, Science, and Governance* (Cambridge: Cambridge University Press, 2003); Paul A. Cohen, *China Unbound: Evolving Perspectives on the Chinese Past* (New York: RoutledgeCurzon, 2003); Jerome Ch'en, "The Communist Movement, 1927–1937," in *The Cambridge History of China*, ed. John K. Fairbank and Albert Feuerwerker (Cambridge: Cambridge University Press, 1986), 13:168–229; James L. Hevia, *English Lessons: The Pedagogy of Imperialism in Nineteenth-Century China* (Durham, N.C.: Duke University Press, 2003); Evan S. Medeiros and M. Taylor Fravel, "China's New Diplomacy," in *Chinese Foreign Policy in Transition*, ed. Guoli Liu (New York: Aldine de Gruyter, 2004); Michael H. Hunt, *The Genesis of Chinese Communist Foreign Policy* (New York: Columbia University Press, 1996). Although Hunt places the CCP's foreign relations within a larger historical perspective, he fails to consider the Unequal Treaties, an issue to which both the Nationalists and Communists devoted time and resources to score points off each other. Similarly, the polemical use of the term *Unequal Treaties* by the CCP and GMD remains an understudied topic in the rich Chinese historiography on the Unequal Treaties. See Li Kan, et al., eds., *Zhongguo jindaishi* [Modern Chinese history], 4th ed. of 1993, 24th reprint (Beijing: Zhonghua shujü, 2001); Tang Ch'i-hua, "'Beiyang waijiao' yanjiu pingjia" [The state of the field on the "Beiyang Diplomacy"], *Lishi yanjiu* 287, no. 1 (2004): 99–113; Wang Jianlang, *Zhongguo feichu bupingdeng tiaoyue de licheng* [The record of abolishing all unequal treaties in China. Original translation of the book title] (Nanchang: Jiangxi renmin chubanshe, 2000); Lee En-han, *Beifa hou de "geming waijiao"* [Revolutionary diplomacy after Beifa] (Taibei: Institute of Modern History, Academia Sinica, 1993); Lin Quan, ed., *Kangzhan shiqi feichu bupingdeng tiaoyue shiliao* [Sources on the relinquishment of the Unequal Treaties during the war resistance period] (Taibei: Zhengzhong shujü, 1984).

3. Hu Sheng, "Yi shi wei jian, ai wo Zhonghua" [History as a mirror—love our Chinese nation], *Renmin ribao* (August 29, 1991) (the ninety-ninth anniversary of the signing of the Nanjing Treaty, the first of the Unequal Treaties imposed upon China by the West). The special CCTV program "Mo'wang ba er'jiu" [Don't Forget August Twenty-Ninth (of 1842)] expressed the same view.

4. Gao Fang, "Jinxiandai zhongguo bupingdeng tiaoyue de lailong qümai" [The origins and development of the Unequal Treaties in modern China], *Nanjing shehui kexue* 2 (1999): 18–28.

5. In his talk entitled "The Spirit of Sun Yat-sen through Twenty-first-century Eyes," given at a conference held in Singapore on March 12, 2003, to commemorate the seventy-seventh anniversary of Sun Yatsen's death, Chinese ambassador to Singapore Zhang Jiuhuan referred to over five hundred Unequal Treaties signed up till 1911. http://www.chinaembassy.org.sg/chn/26595.html (accessed September 29, 2004).

6. Benedict Anderson, *Imagined Communities: Reflections on the Origin and Spread of Nationalism*, 2nd ed. (London: Verso, 1983, 1991); Eric J. Hobsbawm, *Nations and Nationalism since 1780: Programme, Myth, Reality* (Cambridge: Cambridge University Press, 1991); Eric J. Hobsbawm, ed., *The Invention of Tradition* (Cambridge: Cambridge University Press, 1992); John Hutchinson, "Ethnicity and Modern Nations," *Ethnic & Racial Studies* 23, no. 4 (2000): 651–70; Anthony D. Smith, *The Ethnic Origins of Nations* (Oxford: Blackwell, 1986); Anthony D. Smith, *Nationalism* (Cambridge: Polity Press, 2001).

7. Prasenjit Duara, *Rescuing History from the Nation: Questioning Narratives of Modern China* (Chicago: University of Chicago Press, 1996), 10.

8. Anthony Smith, *Nationalism*, 139.

9. Imaginative fictions are just one type of fiction. There are many other types. Peter Lamarque and Stein Haugom Olsen, in *Truth, Fiction, and Literature: A Philosophical Perspective* (Oxford: Clarendon Press, 1994), 175–91, discuss the following types in some detail: logical fictions, epistemological fictions, fictions of convenience, notional objects, and nonentities.

10. The notion of the unequal treaty system, conceptualized by John K. Fairbank, has exerted enormous influence on the understanding of Sino-foreign encounters since the nineteenth century. John King Fairbank, "The Creation of the Treaty System," in *The Cambridge History of China*, ed. John King Fairbank and Denis Twitchett (Cambridge: Cambridge University Press, 1978); Zhang Haipeng et al., eds., *Guochi baitan* [One hundred essays on national humiliation] (Beijing: Zhonghua shujü, 2001); Xiao Zhizhi, *Yapian zhanzheng yü jindai Zhongguo* [The Opium War and modern China] (Wuhan: Hubei jiaoyü chubanshe, 1999); Lu Fanzhi, *Cong Yapian zhanzheng daofeichu bupingdeng tiaoyue* [From the Opium War to the abolition of the Unequal Treaties] (Hong Kong: Yüxiang wenhua fuwush, 1998).

11. See Shao Yi, "Lun gaiding tongshang tiaoyue yü Zhongguo qiantu zhi guanxi" [On the relations between revision of commercial treaties and the future of China], *Waijiaobao*, "Lunshuo," issue 224 (October 19, 1908). See also *Waijiaobao huibian* [Collected documents of the Waijiaobao], reprint of the 1914 Waijiaobao collection issued 1901–1910 (Taibei: Guangwen shujü, 1964), 2:410.

12. Tang Ch'i-hua, *Beiyang "xiuyue waijiao" lunwen xuanji* [Collected writings on the Beiyang "Treaty Revision Diplomacy"] (Taibei: Zhengzhi duxue lishixi, 2004); Tang Ch'i-hua, *Beijing zhengfu yü guoji lianmeng* (1919–1928) [The Beijing government and the League of Nations] (Taibei: Dongda tushu gongsi, 1998); Jin Guangyao, ed., *Beiyang shiqi de Zhongguo waijiao* [The Chinese diplomacy in the Beiyang era] (Shanghai: Fudan daxue chubanshe, 2005).

13. Fariborz Nozari, *Unequal Treaties in International Law* (Stockholm: S-Byran Sundt & Co., 1971), 301.

14. Vienna Convention on the Law of Treaties, Article 4, "Non-retroactivity of the Present Convention" ("The Convention applies only to treaties which are concluded by States after the entry into force of the present Convention with regard to such States"); Article 52, "Coercion of a State by the Threat or Use of Force" ("A treaty is void if its conclusion has been procured by the threat or use of force in violation of the principles of international law embodied in the Charter of the United Nations"). The Convention entered into force in January 1980. See http:// www.un.org/law/ilc/texts/treaties.htm (accessed September 29, 2004). For more information, see chapters 2 and 3.

15. This process has often been depicted in literary form. The political implications of contemporary historical drama in China are explored in Rudolf G. Wagner, *The Contemporary Chinese Historical Drama: Four Studies* (Berkeley: University of California Press, 1990).

16. Lydia H. Liu, "Legislating the Universal: The Circulation of International Law in the Nineteenth Century," in *Tokens of Exchange: The Problem of Translation in Global Circulations*, ed. Lydia H. Liu (Durham, N.C.: Duke University Press, 1999); Lydia H. Liu, *Translingual Practice: Literature, National Culture, and Translated Modernity—China, 1900–1937* (Stanford, Calif.: Stanford University Press, 1995).

17. Douglas Howland problematizes the process of translating Western concepts related to civilization, liberty, sovereignty, and rights in late nineteenth-century Japan. Seeing the issue of translation as more than a mere question of language, he also draws attention to the fact that language cannot be isolated from cultural and political context. Douglas R. Howland, *Translating the West: Language and Political Reason in Nineteenth-Century Japan* (Honolulu: University of Hawaii Press, 2002).

1

Tracing the Contours
of the Unequal Treaties
in Imperial China, 1840–1911

ORIGINS OF THE UNEQUAL TREATIES

Introduction: Some Important Concepts and Issues

For students of modern Chinese history, the *Unequal Treaties* is one of the catchphrases or slogans that is most frequently encountered. However, as pointed out in the introduction, the term itself did not come into use until the first quarter of the twentieth century, and its precise meaning, its range of reference, as well as the significance of the endless repetitions of such a phrase, remain obscure to the present day. What sets the present study apart from previous surveys on similar topics[1] is the attempt to distinguish the legal roots of the Unequal Treaties in the mid-nineteenth century from its various rhetorical and polemical uses since the 1920s. The aim of this chapter is to examine the original texts from which the term developed.[2] The political and cultural factors that gave rise to the phraseology and rhetoricalization of the term *bupingdeng tiaoyue* will be addressed in detail in chapters 3 and 4.

In an attempt to recapitulate the imperial experience of the treaties (1842–1911), I have chosen three sets of treaties that had far-reaching implications: (1) the Treaty of Nanjing of 1842 with its two significant annexes: the General Regulations for British Trade at the Five Ports of Canton, Amoy, Foochowfoo, Ningpo, and Shanghai: the Tariff (*Wukou tongshang zhangcheng: haiguan shuize*, 1843)[3], and the Supplementary Treaty between Her Majesty the Queen of Great Britain and the Emperor of China (*Wukou tongshang fuzhan shanhou tiaokuan*, 1843)[4]; (2) the Sino-British Treaty of Tianjin of 1858; and (3) the New Commercial Treaty of 1902 between Britain and China (also known as the Mackay Treaty, *Makai tiaoyue*).

The origins of what are today understood in China as the Unequal Treaties can be found in the treaties, conventions, and agreements concluded between China and various foreign states whereby unilateral treaty rights and privileges were granted to foreigners, while Chinese failed to enjoy equivalent rights and privileges in those countries.[5] The major countries enjoying "unequal" treaty relations with China were Britain (1842), the U.S. (1844), France (1844), Sweden/Norway (1847), Russia (1851), Prussia (1861), Portugal (1862), Denmark (1863), the Netherlands (1863), Spain (1864), Belgium (1865), Italy (1866), Austria (1869), Japan (1871), Brazil (1881), Mexico (1899), and Switzerland (1918). The most important features of the treaty rights ceded to foreign interests in China were low fixed tariffs, extraterritoriality,[6] concessions and settlements (*zujie*),[7] leased territories, and the non-reciprocal most-favored-nation clause (*pianmian zuihuiguo daiyü*) found in many instruments. While tariff autonomy was restored to China in 1930, extraterritoriality was not revoked until 1943. In their encounters with foreigners in the mid-nineteenth century (1840s–1860s), Chinese emperors and imperial negotiators were led or compelled to grant these special rights in the form of treaties couched in evasive and sophisticated language that was generally incomprehensible to them. Indeed, the conclusion of foreign treaties was usually accompanied by bewilderment on the Chinese side.

Before dealing with specific treaties, some clarification of two key concepts —the unilateral most-favored-nation (MFN) status and extraterritoriality (extrality) in China—is needed. The MFN clause, which had its origins in seventeenth-century European diplomacy, provides a guarantee of equal trading opportunities among states by expanding initially bilateral agreements defining mutual import and export concessions between two countries onto a multilateral basis, involving the extension of trade concession between two countries to other contracting parties. In the case of nineteenth-century China, a crucial deviation from the standard MFN clause involved loss of reciprocal rights. Under the Qing, when trade concessions were made in treaty form to a foreign country, under the terms of the treaty China was consistently obligated to extend the same concessions to other treaty powers, without, however, obtaining reciprocal concessions from the contracting country.

Extraterritoriality in China refers to foreign immunities from Chinese law. Extraterritorial jurisdiction in China was exercised along the following lines. First, Chinese criminals, who committed crimes against Chinese, were to be tried and punished by the Chinese authorities according to Chinese law and procedure. Second, when disputes involved only nationals of a given contracting power, jurisdiction was wholly in the hands of that power. Third, disputes involving the citizens of various foreign powers were determined by the respective foreign authorities according to treaties and agreements concluded among themselves. Fourth, when disputes arose between Chinese and treaty-power nationals, the jurisdiction lay in the court and the law of the defendant's country. In the case of a foreigner being the plaintiff, an "assessor" (usually a junior consular official) of the plaintiff's nationality was allowed to sit alongside the Chinese magistrate during the proceedings in this so-called mixed court to prevent any possible miscarriage of justice.[8]

A Formative Agreement: The Treaty of Nanjing of 1842, the 1843 General Regulations for Trade and Tariff at the Five Ports, and the Supplementary Treaty of 1843

The Unequal Treaties in China took shape through two formative instruments: the Treaty of Nanjing—particularly in its two annexes, the General Regulations for Trade and Tariff of 1843 and the Supplementary Treaty (also known as the Treaty of Bogue) of 1843—and the Sino-British Treaty of Tianjin of 1858. In both of these, the opium trade in China was a key issue.[9]

The Treaty of Nanjing along with its two annexes had very different significance for Britain and Qing China at the time it was signed, as well as later. In the words of Lord Palmerston, later British prime minister, these treaties were landmarks in British commercial expansion in China: "There is no doubt that this event, which will form an epoch in the progress of the civilization of the human races, must be attended with most important advantages to the commercial interests of England."[10] Soon after the conclusion of the Treaty of Nanjing, the *Chinese Repository* exclaimed that such a treaty would surely be received with "lively emotions by all those in England, America, and elsewhere in western lands, who have been watching the progress of the contest."[11] Clearly the British adventurers knew what they wanted and they got it. To Emperor Daoguang, the treaties were simply a nonmilitary means to relieve the Qing empire of an immediate nuisance—the presence of British forces and the prospect of their victory in the lower Yangzi area—by agreeing to British demands. Nonetheless, Emperor Daoguang and Qi Ying (?–1858), the chief Qing negotiator, had little idea of what they were giving away.

On April 7, 1842, Emperor Daoguang appointed Qi Ying as imperial commissioner and ordered him along with Yi Libu to hasten to the Zhejiang coast (the lower Yangzi waters) where over sixty British ships were deployed. Between April and July 1842, Qi Ying was the victim of the emperor's vacillation between military resistance (*jiaoban*) and diplomatic conciliation (*jimi*) as hopes of a successful military defense against the British rose and fell.[12] For their part, the British kept up their attacks and refused to negotiate, as they had little confidence in Qi Ying's diplomatic rank or authority.[13] The first Opium War ended with the fall of Zhenjiang[14] on July 23, 1842 (June 16 of the twenty-second year of Daoguang).[15] This defeat forced the emperor to acknowledge that further military resistance would prove ruinous to the Qing empire. He authorized Qi Ying to make peace, but with no clear objectives other than the withdrawal of British troops. Qi Ying was obliquely advised to "handle matters in accordance with what was necessary."[16] Apparently tormented by the military defeat inflicted on the Qing, the emperor was outraged by the stalling tactics adopted by the British in their insistence on receiving a total indemnity from China before completing the withdrawal of their forces from the lower Yangzi River.[17] In the negotiations that followed, John Robert Morrison and Charles Gutzlaff acted as interpreters for the British, while Zhang Xi, a minor official possessed of intelligence and a clear mind, was the chief negotiator on the Chinese-Manchu side.[18]

The negotiation of the Treaty of Nanjing commenced after the fall of Zhenjiang on July 23, 1842. The Treaty, comprising thirteen articles, was signed on August 29, 1842 (July 24 of the twenty-second year of Daoguang), on the British flagship *Cornwallis* by Qi Ying, Yi Libu, and Henry Pottinger. Its speedy conclusion had involved little bargaining because, although the emperor and his negotiators were anxious about the outcome, they were uncertain about exactly what political and commercial interests they should defend. On August 22, 1842, after reading through Qi Ying's memorial on the draft of the treaty, Emperor Daoguang wrote that he "felt extremely upset." "Considering the millions of lives and the affairs of state at stake here," Daoguang continued, "I feel dispirited—but I have to agree to what is requested as a strategy to get things fixed once and for all."[19] The emperor did not conceal his difficulty in coming to grips with trade and commercial issues, and instructed his envoy accordingly:

> As far as outstanding debts are concerned, you [Qi Ying] should get it across that that country [Britain] has traded hospitably with the interior [China] for two hundred years. Previously, all exchanges of goods and money transactions were arranged by foreign merchants and their compatriots. Our country's officials never had a hand in it. Furthermore, trading is complicated and prices fluctuate. The whole business is trifling and tedious, and it is worse when the different languages used by each country make communication so difficult. These issues are well beyond what our local officials can manage. Thereafter, trade and commerce in different places should go by the old rules and there is no need to make changes.[20]

The major concession offered by the Treaty of Nanjing was the opening of five ports—Guangzhou (Canton), Xiamen (Amoy), Fuzhou (Foochow), Ningbo (Ningpo), and Shanghai—to British citizens for residence and trade without restraint of any kind. Article 3 ceded the island of Hong Kong permanently to Britain. Articles 4, 5, 6, and 7 stipulated that the emperor of China agreed to pay twenty-one million dollars for indemnity, including six million dollars in compensation for the dissolved opium and for the loss of British lives, and three million dollars to cover debts owing to British merchants by Chinese merchants.

The Treaty of Nanjing has been portrayed as extraordinarily significant in shaping modern Sino-foreign relations. However, the text of the treaty was unclear about important questions of trade, tariffs, and the role of British consuls, so that much remained to be worked out in further treaty arrangements. For example, on tariffs, Article 10 stipulated only

> [A] fair and regular tariff of export and import customs and other dues, which tariff shall be publicly notified and promulgated for general information; and the Emperor further engages, that when British merchandize shall have once paid at any of the said ports the regulated customs and dues, agreeable to the Tariff to be hereafter fixed, such merchandize may be conveyed by Chinese merchants to any province or city, in the interior of the empire of China, on paying a further amount as transit duties, which shall not exceed ___ [original] per cent on the tariff value of such goods.[21]

Further, the British consuls in the five treaty ports were only appointed "to be the medium of communication" between the Chinese authorities and British merchants, a formulation that was much too vague to justify a claim to consular jurisdiction involving an exemption from Chinese law under extraterritoriality.[22] Some further important but similarly ambiguous clauses in the 1842 treaty also needed to be amended in the two 1843 treaties, the General Regulations for Trade and Tariff and the Supplementary Treaty. Thus the 1843 treaties go much further in defining a legal framework for extraterritoriality than the Treaty of Nanjing, and it is these two treaties, strictly speaking, that set the pattern for the Unequal Treaties. Such an outcome raises the question why, after the Treaty of Nanjing had already been concluded, Emperor Daoguang ordered Qi Ying to continue negotiating with the British on such unfavorable terms.

The Treaty of Nanjing was a result of Britain's capitalizing on its military victory and Qing China's desire to get the menacing British forces to withdraw, at almost any cost. It satisfied neither the British nor the Chinese. The British were primarily concerned with completing the unfinished business of setting up a legal framework regulating trade and defining the jurisdiction of the British authorities. The Chinese wanted a more detailed treaty in order to preclude future disputes and avoid conflict. However, the Qing court had little experience in either foreign commerce or international law, and this prevented them from defining clear objectives at the negotiation table, even though the Chinese merchants had long and abundant experience as major regional traders. Remarking on the effect on China of the Opium War and the Treaty of Nanjing, a writer in the English-language *Chinese Repository* commented,

> Henceforth, the Centre Kingdom—the celestial empire—ancient and lone secluded China—takes rank among the nations of the earth, and becomes of one family with them. . . . The collision [The Opium War], though not very long, nor

very sharp, gave a shock to the whole empire, such as it had never before experienced. It waked those, charged with the direction of the helm of government,
to such a sense of the impending danger.[23]

The "shock" and "sense of the impending danger" felt by Emperor
Daoguang did not, however, jolt him into providing any specific guidance to
Qi Ying in the continuing negotiations:

> Given the fact that all the barbarian requests have been granted, a speedy solu-
> tion should be reached. The British ought to withdraw from the Yangzi. No de-
> lay should be permitted. . . . As to the other urgent matters that should be at-
> tended to, I order you to negotiate each of them properly. Be patient with
> repetition and trivialities. It is imperative to constantly guard against future
> trouble.[24]

Assisted by Xian Ling and Huang Entong, Qi Ying reached a speedy settlement on trade and diplomatic matters with Pottinger, content to pass over
those small matters to achieve the larger purpose, that is, subduing and con-
ciliating the barbarians.

The English version of the General Regulations for Trade and Tariff was
promulgated in Hong Kong by Henry Pottinger on July 22, 1843, and
reprinted in full as part of the Supplementary Treaty signed on October 8 in
Bogue (Humenzai) by Qi Ying and Pottinger. What is commonly known as
the Treaty of Bogue (*Humen tiaoyue*) was a later document of sixteen articles,
in which the formulations on extraterritoriality were much less clear than
those in the General Regulations for Trade and Tariff.

The General Regulations for Trade and Tariff dealt with the procedure to
be followed from the arrival of merchant ships on the Chinese coast to the
completion of commercial dealings between English and Chinese merchants.
This protocol covered a host of issues: tonnage dues, import and export
dues, examination of goods at customhouses, payment of duties, weights
and measures, lighters and cargo boats, transshipment of goods, subordinate
consular officers, British government cruisers anchoring within the ports,
the security to be given for British merchant vessels, and tariff rates and
scales of duties. Drawn up by the interpreter Robert Thom, the tariff rates to
be levied on imports and exports were remarkably low compared with rates
levied by other countries at the time, which varied between 15 percent and
60 percent.[25] In the case of exports, the tax rate on the most important products, tea and silk, was fixed at 2.5 percent for tea (2.5 *qian* for every 100 *jin,
mei baijin er lian wu qian*); 10 percent for raw silk, silk thread, and silk ribbons;
and 2.5 percent for coarse silk.[26] Only articles not listed in the tariff schedule
were to pay 5 percent ad valorem (*congjia zhibai chouwu*).[27] Thus, the common
conception of the 5 percent ad valorem as the fixed tariff imposed by the
Treaty of Nanjing is in error since the tariff regime specified in the Tariff of
Duties on Foreign Trade with China (attached to the General Regulations for

Trade and Tariff) not only varied with the goods in question, but was also crudely based on *weight* or *number* rather than monetary *value*.

The General Regulations for Trade and Tariff also contained the provision on extraterritoriality.[28] Regulation 13 provided:

> Whenever a British subject has reason to complain of a Chinese, he must first proceed to the consulate and state his grievance. The consul will thereupon inquire into the merits of the case, and do his utmost to arrange it amicably. In like manner, if a Chinese has reason to complain of a British subject, he shall no less listen to his complaint and endeavor to settle it in a friendly manner. . . . *Regarding the punishment of English criminals, the English government will enact the laws necessary to attain that end, and the consul will be empowered to put them in force; and regarding the punishment of Chinese criminals, these will be tried and punished by their own laws, in the way provided for by the correspondence which took place at Nanking after the concluding of the peace.*[29] (My emphasis)

These provisions stand in contrast to Article 9 of the Treaty of Bogue, which is much less clear:

> If lawless natives of China, having committed crimes or offences against their own government shall flee to Hongkong, or to the English ships of war, or English merchant ships for refuge, they shall if discovered by the English officers be handed over at once to the Chinese officers for trial and punishment; or if before such delivery be made by the English officers it should be ascertained or suspected by the officers of the government of China whither such criminals and offenders have fled, a communication shall be made to the proper English officer in order that the said criminals and offenders may be rigidly searched for, seized, and on proof or admission of their guilt delivered up. In like manner, if any soldier, or sailor or any other person—whatever his caste or country—who is [a] subject of the crown of England, shall, from any cause, or on any pretence, desert, fly or escape into the Chinese territory, such soldier or sailor or other person shall be apprehended and confined by the Chinese authorities and sent to the nearest British consular or other government officer. In neither case shall concealment or refuge be afforded.[30]

The Americans extensively studied the contents of the treaties negotiated by the British. The Treaty of Wanghia between the U.S. and the Qing, concluded on July 3, 1844, by Caleb Cushing and Qi Ying, introduced consular jurisdiction as a formal statutory provision in a language of lucid precision. Article 21 stipulated:

> Subjects of China, who may be guilty of any criminal act towards citizens of the United States, shall be arrested and punished by the Chinese authorities according to the laws of China. And citizens of the United States, who may commit any crime in China, shall be subject to be tried and punished only by the Consul, or other public functionary of the United States thereto authorized, according to the laws of the United States. And in order to [secure] the prevention

of all controversy and disaffection, justice shall be equitably and impartially administered on both sides.[31]

At the prompting of the British authorities, a clause setting out the implications of the most-favored-nation status, to be offered unilaterally by China, was added to Article 8 of the Supplementary Treaty at the last minute:

> The Emperor of China having been graciously pleased to grant to all foreign countries whose Subjects, or Citizens, have hitherto traded at Canton the privilege of resorting for purposes of Trade to the other four Ports of Fuchow, Amoy, Ningpo and Shanghai, on the same terms as the English, it is further agreed, that should the Emperor hereafter, from any cause whatever, be pleased to grant additional privileges or immunities to any of the subjects or citizens of such foreign countries, the same privileges and immunities will be extended to and enjoyed by British subjects [*yiti junzhan*]; but it is to be understood that demands or requests are not, on this plea, to be unnecessarily brought forward.[32]

The Sino-British Treaty of Tianjin of 1858

The Sino-British Treaty of Tianjin of 1858, together with the Agreement containing the Rules of Trade and Tariff (abbreviated as Rules of Trade and Tariff) and the Beijing Convention of 1860, marked the consolidation and expansion of the foundation laid down by the Treaty of Nanjing and its two annexes of 1843. The opening up of China exacted by the first Opium War failed to satisfy foreign merchants who felt disappointed "in respect of the results expected from the Treaty of Nanking . . . and the mistake made in limiting the right of ingress to five coastal ports."[33]

In 1856, the *Arrow* Incident and the murder in Yunnan of Abbé Auguste Chapdelaine, a French priest, quickly became stalking-horses for foreign military operations aimed at expanding the limits on trade and abolishing the irregular fees (*likin*) levied on foreign goods, as well as punishing the Qing government for its lack of cooperation in revising previous treaties. On October 8, 1856, the Qing Canton naval force arrested twelve Chinese crewmen aboard the *Arrow*, a Chinese-owned *lorcha* with an expired registration with the British authority in Hong Kong, on suspicion of piracy.[34] The Chinese boarding party allegedly tore down the British flag flying from the mast of the *Arrow*.[35] The British consul in Guangzhou, Harry S. Parkes, pressed Ye Mingchen, viceroy of Guangdong and Guangxi, to release the crewmen and apologize for the disrespect shown for the British flag, but without satisfaction. To punish the recalcitrant Ye, John Bowring, British plenipotentiary and chief superintendent of trade in China, ordered an attack on Guangzhou. On December 29, 1857, the British and French joint forces, commanded by the new British plenipotentiary Lord Elgin and French representative Baron Gros, took over Guangzhou and soon afterward demanded revisions to existing treaties. Having exhausted his military resources, on May 29, 1858, Emperor Xianfeng appointed Gui Liang and Hua Shana as his representatives with full powers to negotiate with Britain, France, the U.S., and Russia, who were then occupying Tianjin, only two hours away from the imperial capital, Beijing.

The Sino-British Treaty of Tianjin and the Agreement containing Rules of Trade and Tariff did not involve much negotiation. Less than one month elapsed between Emperor Xianfeng's authorizing of negotiations for the Treaty of Tianjin on May 29, 1858, and the conclusion of the fifty-six-article treaty on June 25. In the case of the Rules of Trade and Tariff, the negotiations in Shanghai lasted only twenty-four days, from October 14 to November 8, 1858. For the Qing, the signing of the Treaty of Tianjin was merely an expedient to get the foreigners to withdraw their troops threatening Beijing. But waiving foreign taxation in exchange for the abandonment of their other demands proved to be merely an illusion that "failed to move the barbarian chieftains."[36] The imperial negotiators even tried to convince Emperor Xianfeng that signed treaties were not binding. In one memorial, one of the Chinese negotiators, Gui Liang, wrote,

> At present, the treaties of peace with Britain and France cannot be taken as real. These few sheets of paper [the treaties] are simply a means to get [foreign] troops and warships to leave the coast [of Tianjin]. In the future, if Your Majesty desires to break these agreements and the peace, Your Majesty needs only to punish your slave [Gui Liang] for mismanagement. [Those treaties] can henceforth be treated as rubbish.[37]

Central to the "negotiations," if they can be called such, was the issue of the Residence of the British Representative at Beijing, a demand which Emperor Xianfeng personally resented the most. In addition, three other clauses —in the emperor's opinion most injurious to his empire—dealt with inland travel, trade on the Yangzi River, and the issue of indemnity.[38] Although the emperor approved the Treaty of Tianjin with Britain, he continued to harbor a strong desire to have these most unpalatable clauses deleted. On October 18, 1858, Emperor Xianfeng ordered Gui Liang to "search for heavenly inspiration to remedy [the situation] as far as possible."[39] However, the renewal of military conflict in 1860 (see below) ended any hopes that Emperor Xianfeng had for the reversal of what he perceived as the most detrimental provisions of the treaty. Self-appointed diplomatic representation and the agents of commercial expansion triumphed by military means.[40]

Under the terms of the treaty, British diplomats were permitted residence in Beijing under Article 2, "Appointment of Ambassadors," and Article 3, "Residence of [the] British Representative at Peking":

> For the better preservation of harmony in future, Her Majesty the Queen of Great Britain and His Majesty the Emperor of China mutually agree that, in

accordance with the universal practice of great and friendly nations, Her Majesty the Queen may, if she see fit, appoint Ambassadors, Ministers, or other Diplomatic Agents to the Court of Peking. . . . The Ambassador, Minister, or other Diplomatic Agent, so appointed by Her Majesty the Queen of Great Britain, may reside, with his family and establishment, permanently at the capital, or may visit it occasionally, at the option of the British Government.[41]

The Sino-British Agreement containing the Rules of Trade and Tariff was signed in Shanghai on November 8, 1858. It was intended to develop and clarify Article 26 of the Treaty of Tianjin so that

Articles not enumerated in the list of exports, but enumerated in the list of imports, when exported will pay the amount of duty set against them in the list of imports; and similarly, articles not enumerated in the list of imports, but enumerated in the list of exports, when imported will pay the amount of duty set against them in the list of exports. . . . Articles not enumerated in either list, nor in the list of duty-free goods, will pay an *ad valorem* duty of 5 per cent., calculated on their market value.[42]

This agreement, which was in conformity with the tariff rates listed in the Tariff of Duties on Foreign Trade with China attached to the General Regulations for Trade and Tariff of 1843, remained in force for over forty years until it was amended by the Tariff Agreement of August 29, 1902, which set out a revised import tariff regime.[43] The one-off transit dues to be levied on foreign commodities in transit to inland China or to the treaty ports were fixed at 2.5 percent ad valorem. Technically, the whole point of these transit dues was, as John Fairbank has pointed out, "to wipe out the special fees and prerequisites, the whole system of squeeze."[44] However, enforcing this principle was next to impossible once foreign goods were in the hands of local officials. The endless bickering over inconsistent transit dues applied to foreign as well as Chinese goods by local authorities illustrated that "the British were quite unable to prevent the taxation of their goods at points beyond the treaty ports."[45]

Furthermore, this type of commercial friction became interwoven with foreign opposition to *likin*, an internal transit due which in theory was applicable only to Chinese goods. Devised in 1853 by a local official, *likin* was a kind of transit tax levied by provincial governments on goods while en route. Despite the regulations of the Qing central government, local authorities established *lika* (taxation houses) along the roads to collect *likin* at will. The amount of *likin* exacted was variable and unpublished in any official schedule. To resolve such problems, Article 28 of the Treaty of Tianjin and Rule 7 of the trade agreement awarded foreigners the right to pay a single charge of 2.5 percent transit tax on import and export merchandise, and such traders were issued a transit pass exempting them from further taxes along the way.[46] Theoretically, this should have protected foreign goods going through treaty ports into the interior, or from the interior outwards. However, in spite of the treaty agreements, local officials tended either to limit the number of transit passes issued or refuse privileges to those holding them. For years, both Chinese and foreign merchants grumbled about *likin* as a giant obstacle to China's domestic and international trade. Despite attempts to resolve the issue of *likin* in various treaty revisions, such as the negotiations over the Mackay Treaty of 1902, the *likin* was not abolished until 1931.[47]

After the close of negotiations over the Rules of Trade and Tariff, Britain, France, and the U.S. resumed their military campaign and marched toward Beijing with the intention of subduing the Qing court, which had insisted that the ratification of the Treaty of Tianjin should not take place in the imperial capital. On September 21, 1860, the 10,500-strong British Expeditionary Force, assisted by more than 6,000 French soldiers, defeated an army of 30,000 comprising the Qing empire's crack troops at Baliqiao in the suburbs of Beijing. The following day Emperor Xianfeng fled to his summer retreat at Rehe, about one hundred miles from Beijing, and left it to his brother Prince Gong, Yi Xin, to deal with the approaching foreigners. Beijing fell on October 13.[48] Eleven days later, Prince Gong signed the peace treaty known as the Sino-British Convention of Beijing, presented by Lord Elgin, with France, Russia, and the U.S. following suit shortly afterwards.[49] Thus, temporarily at least, the protracted disputes over treaty revisions came to a halt.

The New Commercial Treaty of 1902 between Britain and China: Running Repairs at the Turn of the Century

By 1902, commercial and diplomatic relations with the West, enforced as they were, had been in place for sixty years. What had the Chinese learned from their exposure to treaty rights and negotiations? Was there any real progress to be recorded in negotiations with foreigners, known as "the zone of no-meeting-of-minds"? The Sino-British, Sino-U.S., and Sino-Japanese Commercial Treaties of 1902 and 1903 have so far received scant attention in English-language scholarship despite their significant role in the legal reforms that marked the last ten years of the Qing dynasty.[50] These agreements are important insofar as they allow us to examine how the Chinese conception of bilateral treaties evolved between the 1840s and the early 1900s.[51]

The three Commercial Treaties of 1902 and 1903 signed in Shanghai between Britain, the U.S., Japan, and China were drawn up in compliance with Article 11 of the document known as the Final Protocol for the Settlement of the Disturbances of 1900 concluded between Austria-Hungary, Belgium, France, Germany, Great Britain, Italy, Japan, the Netherlands, Russia, Spain, the U.S., and China. This article stated, "The Chinese Government has agreed to negotiate the amendments deemed necessary by the foreign Governments to the treaties of commerce and navigation and the other subjects concerning commercial relations, with the object of facilitating them."[52] These negotiations for commercial treaties with Britain, the U.S., Japan, Portugal, Germany, and Italy between 1902 and 1907, the last trade treaty revisions in the history of the Qing, were formidable in scope and wearisome in their detail.[53] The upshot was that the Qing government signed new commercial and navigational treaties with Britain, the U.S., Japan, and Portugal, though not with Germany and Italy.[54]

The Chinese delegation was made up of Lü Haihuan (1840–1927), president of the Board of Public Works, and Sheng Xuanhuai (1844–1916), director general of the Chinese Railway Company, assisted by A. E. Hippisley and F. E. Taylor as attachés, both of whom were commissioners in the Chinese Maritime Customs Service, and later by R. E. Bredon, the deputy inspector general, as an assistant delegate.[55] Although junior to Lü, Sheng was personally in charge of the negotiations.[56] Hippisley commented favorably on Sheng's qualifications for the task: "Morally, he may not be a superior man [a Confucian term, *junzi*], but intellectually he is quick, alert, sharp as a Toledo Blade, and with a commercial knowledge that few officials possess."[57]

A shrewd entrepreneur well versed in foreign matters, Sheng pursued the negotiations with extreme prudence. The abolition of *likin* and compensation for its loss—*likin* was one of the main sources of income for Chinese provincial and county authorities—were issues central to the negotiations. Sheng made sure that every move he made was approved by the Foreign Ministry, as well as by Zhang Zhidong and Liu Kunyi, the two powerful Governors-General of Hunan-Hubei and Jiangsu-Jiangxi respectively, both of whom had extensive experience of foreigners.

On the British team, the chief negotiator was Sir James Lyle Mackay, assisted by Charles J. Dudgeon, a merchant based at Shanghai, and Henry Cockburn, secretary of the legation at Beijing.[58] Overall, the Mackay Treaty laid the framework for the series of treaties that followed it, despite the fact that it was received with little enthusiasm by other foreign powers. For example, between June and September 1902, the American delegates at the negotiations—Edwin H. Conger, American minister to China, John Goodnow, the consul-general at Shanghai, and John F. Seaman, the U.S. merchant representative in China—persisted in rejecting what they saw as the British model for "a brand new commercial treaty with China." Instead, the Americans' initial proposal involved emending and revising the text of the 1858 Sino-American Treaty of Tianjin.[59]

In contrast to the Treaty of Nanjing of 1842 and the Treaty of Tianjin of 1858, the negotiations surrounding this particular set of commercial treaties at the turn of the twentieth century exhibited some novel tendencies that are worth further examination. First was the new attitude shown by the Chinese negotiators: far from merely affixing their signatures to documents drafted by foreigners, Sheng Xuanhuai, Zhang Zhidong, and Liu Kunyi displayed a new vigor and made strenuous efforts to turn the situation to China's advantage throughout the negotiations. In dealing with foreign initiatives, senior officials of the Qing constantly kept in view the need to revamp both domestic and foreign taxation regimes.

On January 11, 1902, Britain led off the negotiations with China, which lasted for eight months and resulted in the conclusion of the Mackay Treaty on September 5, 1902. Notably, half of the sixteen-article treaty, plus three sets of annexes, is devoted to the clause on the abolition of the *likin* and internal transit dues. To compensate for the loss of revenue the Qing would suffer from this tax reform, import duties were increased to 12.5 percent ad valorem while export duties were raised to 7.5 percent ad valorem. As a quid pro quo, China guaranteed to exempt foreign goods subject to these new duties from all internal taxation.

Although, as was noted above, the *likin* constituted a considerable income for provincial authorities, it had been a source of annoyance for both Chinese and foreign merchants for forty years as the result of rampant local abuses. For foreigners, the provisions of the new treaty provided an opportunity for the removal of the *likin*. For the Chinese, the abolition of these dues was their trump card in the negotiations over raising the existing flat 5 percent import duty. Since the 1840s, the value of both imported and exported commodities had been expressed in taels of silver at the customhouse. The gold exchange value of these *haiguan*, or customs, taels had been steadily falling—from 80 pence (6.8 pounds) per *haiguan* tael in 1864 to 34 (2.1 pounds) in 1904. To counteract the falling price of silver some Qing officials, such as Sheng Xuanhuai and Shen Baozhen, had already in 1896 put forward proposals that the tariffs be lifted to a uniform 10 percent ad valorem.[60]

Since the viability of the provincial treasury was at stake in this issue, Zhang Zhidong and Liu Kunyi opposed the total elimination of *likin*. They wanted to retain it and other levies on purely internal trade in order to balance the losses caused to provincial governments by the removal of the *likin* on external goods. These internal taxes included an irregular consumption tax on products that were not intended for export, the 2.5 percent native customhouses (*changguan*) duty on native products, and the 10 percent excise tax (*chuchang shui*) on all machine-made yarn and cloth, as well as on all factory products of foreign type. These terms, proposed by the Chinese, were all written into the final treaty.[61]

This newfound assertiveness contrasts with the largely ineffective way in which the Chinese had negotiated treaties in the Daoguang and Xianfeng periods, when agreements with foreigners were often self-deceivingly described as a means of "bringing barbarians under gentle control." A revealing example is Qi Ying's boastful memorial of 1844 to Emperor Daoguang, discovered in 1858 by British troops occupying Guangzhou in the governor-general's office of Ye Mingchen. To his great embarrassment, this document was later gleefully read back to Qi Ying by Horatio Lay, assistant to Lord Elgin in the negotiations for the Treaty of Tianjin:

> Ch'i-ying presents a supplementary memorial: With further reference to the management of the barbarian affairs of the various countries, his receptions of or interviews with the barbarian envoys and his controlling them as the circumstances allowed. Certainly we have to curb them by sincerity, but it has been even more necessary to control them by skillful methods. The methods by which to conciliate the barbarians and get them under control similarly could not but shift about and change their form. . . . There are times when it is possible to have them follow our directions but not let them understand the reasons. Sometimes we can expose everything so that they will not be suspicious, and whereupon we can dissipate their rebellious restlessness. Sometimes we have given them receptions and entertainment, after which they have had a feeling of appreciation. . . . [I]t is difficult to enlighten them with [by] means of reason.[62]

A nascent nationalism suggested another reason for this newfound assertiveness. To Sheng Xuanhuai, Zhang Zhidong, and Liu Kunyi—all of whom had broad experience with foreigners—the negotiation of commercial treaties was also about the reinstatement and defense of political rights (*zhengquan*) and sovereignty (*zhuquan*), as well as financial rights (*caiquan*) and judicial rights (*zhiquan*). Taking Japan as a model, Sheng and Zhang believed that Western-style legal reform would put China on the path to national strength:

> It is only 30 years ago that Japan began to consider judicial reforms and control of foreigners. Japan set out to negotiate with Britain, and Britain granted [Japan's wish to discard extraterritoriality]. Ever since then, Japan has made great headway with legal reform. Where there is a will, there is a way. Now Westerners abide by Japanese law and Japan has become a power in competition with European countries and the U.S.[63]

At a meeting on July 17, 1902, held in a cotton mill in Wuchang, Zhang Zhidong raised the issue of the conditional abrogation of extraterritoriality. Shortly after, he made inquiries of Mackay: "We intend to reform our legal system and will appoint commissioners to prepare for this in the near future. Would you agree that, after our legal system has been overhauled, all foreign nationals [in China] ought to be subject to Chinese law?"[64] Zhang's initiative prompted Article 12 of the Mackay Treaty, a declaration without precedent in China's dealings with the West:

> China having expressed a strong desire to reform her judicial system and to bring it into accord with that of Western nations, Great Britain agrees to give every assistance to such reform, and she will also be prepared to relinquish her extra-territorial rights when she is satisfied that the state of the Chinese laws, the arrangement for their administration, and other considerations warrant her in so doing.[65]

Again, the contrast with previous treaty negotiations is striking. In the eyes of Emperors Daoguang and Xianfeng, treaties with foreign powers could only be regarded as dispiriting defeats for the empire. They had no experience that would enable them to deal with the unprecedented situation where they were facing enemies coming from distant lands across the sea. They did not really understand the purpose and nature of the treaty system imposed on them, and they had virtually no understanding of the terms of the treaties they signed. Military defeat, and the risk of being beheaded by irate emperors for mishandling the situation, made senior Qing officials in Beijing or in the provinces reluctant to deal directly with the foreigners and their demands. Utterly impractical, this strategy of studied avoidance rested on the assumption that the less communication they had with foreign representatives, the less trouble it would involve. Inevitably, it failed to work. The refusal of Ye Mingchen to answer British representative Bowring's requests for treaty revisions in 1854 did nothing to spare the Qing the second Opium War with Britain in 1858. Nor did looking the other way prevent the foreign powers from setting up camp in the capital: as we saw, the issues of communication and compulsory diplomatic representation were settled to the satisfaction of the British in Articles 2 and 3 of the Treaty of Tianjin.

As a third sign of their new spirit of assertiveness, Chinese negotiators at the turn of the century energetically debated the meaning of treaty terms in an effort to limit what previous treaties had permitted—although sometimes such debates could turn to their disadvantage. The dispute, for example, over the definition of *inland waters* (*neigang*) landed Zhang and Liu in semantically perilous waters. The Chinese argued that *neigang* excluded ports on rivers (*yanhe gangkou*) that had no links with the Yangzi River or the oceans. In other words, *neigang* denoted only the few places specified in Section 3 (i) of the Chefoo Agreement of 1876:

> It is farther [further] proposed as a measure of compromise that at certain points on the shore of the Great River [Yangzi River], namely, Ta-t'ung, and Ngan-Ching, in the province of An-Hui; Hu-K'ou, in Kiang-Si; Wu-sueh. Lu-chi-k'ou, and Sha-shih, in Hu Kuang; these being all places of trade in the interior, at which, as they are not open ports, foreign merchants are not legally authorized to land or ship goods, steamers shall be allowed to touch for the purpose of landing or shipping passengers or goods.[66]

However, Mackay insisted that the meaning of *inland waters* was considerably broader, and should be understood as identical to what Section 3 (iv) of the Chefoo Agreement defined as *inland places* (*neidi*).[67] Mackay concluded: "The words *nei ti* [*neidi*], inland, in the clause of Article VII of the Rules appended to the Tariff, regarding carriage of imports inland, and of native produce purchased inland, apply as much to places on the sea coasts and river shores, as to places in the interior not open to foreign trade." After consulting Robert Hart, head of the Inspectorate General of the Chinese

Maritime Customs Service, Zhang and Liu had to accept that "the term 'inland waters' is to be interpreted according to the Chefoo Convention's definition of inland places."[68]

This episode shows that the new vigor that was manifested in the Chinese approach to the tedious eight months of negotiations between Britain and China also demonstrated good faith on the Chinese side in the established scheme of treaties and agreements, which they had no intention of breaching. Even when Chinese initiatives led to unfavorable results, the Chinese proved themselves willing to honor the outcome.

EXPRESSIONS RELATING TO THE UNEQUAL TREATIES

Throughout the nineteenth century, it seems that the term *bupingdeng tiaoyue* was not used by the Chinese. However, related concepts such as sovereignty, reciprocity, tariff autonomy, and extraterritoriality were gradually taken up and introduced into the Chinese language. Prior to 1842, foreigners traded and resided in Guangzhou and Macau purely on sufferance from the Chinese emperors and lacked any legal standing in the eyes of the Chinese authorities. But in the period between the Treaty of Nanjing (1842) and the Treaty of Tianjin of 1858, foreign governments succeeded in forcing the Qing regime to conduct relations with the West on their own terms.[69]

In the early stages, very few Chinese had any inkling of the meaning of the treaty system, a system which fundamentally changed the parameters of the foreign relations pursued by the autarkic Qing regime, and its potential to inflict harm on China. In his work *Tianchao de bengkui: Yapian zhanzheng zai yanjiu* (The fall of the celestial kingdom: A re-examination of the Opium War), Mao Haijian unravels the discrepancies between present-day perceptions of justice and fairness and what Emperor Daoguang and his chief Qing negotiator Qi Ying perceived as unfair and objectionable in the Nanjing Treaties. According to Mao, the vagueness of the Nanjing Treaty paved the way for the British negotiators, led by Henry Pottinger, to limit the rights of the Qing by inducing Qi Ying to enter into negotiations on tariff rates that could only be detrimental to Chinese interests. This led in turn to the signing of the even more unfavorable Bogue Supplementary Treaty.[70] Mao remarks that the Qing Chinese "often felt outraged over some items [in the Nanjing Treaties] which by today's standards have nothing to do with inequity, while they had no opinion about those clauses that are today considered as defining 'unequal treatment.'"[71] Of the thirteen clauses in the Nanjing Treaty, what bothered the senior Qing officials the most was the fact that the queen of England, "a female barbarian," was named side by side with Emperor Daoguan.[72] Other complaints included Clause 2, which allowed the British, "along with their families and establishments," to reside in the five ports.[73]

Qi Ying was fascinated with the "bizarre" customs of Westerners, which often bewildered him, as this report to the emperor shows:

> [T]he barbarians commonly stress the role of their women. Whenever they have a distinguished guest, the wife is certain to come out to meet him . . . on occasions when your slave [Qi Ying] has gone to the barbarians' storied residences to discuss business, these foreign wives have rushed out and saluted him. Your slave was confounded and ill at ease, while they on the other hand were deeply honored and delighted. Thus in actual fact the customs of the various Western countries cannot be regulated according to the ceremonies of the Middle Kingdom. If we should abruptly rebuke them, it would be no way of shattering their stupidity and might give rise to their suspicion and dislike.[74]

In the aftermath of the signing of the Treaty of Nanjing, Chinese references to the treaty regime were occasional and sporadic. Hao Yen-p'ing and Wang Erh-min (Ermin) note that, in the twenty years after the Treaty of Nanjing, there was only one scholar, a *xiucai* (someone who had qualified in the county civil examination), who commented on the changes that had occurred in China's relations with foreigners.[75] Only from the 1870s onward could the sense of humiliation and inferiority brought about by the treaties be discerned in the writings of Qing scholars and diplomatic officials.

First and foremost among these was Guo Songtao (1818–1891), China's first minister to Britain and France (1876–1878). His first-hand exposure to the West and frequent open discussions with Sir Samuel Halliday MaCartney (1833–1906, advisor to the Qing government), led him to share the view that "the West should treat China as an equal" and that "Westerners in China should fall under the jurisdiction of the Chinese local authority, instead of their consuls."[76] On the issue of the tariff rate, Guo noted the inequalities in the series of treaties between the Qing and foreign countries. Compared with the uniform 5 percent ad valorem tariff charged on all foreign merchandise in China, he noted that countries such as England, France, and America all levied much higher taxes on imported commodities, including a 100 percent tariff rate on some items.[77]

Later, the open-minded Qing diplomat, Zeng Jize (1839–1890), Qing minister to Britain, France, and Russia (1878–1885), expressed the same concerns. Drawing a clear line between diplomatic immunity and nondiplomatic privilege, he wrote that "in Western practice, the residential office of a foreign minister is the sovereign territory of that foreign country, over which the host country has no jurisdiction whatsoever." While all diplomatic personnel enjoyed this kind of immunity, "non-diplomatic foreign citizens are not supposed to be exempt from local authorities and laws."[78] On the question of import and export duties, Zeng on several occasions used the terms *ziding* (tariff autonomy), and *zhuquan* (sovereignty). In his communications with foreign officials, he constantly complained about the unfairness, reciprocity (*shibao*), and divestment of sovereignty resulting from the treaties between

China and foreign states. For instance, Zeng argued, under the treaty system, "the British are entitled to establish their legation in China, but there is not a single word about the reciprocal treatment of China."[79]

In 1883, the term *extraterritoriality* (*zhiwai faquan*) first found expression in the Chinese language as *e'wai quanli*, being coined by an influential scholar, Wang Tao (1828–1897). In the section of his work *Taoyuan wenlu waibian*, headed "Abolition of Extraterritoriality," Wang argued that the Qing government was entitled to do away with consular jurisdiction in accordance with Western laws on the grounds that "extraterritoriality, never practiced among European countries, is an exceptional case in Turkey, Japan and China."[80] Wang urged that the Qing regime should proceed through diplomatic channels, rather than by force of arms, violence, and intimidation, to resolve the vexed question of extraterritoriality. On tariff issues, Wang Tao pointed out that the Qing had the right to raise or lower import and export duties as it wished.[81]

Another important figure, Zheng Guanying (1842–1921), in his well-known *Shengshi weiyan*, expatiated on Japan's eradication of consular jurisdiction which followed from the adoption of new criminal laws in line with Western models.[82] Hence, in view of the shortcomings and personality cult of the Qing court system, Zheng Guanying called for legal reforms to persuade foreigners to subject themselves to Chinese law.[83] Huang Zunxian's (1848–1905) translation of extraterritoriality as *zhiwan faquan* was adopted as the modern standard rendering, replacing Wang Tao's original coinage.[84]

During the exacting negotiations that surrounded the commercial treaties between Qing and Britain, Sheng Xuanhuai repeatedly complained of the unfair situation created by the clauses on extraterritoriality that unilaterally granted exemption from Chinese laws to foreigners.[85] In fact, the commercial treaties negotiations of 1902–1907 were debated in *Waijiaobao* by a number of intellectuals, the majority of whom had studied law and politics at Japanese universities.[86] These commentaries aimed to "awaken the incumbent" and "stimulate country-fellows to come up with remedies."[87] Though giving praises to the Chinese representatives, one commentator enumerated the harms and limited benefits of the Sino-British treaty article by article.[88] Shao Yi, another commentator, wrote,

> Unilateral treaties are rooted in unequal relations. One party assumes obligations and the other enjoys privileges and rights, these being [the essence] of treaties of inequity (*bupingdeng zhi tiaoyue*). . . . The guiding principles of the diplomacy between two countries do change from time to time. The transformation [of diplomatic relations] from inequity to equity hinges upon the nature of the policy adopted [by the Qing government] in treaty revisions (*gaiyue*).[89]

An analysis of the Chinese interpretation of the treaties concluded between the 1840s and the 1900s reveals several layers of meaning. By inventing and transmitting terms like *ziding, shibao, zhuquan, e'wai faquan, zhiwai faquan, gaizheng tiaoyue, jiuyue, buduideng zhi tiaoyue,*[90] and *bupingdeng zhi tiaoyue,* influential participants and commentators read the treaties as nonreciprocal, as unfair and extraordinary, and as a violation of China's sovereignty. Their formulations gave a peculiar significance to the difficult-to-interpret and little understood treaty texts, impenetrable to most Chinese at that time. Hence, they provided the framework for a fundamental understanding of China's position on the world scene that was to have repercussions for decades to come. Such awareness, however, was sporadic, and among ordinary Chinese there was a lack of consciousness of China's standing in relation to foreign powers. As a result, in the last part of the nineteenth century and the early 1900s the treaty issue was far less explosive, both politically and socially, than was the case in the first quarter of the twentieth century. Indeed, in the attempt to meet Western legal standards as a quid pro quo for changes to extraterritoriality, imperial officials by and large honored the treaty regime, their ambitions extending no further than the revision of certain contentious clauses.

NOTES

1. Earlier surveys include Hosea Ballou Morse, *The International Relations of the Chinese Empire,* 3 vols. (New York: Longmans, Green, and Co., 1918; Honolulu: University of Hawaii Press, 2004). Citations are to the Longmans, Green, and Co. edition; Hosea Ballou Morse, *The Trade and Administration of the Chinese Empire* (Shanghai: Kelly and Walsh, 1908; Taibei: Chengwen Pub. Co., 1966). Citations are to the Chengwen edition; Wesley R. Fishel, *The End of Extraterritoriality in China* (Berkeley: University of California Press, 1952); Lee, *Beifa hou de "geming waijiao"*; Wang Jianlang, *Zhongguo feichu bupingdeng tiaoyue de licheng.*

2. The major collections of treaties with or relating to China in English are: William Frederick Mayers, ed., *Treaties between the Empire of China and Foreign Powers, Together with the Regulations for the Conduct of Foreign Trade* (Shanghai: J. Broadhurst Tootal, "North China Herald" Office, 1877; Taibei: Chengwen Pub. Co., 1966). Citations are to the Chengwen edition; Godfrey E. P. Hertslet, ed., *Hertslet's China Treaties,* 2 vols. (London: Harrison and Sons, 1908); John V. A. MacMurray, ed., *Treaties and Agreements with and Concerning China,* 2 vols. (New York: Oxford University Press, 1921; Honolulu: University of Hawaii Press, 2004). Citations are to the Oxford University Press edition; Inspector General of Customs, *Treaties, Conventions, etc., between China and Foreign States,* 2 vols. (Shanghai: Statistical Department of the Inspectorate General of Customs, 1917); Waijiaobu, comp., *Zhongwai tiaoyue jibian, 1927–1957* [*Treaties between the Republic of China and Foreign States (1927–1957)*] (Taibei: The Commercial Press Ltd., 1958), 648–49; James Brown Scott, ed., *Treaties and Agreements with and Concerning China, 1919–1929* (Washington, D.C.: Carnegie Endowment for International Peace, 1929). Mayers's selection and reproduction of the treaty texts is of limited value, mainly because some important treaties, such as the 1843 Supplementary Treaty between Britain and China (*Wukou tongshang shanhou fuzhan tiaokuan*) and the General Regulations for British Trade at the Five Ports (*Wukou tongshang zhangcheng: haiguan shuize*), were either condensed—with his own headings—or simply omitted. There are similar problems with Hertslet, *Hertslet's China Treaties.* The most reliable sources of treaty texts are the two volumes published by the Chinese Inspectorate General of Customs (containing treaty versions in both Chinese and the language of the other contractual party) and MacMurray's compilations. With regard to Chinese texts, Wang Tieya's three-volume *Zhongwai*

jiuyuezhang huibian, 1689–1949 [Compilation of former treaties and conventions between China and foreign countries, 1689–1949], 2nd ed. (Beijing: Sanlian shudian, 1982) is notable for its accurate preservation of the originals.

3. Abbreviated as the General Regulations for Trade and Tariff of 1843.

4. Abbreviated as the Supplementary Treaty of 1843, also known as the Treaty of Bogue.

5. Sources from Wu Yügan, *Zhongguo guoji maoyishi* [History of Chinese international trade] (Shanghai: Shangwu yinshuguan, 1928), 90–93; Wang Tieya, *Zhongwai jiuyuezhang huibian*.

6. For the origins of capitulations related to extraterritoriality in international law, see chapter 5. Jurisprudence expert Westel W. Willoughby gives the following definition of extraterritoriality: "When persons—diplomatic officials, for example—are treated from the ordinary jurisdiction of the state within whose territory they are, there exists a situation that can properly be called exterritorial. . . . When a state asserts a jurisdiction over persons or things outside of its own territorial limits, there is presented a case of extraterritoriality." Westel W. Willoughby, *The Fundamental Concepts of Public Law* (New York: Macmillan, 1924), 395.

7. For a comprehensive study of the Shanghai International Concession, see Siu Kong-Sou and Chiu Chin-Tsan, *Shanghai gonggong zujie zhidu* [The status of the Shanghai International Settlement] (Nanjing: Guoli zhongyang yangjiuyuan, 1933).

8. Westel W. Willoughby, *Foreign Rights and Interests in China* (Baltimore, Md.: Johns Hopkins University Press, 1927), chapter 2. Thomas B. Stephens treats the Shanghai Mixed Court, which was unique in China, as a product of Western "translating backward" of its legal system into the Chinese environment. The evolution, rationale, and operation of the Shanghai Mixed Court are discussed in Thomas B. Stephens, *Order and Discipline in China: The Shanghai Mixed Court, 1911–1927* (Seattle: University of Washington Press, 1992). While acknowledging the fundamental inequity of Western treaty rights extracted from China and Japan in the nineteenth century, several authors have argued for a more nuanced and sophisticated view of the practice of extraterritorial jurisdiction in Japan and China. Richard T. Chang has challenged the view that considers the consular courts as generally handing down decisions that were unfair to the Japanese. Richard T. Chang, *The Justice of the Western Consular Courts in Nineteenth-Century Japan* (Westport, Conn.: Greenwood Press, 1984), 135. Like Chang, Eileen Scully in a recent study disagrees with the "West-versus-the-rest paradigm of colonial studies," which focuses exclusively on the immunity of foreigners from native law-enforcement and the inequality of coerced state-to-state treaties. Her own area of inquiry focuses on the struggle over the rights and responsibilities of citizenship between American expatriates in China and their home government. Eileen P. Scully, *Bargaining with the State from Afar: American Citizenship in Treaty Port China, 1844–1942* (New York: Columbia University Press, 2001), 2.

9. The Opium Wars were the two trade wars fought in 1839–1842 and 1856–1860 (the latter was also known as the Arrow War) between China and the Western powers as the result of China's attempts to curb opium smuggling. British merchants had been exporting opium illegally to China and the resulting widespread drug addiction had serious social and economic consequences. The Chinese Qing government (1664–1912) dispatched Commissioner Lin Zexü to Guangzhou (Canton) to handle the crisis. Lin confiscated and destroyed more than twenty thousand chests of opium in the Canton area. As a result, British merchants appealed to the British government to take action by sending sixteen warships to attack important cities including Canton, Nanjing, and Zhenjiang. The defeated Qing government was forced to sign the Treaty of Nanjing and two other annexed agreements in order to end the hostilities in 1842–1843. The second Opium War broke out in 1856, triggered by the Chinese search of a Chinese-owned but British-registered ship, the *Arrow*. For details, see the discussions below. "Opium Wars," *The Columbia Encyclopedia*, 6th ed. (New York: Columbia University Press, 2001–2004) http://www.bartleby.com/65/ (accessed July 30, 2004); John King Fairbank, *Trade and Diplomacy on the China Coast: The Opening of the Treaty Ports, 1842–1854* (Stanford, Calif.: Stanford University Press, 1969).

10. Palmerston to J. A. Smith, November 28, 1842; Fairbank, *Trade and Diplomacy*, 83; Harry Tucker Easton, *The History of a Banking House (Smith, Payne and Smiths)* (London: Blades, East & Blades, 1903), 29.

11. *Chinese Repository*, vol. 11, no. 10 (October 1842): art. 5.

12. Fairbank, *Trade and Diplomacy*, chapter 6.

13. Qi Ying reported on British delaying tactics in a memorial dated August 1, 1842. Zhongguo diyi lishi dang'an'guan, ed., *Yapian zhanzheng dang'an shiliao* [Archival sources on the Opium War] (Tianjin: Tianjin guji chubanshe, 1992), 5:786.

14. An important city port on the Yangzi River in Jiangsu Province.

15. For the conversion of Chinese lunar dates, see Zheng Hesheng, ed., *Jinshi zhongxi shiri duizhaobiao* [Lunar and solar calendars in modern history: A comparative study] (Beijing: Zhonghua shujü, 1980).

16. On July 3, 1842 (May 25 of the twenty-second year of Daoguang), Emperor Daoguang ordered Qi Ying not to meet with the British in person, as "barbarians are too deceptive to be trustworthy." If there is something that needs to be addressed, contact with the British should be made only through Chen Zhigang [a lowly officer] in order to avoid being compromised. If the British reply contains excessive demands that are difficult to comply with, focus on defense together with Niu Jian [governor-general of Jiangsu and Zhejiang Provinces]. Destroy the enemy whenever you can, stop the enemy whenever the opportunity presents itself. It is imperative not to harbor any indecisiveness." Zhongguo diyi lishi dang'an'guan, *Yapian zhanzheng dang'an shiliao*, 5:537. On July 26, 1842 (June 19 of the twenty-second year of Daoguang), Daoguang contradicted himself by ordering Qi Ying and Yi Libu to make efforts to conciliate and to handle matters in accordance with what was necessary. *Yapian zhanzheng dang'an shiliao*, 5:742. The following day, after receiving their report on the fall of Zhenjiang, Daoguang authorized Qi Ying to once again concentrate on negotiations and to handle the situation with greater urgency. *Yapian zhanzheng dang'an shiliao*, 5:743.

17. For Qing Ying's memorial and Daoguang's remarks on the treaty negotiations of August 17, 1842, see Zhongguo diyi lishi dang'an'guan, *Yapian zhanzheng dang'an shiliao*, 6:75.

18. Zhang Xi's *Fuyi riji* [Diary of negotiations with the barbarians] is considered the most detailed and lively account of the events surrounding the Treaty of Nanjing of 1842; it is reprinted in *Yapian zhanzheng dang'an shiliao* [Archival sources on the Opium War], vol. 5 (Shanghai: Shanghai renmin chubanshe, 1987). Also see Teng Ssu-yü's translation of *Fuyi riji*, *Chang Hsi and the Treaty of Nanjing, 1842* (Chicago: University of Chicago Press, 1944); Mao Haijian *Tianchao de bengkui: Yapian zhanzheng zai yanjiu* [The fall of the celestial kingdom: A reexamination of the Opium War] (Beijing: Sanlian Shudian, 1995), 456.

19. Zhongguo diyi lishi dang'an'guan, *Yapian zhanzheng dang'an shiliao*, 6:114.

20. Zhongguo diyi lishi dang'an'guan, *Yapian zhanzheng dang'an shiliao*, 6:114–15.

21. Hertslet, *Hertslet's China Treaties*, 10.

22. Hertslet, *Hertslet's China Treaties*, 8.

23. "Art. 1. Present condition of the Chinese empire, considered with regard both to its domestic and foreign relations, especially as affected by the late war and treaty," *Chinese Repository* 12, no. 1 (January 1843).

24. Daoguang's edict to Qi Ying, August 31, 1842. Zhongguo diyi lishi dang'an'guan, *Yapian zhanzheng dang'an shiliao*, 6:165.

25. Wunsz King, ed., *V. K. Wellington Koo's Foreign Policy: Some Selected Documents* (Arlington, Va.: University Publications of America, 1976), 39.

26. 1 *jin* = 10 *liang* = 100 *qian*. Although expressed by different systems of weights and measures, the rates in the Chinese text (Wang Tieya's *Zhongwai jiu yuezhang huibian*, 1:43–50) adopt *jin*, *liang*, and *qian*, and correspond to those in pecul (*dan*) and catties (*jin*) published in English in *The Chinese Repository*, vol. 12, no. 7 (July 1843): art. 7, and Stanley F. Wright, *China's Struggle for Tariff Autonomy: 1843–1938* (Shanghai: Kelly & Walsh, 1938), 15. 1 *dan* = 100 *jin* = 10,000 *liang*. For the complete Chinese and English versions of the Tariff of Duties on Foreign Trade with China, see Inspector General of Customs, *Treaties, Conventions, etc.*, 359–82.

27. Ad valorem (according to the value) refers to taxes or charges imposed at a fixed percentage of the value as stated in an invoice.

28. Item 8 of Qi Ying's alleged twelve-article proposal for discussion sent to Henry Pottinger and dated September 1, 1842, suggests that it was Qi Ying who initiated the inclusion of extraterritorial rights in the later treaty negotiations. See Sasaki Masaya, *Ahen Sensō no kenkyū. Shiryō hen* [A Study of the Opium War (Sources)] (Tokyo: Kindai Chūgoku Kenkyūlinkai,1964), 217–19. The authorship of the proposal is questionable as Item 8 seems too sophisticated to have been written by Qi Ying, who was not well versed in law and commerce. As a point of reference, the drawing up of both the Chinese and English texts of the Treaty of Nanjing and the Supplementary Treaty of 1843 relied in each case on one man, respectively John Robert Morrison and Robert Thom. On January 4, 1843, Lord Aberdeen wrote in a note to Henry Pottinger: "On this point of jurisdiction as regards the criminal and civil cases, I would call your attention to the expediency of obtaining in as formal a manner as circumstances will permit, the assent of the Chinese government to the absolute jurisdiction of the British authorities over British subjects in the one class, and to their concurrent jurisdiction of the Chinese officers in the other class, when a Chinese subject is one of the parties." Yu-hao Tseng, *The Termination of Unequal Treaties in International Law: Studies in Comparative Law of Nations* (Shanghai: The Commercial Press, 1931), 271.

29. Fairbank perhaps underestimated the legal significance of such a provision as he failed to mention it in his study of the opening of the treaty ports. Fairbank, *Trade and Diplomacy*, 121.

30. *Chinese Repository*, vol. 13, no. 9 (September 1844) (Hong Kong: Printed for the proprietors).

31. Mayers, *Treaties between the Empire of China and Foreign Powers*, 80–81.

32. Mayers, *Treaties between the Empire of China and Foreign Powers*, 80–81.

33. Nathan A. Pelcovits, *Old China Hands and the Foreign Office* (New York: American Institute of Pacific Relations, 1948), 14–15.

34. A *lorcha* is a small vessel with a Western-style hull and Chinese-style masts and sails. Frances Wood, *No Dogs and Not Many Chinese: Treaty Port Life in China, 1843–1943* (London: John Murray, 2000), 83.

35. Hosea Ballou Morse, Mao Haijian, and Immanuel Hsü all offer different accounts of this incident. Despite the fact that the *Arrow's* registration with the British authorities had expired, Morse argues that the most serious offence committed by the Guangdong government was "the arrest of the crew without a warrant from the consul." Morse asserts that the Chinese hauled down the British flag on purpose, rather than as a result of the confusion on deck. Morse, *International Relations of the Chinese Empire*, 1:422–27. Mao disputes the allegation that the British flag was deliberately torn down by the Chinese. Mao Haijian, *Kuming tianzi* [Ill-fated son of heaven] (Shanghai: Shanghai renmin chubanshe, 1995), 165. A neutral interpretation is proposed in Immanuel C. Y. Hsü, *China's Entrance into the Family of Nations: The Diplomatic Phase, 1858–1880* (Cambridge, Mass.: Harvard University, 1960), 21.

36. Gui Liang et al., memorial to Emperor Xianfeng on foreign tax exemptions dated September 11 of the 8th Year of Xianfeng; Qi Sihe et al., eds., *Di erci Yapiang Zhanzheng* [The second Opium War] (Shanghai: Shanghai renmin chubanshe, 1978–1979), 3:541–44.

37. Jia Zhen et al., eds., *Xianfeng chao chouban yiwu shimo* [A complete account of the management of barbarian affairs under the Xianfeng regime] (Beijing: Zhonghua shujü, 1979), 3:966.

38. Qi et al., *Di erci Yapiang Zhanzheng*, 3:544.

39. September 12 of the 8th Year of Xianfeng. Qi et al., *Di erci Yapiang Zhanzheng*, 3:544.

40. Lassa Oppenheim, *International Law, A Treatise*, 7th ed., ed. Hersch Lauterpacht (London: Longmans, Green, and Co., 1948–1952), 1:700.

41. Hertslet, *Hertslet's China Treaties*, 1:19–20 (in part 1).

42. Hertslet, *Hertslet's China Treaties*, 1:36 (in part 1).

43. As a result of the devaluation of the customs taels (see below), the 5 percent ad valorem tariff had plummeted to less than 3 percent in the forty years since 1860. As a result, the 1902 revised tariff agreement stated that "the existing Tariff on goods imported into China should be

increased to an effective five per cent. . . . All Duties levied on Imports *ad valorem* should be converted as far as feasible and with the least possible delay into specific Duties, this conversion to be effected in the following manner: The average value of merchandise at the time of landing during the three years 1897, 1898, and 1899, that is to say, the market price less the amount of Import Duty and incidental expenses to be taken as the basis for the valuation of such merchandise." MacMurray, *Treaties and Agreements*, 339–40. This meant that all ad valorem duties were to be converted into specific monetary values, equivalent to 5 percent (i.e., the so-called effective 5 percent, *qieshi zhibai chouwu*) of the average value of specific goods in 1897, 1898, and 1899. This effective 5 percent ad valorem duty was made applicable to many classes of goods formerly imported duty free.

44. John King Fairbank, "The Creation of the Treaty System," 221.

45. Fairbank, "The Creation of the Treaty System."

46. Wang Tieya, *Zhongwai jiuyuezhang huibian*, 1:99–100, 1:117–18; Hertslet, *Hertslet's China Treaties*, 1:27–28 (in part 1), 1:38–39 (in part 1).

47. Chen Xiukui, ed., *Zhongguo caizheng shi* [The economic history of China], vol. 2 (Taibei: Zhengzhong shujü, 1968); Luo Yüdong, *Zhongguo lijinshi* [The history of the Chinese *likin*], 2 vols., reprint ed. (Taibei: Wenhai chubanshe, 1979).

48. For Chinese eye-witness accounts of British and French plundering and destruction in the Beijing area, see *Gengshen yifen jilue* [Records of barbarian matters for the Year of Gengshen], *Gengshen beilue* [Record of the North for the Year of Gengshen], *Gengshen yingyi rukou dabian jilu* [Brief account of the disaster caused by the invasion of the British barbarians], and *Qing Xianfeng shinian Yingfabing rujing fenhui Yuanmingyuan an* [An account of the British and French destruction of Yuanmingyuan in the tenth year of the Qing Xianfeng], etc. Qi et al., *Di erci Yapiang Zhanzheng*, vol. 2. For a recent English study of the looting of Yuanmingyuan, see James L. Hevia, *English Lessons: The Pedagogy of Imperialism in Nineteenth-Century China*, chapter 4.

49. Li Wenhai and Kuang Jixian, eds., *Jindai Zhongguo bupingdeng tiaoyue xieshi* [True records of the unequal treaties in modern China] (Beijing: Zhongguo renmin chubanshe, 1997), 239–333.

50. Douglas R. Reynold connects the Sino-U.S. Commercial and Navigation Treaty of 1903 with the Qing's Xinzheng reforms. Douglas R. Reynold, *China, 1898–1912: The Xinzheng Revolution and Japan* (Cambridge, Mass.: Harvard University Press, 1993).

51. No monographs in English have been published as yet on this set of treaties, although both Michael Hunt and Warren Cohen address in passing the provisions of the Sino-American Commercial Treaty relating to Manchuria. W. Cohen, *America's Response to China*, 51–52; Michael H. Hunt, *Frontier Defense and the Open Door: Manchuria in Chinese-American Relations, 1895–1911* (New Haven, Conn.: Yale University Press, 1973), 68–76. Useful works in Chinese are Wang Ermin, *Wanqing Shangyue waijiao* [The diplomacy of the commercial treaties between China and foreign powers during the late Qing Period] (Hong Kong: The Chinese University of Hong Kong Press, 1998); Cui Zhihai, "Shilun 1903 nian Zhongmei Tongshang xingchuan xüding tiaoyue" [On the revised Sino-U.S. Commercial and Navigational Treaty of 1903], *Jindaishi yanjiu* 5 (2001): 144–76; Ding Mingnan et al., eds., *Diguo zhuyi qinhuashi* [History of Imperialist aggression towards China], vol. 2 (Beijing: Renmin chubanshe, 1986), chapter by Zhang Zhenkun.

52. As foreigners increased their presence in China, strong anti-foreign feelings spread among the Chinese. In 1900, this hostility flared up in the Boxer Uprising in northwest Shandong. The Boxers practiced martial arts with the conviction that, being possessed by spirits, they had a magical invulnerability to weapons. With some encouragement from the conservatives in the Qing court, the peasant Boxers went into Beijing and Tianjin killing foreigners, ripping up railway tracks, and besieging foreign legations. In August 1900, a international army of twenty thousand defeated the Boxers in Beijing. Empress Dowager Cixi fled from the capital. In 1901 the Boxer Protocol was signed between China and foreign countries. Major terms of the 1901 Protocol are: erecting monuments to the memory of two hundred dead foreigners; executing high officials who supported the Boxers; forbidding arms and permanent foreign guards in Beijing; indemnity—450 million taels (the Qing's annual income was only 250 million taels);

reforms in all aspects including in law. MacMurray, *Treaties and Agreements*, 1:278–94; Wang Shu-hwai, *Gengzi peikuan* [The Boxer Indemnity] (Taibei: Institute of Modern History, Academia Sinica, 1974); Paul A. Cohen, *History in Three Keys: The Boxers as Events, Experience, and Myth* (New York: Columbia University Press, 1997); Joseph Esherick, *The Origins of the Boxer Uprising* (Berkeley: University of California Press, 1987).

53. As a nonsignatory power to the 1901 Boxer Protocol, Portugal's participation in the commercial treaty revisions was an exception. The real intention of the Portuguese was to alter the boundaries of its colony Macau, granted in perpetuity by the Treaty of Friendship and Commerce of 1887 between Portugal and China. After its demand was rejected by the Qing government, Portugal later claimed to have relinquished it in exchange for negotiations aimed at enhancing its trade interests in China. The two rounds of negotiation took place from May 12 to October 15, 1902, and from June to November 1904, resulting in two treaties signed by Castello Branco, Portuguese minister to China, Prince Qing, and Sheng Xuanhuai. The Portuguese parliament, however, rejected both treaties—first because they failed to provide for any alteration of the borders of Macau, and second because the parliament concluded that its negotiators had made excessive compromises in the Guangdong-Macau Railway contract and over the rights of the Chinese Maritime Customs at Macau. Hertslet, *Hertslet's China Treaties*, 423–24 (in part 2); Shen Tongsheng, comp., *Guangxü zhengyao* [Documents of the Guangxü regime], reprint ed. (Taibei: Wenhai chubanshe, 1961), 1844; Zhongguo jindai jingjishi ziliao congkan bianji weiyuanhui, *Xinchou heyue dingli yihou de shangyue tanpan* [The commercial treaty negotiations in the aftermath of the Boxer Protocol of 1901] (Beijing: Zhonghua shujü, 1993), Maritime Customs archives, translated negotiation transcripts, chapter 4; Stanley F. Wright, *Hart and the Chinese Customs* (Belfast: W. Mullan, 1950), 764.

54. Averse to following the British treaty model, which the Chinese had accepted, both Germany and Italy dropped out of the negotiations. The German representative was W. Knappe, consul in Shanghai. At the meeting of October 7, 1905, with the Chinese, Knappe read out a telegram from Berlin: "The Chinese side has struck out all items proposed by Germany and admitted only those already accepted in the British and American treaties. The German government will not tolerate this situation." Translated from Chinese, Zhongguo jindai jingjishi ziliao congkan bianji weiyuanhui, *Xinchou heyue dingli yihou de shangyue tanpan*, minutes of the tenth meeting of the Sino-German negotiations for treaty revision, October 7, 1905, 313. Germany's withdrawal was partly motivated by its objection to the British monopoly on trade in the Yangzi River area. The negotiations for the Sino-Italian treaty were aborted for the same reason. Zhongguo jindai jingjishi ziliao congkan bianji weiyuanhui, *Xinchou heyue dingli yihou de shangyue tanpan*, minutes of meetings nos. 1–3 of the negotiations for the Sino-Italian treaty, May 15, July 26, and October 9, 1906, F. E. Taylor to Robert Hart, Inspector General of the Chinese Maritime Customs, 334–42.

55. Zhu Shoupeng, ed., *Guangxü chao donghualu* [Documents of the Guangxü regime] (Beijing: Zhonghua shujü, 1958), 4:109.

56. In 1870 Sheng joined the staff of the Qing statesman Li Hongzhang (1823–1901), responsible for economic affairs. Later in the 1870s, Sheng took control of the important China Merchants' Steam Navigation Company and soon afterwards, of the Imperial Telegraph Administration. Other official, semiofficial, and private businesses successfully managed by Sheng included the Hau-sheng Spinning and Weaving Company and the Han-yang Iron Factory. In addition, from 1879 to 1896, Shang held various positions in the Chinese Maritime Customs in Tianjin and Shangdong. Chen Xülu et al., eds., *Zhongguo jindaishi cidian* [Dictionary of modern Chinese history] (Shanghai: Shanghai cishu chubanshe, 1984), 620–21.

57. Hui-min Lo, ed., *The Correspondence of G. E. Morrison: 1895–1920*, 2 vols. (Cambridge: Cambridge University Press, 1976), 1:181. Lü Haihuan was Minister to Germany and Holland during the period 1897–1901.

58. Zhu S., *Guangxü chao donghualu*, 4:109. The British treaty thus became known as the Mackay Treaty. Mackay was a former member of the Legislative Council of the Viceroy of India, and was at the time director of the British Steam Navigation Company.

59. Zhongguo jindai jingjishi ziliao congkan bianji weiyuanhui, *Xinchou heyue dingli yihou de shangyue tanpan*, minutes of meetings nos. 1–2 of the negotiations for the Sino-American treaty, June 27, 1902, and September 9, 1902, 147–59.

60. Sheng Xuanhuai, *Yüzhai cungao* [Collected works of the folly study], reprint ed. (Taibei: Chengwen chubanshe, 1966), 1:49–51. The Chinese Inspectorate General of Customs, *Documents Illustrative of the Origin, Development, and Activities of the Chinese Customs Service*, 7 vols. (Shanghai: Statistical Department of the Chinese Inspectorate General of Customs, 1937–1940), 2:132.

61. Wang Ermin and Chen Shanwei, eds., *Qingmo yiding zhongwai shangyue jiaoshe: Sheng Xuanhuai wanglai handian gao* [Documents relating to commercial treaty negotiation between China and the West in the late Qing: Correspondence and telegrams of Sheng Xuanhuai] (Hong Kong: Chinese University of Hong Kong, 1993).

62. The translation is by Ssu-yu Teng and John K. Fairbank. See Ssu-yu Teng and John K. Fairbank, *China's Response to the West: A Documentary Survey, 1839–1923* (Cambridge, Mass.: Harvard University Press, 1954, 1979), 36–42.

63. Wang Yanwei, comp., *Qingji waijiao shiliao* [Diplomatic sources of the late Qing] (Beijing: Shumu wenxian chubanshe, 1987), 3 (no. 150): 2565.

64. Translated from Chinese, *Xinchou heyue dingli yihou de shangyue tanpan*, minutes of the nineteenth meeting of the Sino-British negotiations for treaty revision (July 17, 1902), 137.

65. MacMurray, *Treaties and Agreements*, 1:351.

66. Mayers, *Treaties between the Empire of China and Foreign Powers*, 47.

67. Mayers, *Treaties between the Empire of China and Foreign Powers*, 47.

68. The Chinese Inspectorate General of Customs, *Documents Illustrative of the Chinese Customs Service*, vol. 2 (circular no. 486): 139.

69. Commenting on the irony inherent in the treaty system, Frances Wood writes: "Paradoxically, the treaty ports never really fulfilled the ends of those who fought to establish them. Their very existence contradicted the principle of free trade upon which they had been founded. Traders lobbying for the opening of China to foreign trade may have envisaged them as secure bases from which to conquer undreamt-of-markets, but the Chinese saw them as areas of confinement." Wood, *No Dogs and Not Many Chinese*, 6. Mainland Chinese scholar Li Yümin notes the ironic result of the forced entry of Westerners into the middle kingdom: "The new treaty system which signified the new era of Sino-foreign relations began to undermine the celestial system, which, however, did not result in Sino-foreign relations based on equality. On the contrary, the Powers used the treaty system to bring China into their sphere of dominance and thus established real inequality in China-foreign relations." Li Yümin, *Jindai tiaoyue zhidu* [The modern treaty system] (Changsha: Hunan shifan dauxue chubanshe, 1995), 12.

70. With regard to the tariff rate applicable to customs duties, Article 10 of the Nanjing Treaty reads: "His Majesty the Emperor of China agrees to establish at all the ports which are, by the second article of this Treaty, to be thrown open for the resort of British merchants, a fair and regular Tariff of Export and Import Customs and other dues, which Tariff shall be publicly notified and promulgated for general information." There was no mention of who should decide the tariff rate, nor any mention of the need for further negotiations on the issue. Mayers, *Treaties between the Empire of China and Foreign Powers*, 1–5.

71. Mao H., *Tianchao de bengkui*, 483; Mao Haijian, *Jindai de chidu: Liangci Yapian Zhanzheng junshi yü waijiao* [A modern assessment: military and diplomatic aspects of the two Opium Wars] (Shanghai: Sanlian shudian, 1998).

72. Li Xingyuan, *Li Xingyuan riji* [Diary of Li Xingyuan] (Beijing: Zhonghua shujü, 1987), 1:428. In his diary, Li commented on the Nanjing Treaty: "I read through the agreement [the Nanjing Treaty] from the South and gasped for breath. The celestial kingdom is abundant in everything. Why should we then suffer such a mishap as to have a female barbarian listed side by side with His Majesty?" Mao H., *Tianchao de bengkui*, chapter 7.

73. Yao Weiyuan, *Yapian zhanzheng* [The Opium War] (Wuhan: Hubei renmin chubanshe, 1983), 5:382; Mao H., *Tianchao de bengkui*, chapter 7; Mayers, *Treaties between the Empire of China and Foreign Powers*, 1–5.

74. Translation by Teng Ssu-yu and John K. Fairbank. Teng and Fairbank, *China's Response to the West*, 38–39.

75. Hao Yen-p'ing and Wang Erh-min (Ermin), "Changing Chinese Views of Western Relations, 1840–1895," in *The Cambridge History of China*, ed. John K. Fairbank, 11:142–201 (in part 2).

76. Zhong Shuhe et al., eds., *Guo Songtao Lundun yü Bali riji* [Guo Songtao: The London and Paris Diaries] (Changsha: Yuelu shushe, 1984), 199 et passim.

77. Zhong et al., *Guo Songtao Lundun yü Bali riji*, 706–7.

78. Yang Xiangqun et al., eds., *Zeng Jize chushi yingfa riji* [Zeng Jize's diary in England, France, and Russia] (Changsha: Yuelu shushe, 1985), 164–65.

79. Yang X. et al., *Zeng Jize chushi yingfa riji*, 261–62, 318–19.

80. Wang Tao, *Taoyuan wenlu waibian* [Supplementary collection of the writings of Wang Tao] (Shanghai: unknown publisher, 1897), 3:27–29.

81. Wang Tao, *Taoyuan wenlu waibian*, 1:28.

82. *Shengshi weiyan* [Warnings to a prosperous age], in Xia Dongyuan, ed., *Zheng Guanying ji* [Collected writings of Zheng Guanyin] (Shanghai: Shanghai renmin chubanshe, 1982).

83. Xia, *Zheng Guanying ji*, 422.

84. Huang Zunxian, *Riben guozhi* [National history of Japan] (Shanghai: Tushu jicheng yinshujü, 1898), 210; Yen-p'ing Hao and Erh-min Wang, "Changing Chinese Views of Western Relations," 11:142–201.

85. Zhongguo jindai jingjishi ziliao congkan bianji weiyuanhui, ed., *Xinchou heyue dingli yihou de shangyue tanpan*, 13. Also see Wang Ermin and Chen Shanwei, *Qingmo yiding zhongwai shangyue jiaoshe*; Wang Ermin, *Wangqing shangyue waijiao*, part 2, chapter 1.

86. *Waijiaobao*, published in Shanghai, edited by Zhang Yuanji, was in circulation 1902–1911. See Wang Huilin, and Zhu Hanguo, eds., *Zhongguo baokan cidian (1815–1949)* [Dictionary of Chinese newspapers and periodicals] (Taiyuan: Shuhai chubanshe, 1992), 19.

87. Editorial, "Lun Zhongying shangyue," [On the Sino-British commercial treaty] *Waijiaobao*, "Lunshuo," issue 23, 1902 (dates unknown). See *Waijiaobao huibian* [Collected documents of the *Waijiaobao*], reprint of the 1914 *Waijiaobao* collection issued 1901–1910 (Taibei: Guangwen shujü, 1964), 1:163–64.

88. *Waijiaobao huibian* [Collected documents of the *Waijiaobao*], reprint of the 1914 *Waijiaobao* collection issued 1901–1910 (Taibei: Guangwen shujü, 1964), 1:163–64.

89. Shao Yi, "Lun gaiding tongshang tiaoyue yü Zhongguo qiantu zhi guanxi" [On the relationship between commercial treaty revisions and China's future]. See *Waijiaobao huibian*, 2:410.

90. *Waijiaobao huibian*, 2:404.

2

Implementing and Contesting International Law: The Unequal Treaties and the Foreign Ministry of the Beijing Government, 1912–1928

Much of the considerable literature in both English and Chinese on the history of the Unequal Treaties focuses attention on the efforts of the Beijing government (1912–1928, *Beijing zhengfu*, usually known as *Beiyang zhengfu*, or the first Republic) to revise the treaties concluded with foreign countries.[1] This chapter argues that there are two complementary aspects of this process that have so far been ignored: China's legal justification of its claims to annul the Unequal Treaties needs to be set alongside the dynamics of the day-to-day handling of foreign affairs. The pursuit of treaty adjustments at the state-to-state level must be understood against the background of the daily business of managing foreigners at the local level. Adopting such a perspective allows us to see that the Beijing government's approach to the treaty issue was partly anchored in the imperial past and partly revolved around a number of unsolved problems in international law. In other words, the Beiyang Foreign Ministry's position on so-called treaty ports imperialism[2] represented neither a drastic rupture from the established practice of fulfilling treaty obligations nor a total rejection of the role of international law in resolving international conflicts. Its simultaneous adherence to the treaty regime and attempts to challenge international law reflected the fact that the management of foreign relations in the Beijing government was concentrated in the hands of a foreign-trained elite that was very different from the inadequate leadership that marked the imperial Qing (1644–1912).

THE *TSUNGLI YAMEN, WAIWUBU,* AND *WAIJIAOBU*: AN INSTITUTIONAL CONTEXT

The *Tsungli Yamen* and *Waiwubu*

Before dealing with the management of treaty issues in the era of the Beijing government, it is necessary to place the Beiyang Foreign Ministry in its institutional context.[3] The Foreign Ministry of the Beijing government (*Waijiaobu*) had its origins in two predecessor organizations: the *Tsungli Yamen* (the Office of the General Management of Foreign Affairs, 1861–1901) and the *Waiwubu* (the Ministry of Foreign Affairs, 1901–1911)[4], which together constituted an institutional witness to China's modern experience with foreign countries.

By an imperial edict passed on January 20, 1861,[5] at the urging of Prince Gong, the Qing court agreed to create a new government department, *Zongli Geguo Shiwu Yamen* (the Office of the General Management of the Affairs of All Countries), usually known as the *Tsungli Yamen* or *Zongshu* (General Management), to deal specifically with foreign relations.[6] In the same year, the Qing regime reluctantly granted foreign legations the right of residence at Beijing. To avoid undermining the imperial "essential system" in any way, Prince Gong proceeded cautiously in selecting an appropriate location for the office of the *Tsungli Yamen*.[7] The office of the Board of Rites was crossed off the list of possible sites as the *Tsungli Yamen* lacked the status of this august institution and would damage the Board's "image" as the place where proper imperial rites and ceremonies were especially respected. The rationale was that the *Tsungli Yamen* "cannot have a standing equal to that of other government agencies, thus preserving the distinction between China and foreign countries."[8]

All the members of the *Tsungli Yamen*, who held many other posts concurrently, were temporarily deputed to this office. The most senior officials of the *Tsungli Yamen* were the *zongli dachen* (ministers of the *Tsungli Yamen*), numbering between three and twelve. Below the ministers were the *zhangjing*, or secretaries, who were drafted from other administrative bodies. For the forty years of the *Tsungli Yamen*'s existence, the lack of a clear division of labor in the department, the shirking of responsibilities, and the department's ignorance of the outside world and of foreign languages became a target of criticism for foreigners in China.[9]

In 1901, the foreign powers were at last able to bring about a long-awaited "reform" of the *Tsungli Yamen* in the Boxer Protocol of September 7, 1901. Article 12 of the Protocol firmly established the prestigious status of the Ministry of Foreign Affairs for the following half century:

> An Imperial Edict of the 24th of July, 1901 (Annex No. 18) reformed the Office of Foreign Affairs (Tsungli Yamen) on the lines indicated by the Powers, that is to say, transformed it into a Ministry of Foreign Affairs (Wai-wu Pu [original English text]), which takes precedence over the six other Ministries of State.[10]

Yi Kuang, Prince Qing, was designated as president of the Ministry of Foreign Affairs, becoming known as the *zongli qinwang* (minister and prince). The other major officials, in order of rank, were *huiban dachen* (assistant president), *huiban dachen jian shangshu* (assistant president and secretary), *zuo silang*, and *you silang* (senior and junior councillor, respectively).[11] The routine business of the Ministry was managed by four departments (*si*), one chancery (*ting*), and five divisions (*chu*), each dealing with one of the major foreign powers. In contrast with the previous messy division of duties in the *Tsungli Yamen*, the four departments—Protocol, Technical Affairs, Commerce and Finance, and General Affairs—were apparently set up according to the nature of the tasks they had to perform, tasks which were fairly narrowly defined. The five divisions—relating to Russia, Germany, France, Britain, and Japan—remained substantially the same as the original four sections of the *Tsungli Yamen*. With regard to the professional background of the staff, according to Cao Rulin, up until 1907 the majority had qualified in the traditional civil service exams but lacked any knowledge of foreign languages.[12]

The formalization and relative rationality of its constituent parts gave the Ministry of Foreign Affairs some resemblance to its European counterparts. Nonetheless, it would be a mistake to assume that this reform, driven by pressure from the Western powers, was a total success. Prince Qing, the president of the Ministry, visited his office only once a year as his duties as prime minister took most of his time. And the assistant president, Na Tong, spent only an hour a week working in the Ministry.[13]

In 1907, the appointment of Yuan Shikai as assistant president in some respects changed the lethargic practices of the Ministry.[14] Yuan was the first senior official actively to take charge of foreign affairs. Highly respected by the foreign legations, especially Sir John Jordan (the British minister to Beijing), as a progressive, realistic, and skillful politician, Yuan both introduced and promoted into the Ministry of Foreign Affairs a number of young men educated in Japan and America, including Tang Shaoyi, Zhou Ziqi, Sao-ke Alfred Sze, W. W. Yen, Wellington Koo, Liang Dunyang, and Wei Chenzu. Yaun's pragmatic decision to recruit this group of foreign-educated staff to the Ministry proved most useful to the leaders of the Beijing government after his death in 1916.

The Composition of the *Waijiaobu* (The Foreign Ministry) and Its Place in the Beijing Government (1912–1928)

The Revolution of 1911 and the birth of a constitutional government in Beijing ended the last Chinese imperial dynasty, the Qing, and put China on a new path to an experiment in democracy.[15] In the course of the sixteen years of its life, the Beijing government produced seven heads of state and forty-six cabinets that coexisted with different political factions, as well as with the National Party (GMD) government in Guangzhou.[16] As the sole government in China to be recognized by the foreign powers, the Beijing government had a unique position of legitimacy. Preceded by the Qing, and followed by a Nationalist government controlled by a single party (1928–1949), the Foreign Ministry of the Beijing government provided the structural prototype for its successors, including that established by the People's Republic of China (1949–present).

Scholars commonly characterize the Beijing government as a "phantom republic" or "comic theater."[17] Nonetheless, below the surface, we can discern some consistent patterns or characteristics that were working against this stereotype. For instance, despite the instability produced by forty-six successive cabinets, the top post in the Foreign Ministry was monopolized by five professionals who had been working in foreign relations for most of their adult lives. Lu Zhengxiang (1871–1949) served as foreign minister fourteen times in total, W. W. Yen (1876–1950) five times, Wellington Koo (1888–1986) eight times, C. T. Wang (1882–1961) five times, and Sao-ke Alfred Sze (1876–1958) twice.[18]

A further pattern of political consistency can be discerned in the recruitment of young, foreign-educated graduates. In the forty-six cabinets of the Beijing government, the percentage of foreign-trained members was high, ranging from 79.5 percent to 46.8 percent during the years 1912–1921.[19] As for the Foreign Ministry, of the fourteen men who held the post of foreign minister, nine had received their education in America, Britain, Japan, or Germany, one (Lu) had received both foreign and Chinese training in China's traditional and new-style schools, and the three classically educated incumbents—Sun Baoqi, Hu Weide, and Wang Daxie—all had served in the foreign affairs office of the Qing government, as well as on consular service overseas in their early days.[20] Skillfully implementing their shared ideas on foreign policy, these diplomats came to be known to both foreigners and Chinese as the "young China group" or "the foreign-affairs clique," labels with positive connotations for all parties.[21] Led by Koo, Sze, Yen, and Wang, they garnered high praise from their contemporaries and later historians alike as "the most successful civilian leaders in China . . . they were able to achieve results completely out of proportion to the power of China."[22]

A third major factor was the mystique that surrounded the foreign ministry elite. With their overseas experience and their knowledge of foreign languages they gave a professional stamp to the Ministry, and won for it a reputation as a specialized and competent technocratic organization.

Despite his frail health, Lu Zhengxiang was appointed the first foreign minister in the first elected Republican cabinet under Tang Shaoyi. Educated in the Shanghai Language School and the *Tongwenguan*,[23] Lu had spent almost two decades overseas from his first appointment to St. Petersburg as an interpreter in 1890 to his recall to take up the post as foreign minister in 1912. His other important posts under the Qing had included secretary to the Chinese Legation in Russia (1895), delegate to the Hague Conference (1899), Minister to the Netherlands (1905), delegate to the second Hague Conference

(1907), and minister to Russia (1911).[24] In the politically unstable years 1912–1921, he held the post of foreign minister in fourteen out of twenty cabinets. In 1919, as foreign minster, Lu led the Chinese delegation at the Paris Peace Conference (discussed below). In 1922, he was appointed minister to Switzerland, where he lived a leisured and quiet life until the death of his Belgian wife in 1926. Soon after, he entered the monastery of St. André in Bruges, Belgium, and remained there for the rest of his life.

In concert with Vice Minister W. W. Yen, Lu made strenuous efforts to put the Foreign Ministry "on a basis much like the foreign ministry of any Western nation,"[25] with its scope and activities codified in a whole set of new laws and regulations. According to the organizational structure of the Foreign Ministry promulgated on October 8, 1912, the Foreign Ministry was to operate under a single responsible minister assisted by a vice minister and was to be divided into four departments: General Affairs, Political Affairs, Commercial Affairs, and Protocol.[26] Directly responsible to the minister and vice minister, four secretaries and four councillors were charged with law enforcement as well as treaty issues.[27]

Lu also took the initiative to regularize, formalize, and publicize the procedure for selecting foreign service officials. As a result, on September 30, 1915, Regulations Governing the Diplomatic and Consular Service Examinations were implemented.[28] On January 27, 1916, the Beijing government promulgated the Ordinance on the Diplomatic Consular Examinations, and in June the first examination was held in Beijing. Three years later, government statute No. 9, the Ordinance on the Diplomatic and Consular Examinations, was put into effect, modifying the original government regulations of 1915. The basic prescription for the foreign service entry examinations remained consistent over the years of the Beijing governments.[29] The No. 2 Chinese Historical Archives in Nanjing have preserved some candidates' resumes and examination answers.[30]

In contrast to Lu, the four other leading members of the foreign ministry group, Sao-ke Alfred Sze, W. W. Yen, Wellington Koo, and C. T. Wang, all possessed degrees from American universities. These exceptional individuals served in the diplomatic service for almost the entire life of the Beijing government and the Nationalist government in Nanjing (1928–1949) which succeeded it.[31] Sze graduated from St. John's University, an American missionary school in Shanghai, under the presidency of Dr. Hawks Pott. In 1892, at the age of sixteen, Sze was attached to Yang Ru, the Qing government's minister plenipotentiary to the U.S., Spain, and Peru, as a student interpreter.[32] In 1897, after his resignation from the legation, Sze enrolled as a student at Cornell University, where he received his B.A. in 1901 and M.A. in literature in 1902. As minister plenipotentiary to Great Britain, he was appointed senior delegate to the Paris Peace Conference in 1919, where China (or, more accurately, the Beijing government) requested that Japan return to China the territory it had occupied in Shandong

Province (which previous to the Japanese occupation had been leased to the Germans). In 1921, Sze transferred to Washington as minister plenipotentiary, and later headed the Chinese delegation of 120 members at the Washington Conference where he put forward the famous "ten-point program," which included the restoration of tariff, jurisdictional, and administrative rights to China. When the Chinese Legation became an embassy in 1933, he was appointed the first ambassador to the U.S., a post which he held until his retirement in 1937.

Like Sze, W. W. Yen was also a returned student.[33] After earning a B.A. in liberal arts and law in 1900 from the University of Virginia, Yen returned to China and taught English at St. John's University in Shanghai for six years before beginning his career as a diplomat. As China's envoy to Denmark, he represented China at the Paris Peace Conference and repeatedly held the posts of both prime minister and foreign minister in the Beijing government. A patriotic statesman, Yen was one of the main negotiators at the Beijing Special Tariff Conference where a determined effort was made to realize China's long-time aspirations for tariff autonomy. During the Manchurian crisis of 1931, he headed the Chinese delegation at the League of Nations in Geneva. Later he was appointed China's first Ambassador to Moscow.

Among the diplomats of the Beijing government, Wellington Koo's skills and charisma made him stand out.[34] He studied at Columbia University and received his M.A. in 1909 and Ph.D. in political science and international law in 1912 under the direction of John Bassett Moore (1860–1947), an eminent American jurist specializing in international law. Koo enjoyed great favor with successive governments. In 1915, three years after beginning a career in the Foreign Ministry and at the age of twenty-seven, he was promoted to the position of minister to the U.S. After World War I, he was a leading member of the Chinese delegation to the Paris Conference. In the aftermath of the Mukden Incident of 1931, as Minister to Paris, Koo represented China on the Lytton Commission of Inquiry and later at the League of Nations in Geneva, where he demanded support for China against Japan's invasion of Manchuria. During 1943, as Chinese ambassador to the Court of St. James, Koo negotiated two significant treaties with Britain and the U.S. over the relinquishment of extraterritoriality. After retirement from his post as the Nationalist government's ambassador to Washington in 1956, Koo was elected as one of the judges of the International Court of Justice at the Hague, a position which he held until 1966.

Like the other three diplomats who first served the "legitimate" Beijing government and then shifted their allegiance to the Nationalist government with the former's collapse in 1928, C. T. Wang's political inclinations fluctuated. He represented the Nationalist Guangzhou government on the Chinese delegation at the Paris Peace Conference and later served in the Beijing government. Wang received his early education at the Anglo-Chinese missionary school in Shanghai under Walter Moule.[35] Later, he went to Yale University, where he studied liberal arts, and received his B.A. in 1910. After a year of graduate study, he returned to China with an appointment as secretary of the YMCA in Shanghai. After returning briefly to the U.S. as a member of the Chinese delegation at the Washington Conference, he headed the Shandong Rehabilitation Commission dealing with the transfer from Japan of the Jiaoji Railway and the leased territory—arrangements negotiated through the Washington Conference. As the Beijing government's minister of foreign affairs in the early 1920s, he handled Sino-Soviet relations and was appointed as chief delegate to the Beijing Special Tariff Conference. From June 1928 to September 1931, as foreign minister of the Nationalist government, he negotiated and signed more than forty treaties and agreements on tariff autonomy and the relinquishment of extraterritoriality.

The internationalism, pragmatism, party neutrality, and wealth of these Beiyang diplomats, as well as their close ties with "boorish" militarists, not only redefined the image of Chinese diplomacy at the time but have also captured the contemporary Chinese imagination. Chinese fascination with the so-called *Waijiao Xi* (the Clique of Diplomacy),[36] in particular with Wellington Koo, C. T. Wang, W. W. Yen, and Lu Zhengxiang, is striking. The wealth of publications on this group that has appeared in recent years reflects current Chinese interest in the Foreign Ministry elites in relation to contemporary diplomacy.[37] These patriotic first Republican diplomats have come to represent the model for Chinese who are searching for more rapid and effective ways to allow China to conform to international standards.

NARRATIVES OF THE TREATIES: THE FOREIGN MINISTRY (*WAIJIAOBU*) AND THE UNEQUAL TREATIES

In this part of the study, I examine the ways in which the Unequal Treaties were perceived by the Foreign Ministry of the Beijing government.[38] Their discourse on the treaties embodied, to some degree, the inheritance of the cooperative strategy adopted by the Qing, as well as their keen interest in the phenomenon known as the study of the Unequal Treaties (*bupingdeng tiaoyue xue*). During the first quarter of the twentieth century, the study of the treaties gathered momentum in China. Two elements were given special emphasis in the reexamination of treaties: the specific provisions stipulated in a given treaty and the circumstances around its signing. The other important factor was the use of the treaties by first Republican officials to put pressure on foreign countries to carry out their treaty obligations. This in its turn created the conditions for a well-argued resistance to foreign demands.

From the legal perspective, the negotiations that surrounded the Unequal Treaties were bidimensional. On the one hand, the Foreign Ministry of the first Republic took a hard line on implementing treaty provisions in its resistance to excessive foreign demands. On the other hand, the corps d'elite diplomats consistently challenged the standard interpretation of international law by arguing that imposed treaties were invalid.

Sources of Authority: The Foreign Ministry and Its Local Diplomatic Organs

While pursuing the adjustment of the treaty system in international forums, the Foreign Ministry also had to deal with the various agencies responsible for the implementation of treaty obligations and rights at the local level. A closer look at the working relationship between the Foreign Ministry and these local agencies provides an opportunity for examining how these treaty obligations and rights were actually implemented at the local level, a topic rarely discussed by historians in any detail.

As a result of the traditional rule of *junzi wu waijiao* (no diplomacy for unauthorized subjects), the management of foreign relations at the local level had historically consisted in the practice of avoidance: one simply did not deal with foreigners. At the inception of Sino-foreign relations during the Qing dynasty in the mid-nineteenth century, local officials, haunted by a lingering fear of all matters foreign, were inclined to adopt this practice and simply "pass the buck." In consequence, diplomatic power rested with one or two imperial commissioners who also held the concurrent position of governor of Guangdong and Guangxi—powerful figures like Qi Ying, Xü Guangjin, and Ye Mingchen, discussed in chapter 1.

Given the increase in the number of treaty ports, on January 31, 1861,[39] Prince Gong proposed the creation of two new positions of *nanbeiyang tongshang dachen* to manage foreign affairs on a multi-provincial level in north and south China, respectively.[40] These two imperial commerce commissioners were again concurrent appointments, normally held respectively by the governor of Zhili based in Tianjin and the governor or governor-general of Liangjiang/Jiang Su in Shanghai. Chong Hou and Xue Huan gained the first two appointments to these posts, while Li Hongzhang proved the most powerful *beiyang dachen*. Technically, the *nanbeiyang dachen* were supposed to function as branch offices of the *Tsongli Yamen*. In reality, this decentralized system based on concurrent appointments increased the power of provincial governors in foreign relations. The apex of this development was the event known as the Independence of Southeast China. In 1900, when the Boxer Movement broke out into open rebellion, the Qing governors in south China—Zhang Zhidong, Liu Kunyi, and Li Hongzhang—took concerted action to negotiate with the foreign powers directly in order to maintain peace and protect the lives of foreigners in southeast China.[41]

In 1910, an Office of Negotiations—or *Jiaoshe Si*—headed by an official known as *jiaoshe shi* became the Foreign Ministry's designated organ at the provincial level. It was directly controlled by the Foreign Ministry.[42] This development was a big step toward centralization and standardization of the management of foreign affairs at the provincial level.

After the founding of the Republic of China in 1912, this effort continued. In 1913, the local handling of foreign matters was brought within the jurisdiction of *Jiaoshe Shu* (Bureau of Negotiations), led by *jiaoshe yuan* (commissioner of negotiations), *jiaoshe zhuanyuan* (special commissioner of negotiations) and *tepai yuan* (special commissioner). The Bureau of Negotiations had local stations in the provinces and ports and was directly subordinate to the Foreign Ministry.[43] In each provincial capital there was a *tepai jiaoshe zhuanyuan* (special commissioner of negotiations), and each port had a *jiaoshe yuan*. The structure of the Bureau of Negotiations was parallel to that of the central government. Under the special commissioner of negotiations were the bureau secretary and divisions such as General Office, Office of Commercial Affairs, Protocol, and Office of Political Affairs.[44] The new system strengthened the Foreign Ministry's guiding role in diplomatic matters in relation to local governments. In the politically unstable first Republic, the conduct of diplomacy was more centralized than is commonly assumed.

From the founding of the first Republic in 1912, a group known as the Association for Treaty Studies, set up under the aegis of the Foreign Ministry, held a biweekly seminar to evaluate treaty-related problems reported by local provinces, diplomatic commissioners, and agencies. The more than a dozen available reports submitted by the Treaty Studies Association offer an accurate reflection of the nature of "treaty studies," as well as the inner workings of the Foreign Ministry.[45] First, in the light of lessons learned from past experience, there was a clear emphasis on interpreting treaties and enforcing their provisions in the most precise and narrow sense. In response to a request from its Shanghai agency, the Treaty Studies Association contemplated a case in which British subjects in Baoshan (Shanghai) refused to comply with local regulations to apply for a license for new building construction. The Association debated whether extraterritoriality or local regulations should be applied in such a case. In the end, it offered the following justification for overruling the British action:

> The interpretation of treaties is an entirely different matter from the interpretation of laws because it cannot be simply confined to language itself. It is imperative to take account of both the circumstances of the treaty signing and the intention of the treaty signatories. In addition, in cases where national sovereignty is in jeopardy, interpretations must be given in the most strict and narrow way possible. This is the norm observed in international law.[46]

The Association's reports pointed out that ambiguity had been a problem in all the treaties that China had signed with foreign countries. By contrast, accuracy and precision had always been painstakingly pursued in treaty negotiations concluded by foreign countries among themselves.[47]

As noted above, interpreting and implementing treaties in the unstable political climate of the first Republic was a much more centralized business than is commonly assumed. Diplomatic authority was, to a much greater extent than in the Qing period, vested in the Foreign Ministry. This is demonstrated in the concrete guidance and advice given by the Foreign Ministry to local administrations and diplomatic commissioners on diplomatic matters. In their concluding remarks on the case discussed above, the Association for Treaty Studies recommended that "the Shanghai diplomatic commissioner ought to use this report [by the Association] to expose Britain's wrongdoing."[48] Appraising a different case in which the governor of Anhui had approved tax exemptions for Japanese rice merchants without consulting the central authority, the Association was trenchantly critical: "Was the Governor of Anhui ever authorized to issue this tax exemption permit? This is a blatant transgression of power."[49]

Such local cases were also regularly published in *Waijiao gongbao*, a journal which appeared from 1921 to 1928 and was compiled and edited by the Foreign Ministry. Its first issue reported details of a case brought against a Chinese Catholic named Xü Jixing in Baihe County, Shaanxi Province, who was allegedly involved in kidnapping. In its communications with the governor of Shaanxi Province, the Foreign Ministry instructed that everyone, regardless of his or her religious beliefs, should obey the law and that the church could have no role in sentencing. Given the conflicting allegations made by the Catholic and non-Catholic parties to the case, the Foreign Ministry simply advised local officials to proceed with the investigation on the basis of existing treaties.[50]

Another case reported in *Waijiao gongbao*, this time from Xiakou County, Hubei Province, involved the rights of legal representation for foreign plaintiffs in a preliminary trial. In 1924, Hubei Province's special commissioner of negotiations questioned whether foreign attorneys should be permitted at the hearings held by the Bureau of Negotiations in Xiakou County. In the words of the special commissioner, this situation involved "important questions of national sovereignty." In response, the Foreign Ministry instructed that while no foreign lawyers would be allowed to appear on such an occasion, precedent permitted the presence of a foreign agent.[51]

In 1926, a mixed case in the jurisdiction of the Yantai *Jiaoshe Shu* (Bureau of Negotiations in Yantai, Shandong) involved an American merchant who brought a suit against three Chinese merchants for outstanding debts. The facts of the case were as follows: Chinese merchant A had approached the American to borrow a certain amount of money on the security of Chinese B's property, with Chinese C as guarantor. Later A and C could not pay off the arrears and C went into hiding, leaving B held accountable. The Bureau of Negotiations inquired about the procedure followed in the second trial, which took place after a preliminary court hearing presided over by the county magistrate.

The Foreign Ministry's inquiry into the case focused on three main questions. First, the Bureau asked whether it was allowed to summon witnesses and hold hearings if it had doubts about the documents submitted to the court. Second, at the preliminary hearing, a Chinese agent representing the American merchant had made a declaration to the effect that the plaintiff would relinquish his right to request a consular assessor in the mixed court.[52] Accordingly, the magistrate did not invite the American consul to observe the trial. The Bureau of Negotiations was undecided whether foreign consuls should be present at court hearings initiated by it. Third, if (as he claimed) the American merchant did not recognize the verdict of the county court on the pretext that he had not been notified of the case beforehand, should the Bureau accept such a claim? On May 13, 1926, the Foreign Ministry replied that the Yantai Bureau of Negotiations was entitled to hold hearings if necessary. As to the last two questions, the Foreign Ministry advised that, even if the American consul demured, the Bureau should still do what it felt was needed.[53]

This case provides some insight into the relationship between the central and local levels in the management of foreign affairs under the Beijing government. Through the specialized knowledge gained from its practice of continuously examining and interpreting existing treaties—knowledge channeled to the regions through its local agency, the Bureau of Negotiations—the Foreign Ministry became the source of authority on all questions relating to the treatment of foreign nationals. The principles of *Zhaoyue* (go by the treaties) and *Shouyue* (stick to the treaties) that the Foreign Ministry followed in carrying out its bilateral obligations at the local level presented a marked contrast to its contemporaneous state-to-state initiatives.

Contesting International Law

In this section, the focus shifts to the ways in which the Foreign Ministry of the Beijing government dealt with treaty issues at the level of state-to-state relationships. The Chinese desire to remove extraterritoriality and gain tariff autonomy at the end of the nineteenth century has been discussed at length in chapter 1. In the first twenty years of the twentieth century, these goals continued to be expressed in diplomatic negotiations with increasing frequency but with a significant shift of emphasis.

One of the earliest systematic discussions by a Chinese on foreign rights and treaties in China was Wellington Koo's Ph.D. dissertation, *The Status of Aliens in China*. In his thesis, Koo described and analyzed the origins and formulation of the many different kinds of right—of residency, trade, travel, preaching, and extraterritorial jurisdiction—that foreigners in China had been granted.[54] Adopting a legal perspective, Koo pointed out that the Treaty of Nanjing "confers for the first time a definite status on the alien in China."[55] He also remarked on the injustice done to China and the inequality imposed on China through the treaties: "Foreigners in China enjoyed very many rights and privileges which are not accorded to aliens in other countries."[56] To Koo, the reasonableness of reciprocal practices in relations between nations was obvious:

> Mutual forbearance and reciprocal concession are no less the best policy in the intercourse between nations than in the relations between individuals; and history has shown that few international questions of an important character have been peacefully settled without observing these apparently commonplace principles.[57]

The notion of international equality and ways for China to achieve it were also keenly canvassed in diplomatic circles. The recruitment examinations for the diplomatic and consular services set by the Foreign Ministry included questions on how the nation should prepare for the abolition of consular jurisdiction. Mooting the question of extraterritoriality in an examination held immediately after World War I, Xü Mo, a candidate who scored a remarkable 95 percent, considered that "consular jurisdiction in China is an anomaly, an exception from international law. It is nothing more than a derogation [of] the [s]overeign rights of China. It is a stain on the civilization of four hundred million people."[58] In Xü's opinion, there were two interrelated ways to "cancel" or "revise" the existing "unequal treaties" (original English text): judicial reform—the drafting and promulgation of civil and commercial codes as well as other important laws—and diplomatic measures necessary "to present our case to the foreign governments or to the League of Nations, if it has then come into existence."[59] In his answer, Xü also alluded to the implications of the Great War for China: "Now the Great War—a war fought for liberty and equality of individuals as well as nations—is over. China . . . is a victor at present, and should therefore be accepted as an equal sister of the Family of Nations."[60] Xü later entered the foreign service and was posted to the Chinese embassy in the U.S.[61]

The Foreign Ministry's legal justification for its multilayered approach to the treaty issue has long been an unsolved problem of legal and political history. In his dissertation, "The Age of Innocence: The First World War and China's Quest for National Identity," Xü Guoqi sees World War I as a watershed for China because "it was the first time that China took major initiatives to participate in world affairs in order to serve its three main purposes: to get back Shandong, to recover the sovereignty it had lost since the Opium War and to join the world as an equal member."[62] According to Xü, this new type of diplomacy represented "China's search for a new national identity, its hope to join the world system, and China's departure from its tradition and self-imposed isolation and all that isolation implied."[63] Xü holds that China's participation in World War I on the side of the Allies was motivated by its legitimate goals of checkmating Japan by forging an alliance with the

U.S., Britain, and France, attending the postwar peace conference, and joining the international system.[64]

After Japan forced China to accept the Twenty-one Demands,[65] in Xü's words, "the Waijiaobu resolved in early 1915 to make membership in the postwar peace conference as a top priority issue."[66] An alternative view is offered by Frederick Dickinson who treats the Japanese démarche in World War I as the product of domestic political conflict primarily between foreign minister Katō Takaaki and elder statesman (genrō) Yamagata Aritomo. Dickinson argues that Japanese foreign policy-making reflected competing versions of national identity in the Japanese context. Japan's disappointment at the outcome of the Paris Peace Conference mirrored a clash between different outlooks on world politics, that is, between Wilsonianism and the Old Power Diplomacy, which Japan had been trying to emulate in Asia.[67] As a part of his argument, Dickinson rejects the conventional view of the Twenty-one Demands as exceptionally harsh to China, maintaining that they represented nothing new or even "particularly harmful" when compared with all the privileges and rights already enjoyed by other powers in China.[68]

The legal challenges mounted by the Foreign Ministry to the "standard" interpretation of the treaties as a source of international law, however, receive no attention in the otherwise admirable studies by Xü and Dickinson. In formulating its challenges, the Beijing government had recourse to the concept of the invalidity of forced treaties and the doctrine of *rebus sic stantibus* which had not been a generally accepted principle of international law. In fact, contemporary specialists in international law are inclined to greatly limit the application of *rebus sic stantibus*.[69] To make sense of this question, we must turn to the wider development of the issues of treaties signed under duress and *rebus sic stantibus* in international law.

Any contemporary discussion of treaties as a source of international law must start with the 1969 Vienna Convention on the Law of Treaties. The commentary on the Convention drafted by the International Law Commission provides a guide to the provenance of the articles as well as to their interpretation.[70] The legal grounds for considering a treaty invalid are set out in Article 52: "A treaty is void if its conclusion has been procured by the threat or use of force in violation of the principles of international law embodied in the Charter of the United Nations."[71] However, there has been no consensus about the meaning of "force" and "threat." Some parties argue that the coercion of a state by force can be political, economic, or military in character. Furthermore, the Convention has limited use since it only applies to treaties made after it came into force on January 27, 1980.[72] In relation to contemporary rules against the use of force in international relations, the standard interpretation of Article 52 is that "if a treaty was procured by force at a time when force was not illegal, the validity of the treaty is not affected by subsequent changes in the law which declares that force is illegal and that treaties procured by force are void."[73] However, the legality of treaties procured by the threat or use of force against one of the parties has remained equivocal in international law. According to Mark Janis, the doctrine of international law

> has considerable difficulty in accounting for the unilateral termination of treaties, although as a matter of practice treaties are regularly denounced by states unilaterally. Typically, unilateral denunciations are justified by an appeal to changed circumstances; that is, the legal concept of *rebus sic stantibus* is implicitly incorporated by the denouncing state into the international agreement.[74]

The doctrine of *rebus sic stantibus* literally means "things remaining as they are." In other words, "every treaty contained an implied term that it should remain in force only as long as circumstances remained the same (*rebus sic stantibus*) as at the time of conclusion."[75] Its operation "rests on the assumption that a treaty may be denounced if circumstances change profoundly from the ones prevailing at the time of the treaty's conclusion."[76] In practice, given the difficulty of establishing an argument of changed circumstances acceptable to the other parties involved, the legal status and value of *rebus sic stantibus* has been controversial in international law.[77] The modern consensus has been that the rule of the change in fundamental circumstances "applies only in the most exceptional circumstances; otherwise it could be used as an excuse to evade all sorts of inconvenient treaty obligations."[78] As Hans Kelsen noted in 1952, "no international tribunal has, until now, unreservedly confirmed the existence of this rule [*rebus sic stantibus*]."[79] Although the term *rebus sic stantibus* was not adopted in the 1969 Vienna Convention on the Law of Treaties, the concept of "a fundamental change of circumstances" was substantiated in Article 62.

Armed with the legally ambivalent concepts of the Unequal Treaties and *rebus sic stantibus*, the Foreign Ministry contested accepted interpretations of international law at the Paris Peace Conference. With the end of World War I in 1918, China—as represented by the Beijing government, the only governmental authority recognized by foreign powers—was invited to participate in the conference as one of the victors. As head of the Chinese delegation, Lu Zhengxiang, minister of foreign affairs, appointed a number of diplomats to attend the Peace Conference, including Wellington Koo, minister to the U.S.; Sao-ke Alfred Sze, minister to London; Wei Chenzu, minister to Brussels; and W. W. Yen, minister to Germany (transferred to Denmark following the suspension of diplomatic relations with Germany). To preserve the facade of national unity, Lu also invited C. T. Wang—the Guangzhou Nationalist government's representative in the U.S.—Wu Chaoshu—vice minister of foreign affairs in the Guangzhou regime—and Chen Youren to join the delegation on behalf of the southern government.[80]

The Chinese representatives at the Paris Peace Conference emphasized two major issues.[81] First and foremost was the Shandong question: China demanded the restoration of Germany's leased territory and rights in Shandong province in eastern China.[82] In addition, China requested the termination of the treaties and agreements that had allowed Japan to acquire all of Germany's former privileges in Shandong.[83] Second, the so-called Questions for Readjustment (also known as the Seven Aspirations) were submitted by China to the conference.[84] The seven questions included the renunciation of "spheres of influence" in China, the withdrawal of foreign troops and police, and of foreign post and telegraph offices, the abolition of consular jurisdiction, the relinquishment of leased territories, and the restitution of tariff autonomy.[85]

Applying principles of international law, the Chinese team led by Lu, Koo, Sze, Wang, and Yen underscored the unreasonable and inconsistent elements making for partiality and injustice in each of these cases to justify China's grievance. For instance, the multiplicity of national laws in effect in China caused not only controversy but also inequality of treatment and sentencing. Under this treaty right, claims made against English nationals would be heard in the English courts, those against Americans in the American courts, and so forth. Different laws embodied differing standards and interpretations of what constituted an offense, often producing markedly divergent court decisions in the same legal case.

The Chinese delegates noted that extraterritoriality "is not and was not based upon any principle of International Law, but was merely created by the Treaties."[86] They considered it unfair that, under the most-favored-nation clause, "any one Power is entitled to claim whatever rights or privileges are granted to another Power, but in return China receives no reciprocal treatment." Hence, the Chinese argued, nonreciprocity violated international law in which "tariff concessions are always made on a mutual and compensatory basis."[87] The treaties were characterized as obstructions on an international scale to the "free development" of China. Citing the major developed countries as points of reference, the Chinese delegation in their "Questions for Readjustment" argued that the uniform 5 percent ad valorem tariff was harmful to China's revenue and economy.[88] Under this tariff regime, all goods ranging from luxuries to necessities were taxed at the same rate, an arrangement contrary to the general practice in force among the community of nations.

At the same time, the Chinese delegates stressed China's willingness to cooperate with the treaty powers over the reestablishment of relations on the condition that any concessions granted through negotiations must be mutual. In all the major documents submitted by China to the Paris Conference, the theme of China's willingness to conform to international norms and fulfill its international obligations was prominent. The delegates' memorandum on "Abolition of Consular Jurisdiction," for example, based its call for the abolition of extraterritoriality on the improvement of the legal system in China.

On June 28, 1919, the Peace Treaty was signed at Versailles by all the negotiating countries with the single exception of China, which protested against the arbitrary settlement of the Shandong question. Japan succeeded in getting approval for all its claims to Shandong on the basis of a number of secret agreements, the Twenty-one Demands of 1915, and the exchange of notes between China and Japan in September 1918. Although the Questions for Readjustment were deemed important, they were considered to be beyond of the scope of the conference.

China's case was brought up again at the Washington Conference of 1921–1922. Adopting an approach similar to that taken at the Paris Conference, the Chinese representatives Sze, Koo, and Wang Chonghui described the old treaty regime (*jiuyue*) as unjust, imposed by the strong upon the weak. On November 21, 1921, at the first meeting of the Conference's Pacific and Far East Committee, Sze, on behalf of the Chinese delegation, presented a statement proposing ten general principles to be followed in determining questions regarding China. These included respect for the territorial integrity of China; the removal of existing limitations on China's political, jurisdictional, and administrative freedom of action; application of the Open Door Policy to the whole of China; and the establishment of procedures for the peaceful settlement of international disputes in the Pacific and Far East regions.[89] Koo argued that "the existing treaty provisions, by which the levy of customs duties, transit dues, and other imposts are regulated, constitute not only a restriction on China's freedom of action but an infringement of her sovereignty."[90] On the other hand, the Chinese representatives offered to make the removal of the existing treaty regime conditional on a quid pro quo that promised political stability and juridical reform.[91]

Although emphasizing the treaties as obstacles to China's development, the documents submitted to the Paris and Washington conferences echoed the muted observations of earlier Qing officials. Following in the footsteps of these nineteenth-century scholar-bureaucrats, the first Republican Foreign Ministry's approach to the controversial treaty issues was moderate in both tone and substance. One point, nonetheless, should be made here: the Beijing government's professional diplomats were the first to make a provocative case against international treaties signed under duress. Up until this point, unequal treaties had been an understudied branch of international law. International jurist Albert H. Putney pointed out the deficiencies of the existing laws in 1927:

> Whatever kind of unequal treaty we refer to, I do not think that there is any principle of international law, or that any such view has ever been laid down, that on account of the inequality of the treaty the party suffering under the inequality has a right to abrogate it for this reason alone, any more than a person who has made a bad bargain is allowed to rescind his contract for that reason.[92]

Putney observed that the invalidity of unequal treaties was not then "a matter of strict legal right . . . it is still a question of diplomacy, and, to a large extent, a question of force, as to what a country is able to secure."[93]

In their writings, the celebrated jurists Hugo Grotius, Samuel Pufendorf, and Emmerich de Vattel all made reference to equal and unequal treaties. In his treatise *De Jure Belli Ac Pacis Libri Tres* (1625), Grotius, the "father" of international law, categorized treaties into those concluded on either equal or unequal terms. He recognized unequal treaties with an inferior party as "arrangements imposed by command," which were either accompanied by impairment of sovereignty or concluded without such impairment. According to Grotius, "Unequal Treaties . . . are wont to be made not only between victors and vanquished . . . but also between more powerful and less powerful peoples that have not even engaged in war with each other."[94] The German scholar Pufendorf, in his *De Jure Naturae et Gentium* of 1672, defined unequal treaties as those in which "the things promised by the two parties are unequal, or when either party is made inferior to the other."[95] While the question of unequal treaties was canvassed, these early writers all noted that imposed peace treaties should be observed as a valid means to end hostilities. The same conclusion was justified by the eighteenth-century Swiss jurist Emmerich de Vattel on the grounds that "to authorize [a rule invalidating imposed treaties] would amount to an attack upon the common safety and welfare of Nations; the principle would be condemned as abhorrent by the same reasons which made the faithful observance of treaties a universally sacred duty."[96] In practice also, "the sovereignty and equality of States found little recognition in the numerous conferences which were held to regulate these affairs or in the decisions which were reached."[97]

It was China that was to prove the challenger here. At the Paris Peace Conference of 1919, China made the case against the 1915 Twenty-one Demands forced on it by Japan. For the first time in the practice of the law of nations and law of war, China invoked the principle of the inequality of treaties signed under threat as a reason for declaring such treaties legally void. What is particularly interesting, however, is the *effect* that China's proactive role had on the further development of international law in this area.

One example can be given here. At the twenty-first annual meeting of the American Society of International Law held in April 1927, the fourth session was devoted to the termination of the Unequal Treaties in China.[98] Frank E. Hinckley, then lecturer in international law at the University of California, remarked that treaties in relation to consular authority were not uncommon, and could be either very general or very detailed in their arrangements. For instance, the 1815 treaty between the U.S. and Great Britain and that between the U.S. and Japan concluded in 1911 both provided for the appointment, by each of the contracting parties, of consuls in all ports, cities, and other specified places in the other's country. Hinckley argued that, in the case of China, maintaining consular jurisdiction could be of questionable value as Chinese opposition to extraterritoriality might prove an obstacle to general consular authority. As a result, Hinckley proposed the termination of "the peculiar and really lesser provisions of the so-called unequal treaties with China" and argued that observers should "have confidence that the great and lasting desire of the Chinese people for international equality will be fruitful of equality in international practice. In that good will and practice the most useful agency will be the normal authority well established in international law."[99] In this way China's discourse of the Unequal Treaties generated new studies of an overlooked branch of international law among jurists.

In *Wilson and China: A Revised History of the Shandong Question,* Bruce Elleman discusses the controversies surrounding the Shandong Question at the Paris Peace Conference, including the myth of Wilson's betrayal of China.[100] Elleman, however, overlooks the complex legal ramifications of China's case at the Paris Conference and thus ignores the nuances and real significance of the arguments made by China against forced treaties.

The polemical campaign waged by the Foreign Ministry against the Unequal Treaties contested fundamental principles of international law by invoking the doctrine of *rebus sic stantibus.* In February 1926, Sao-ke Alfred Sze, then minister to the U.S., called for rapid action by the foreign powers to avoid aggravating "the feelings of the already justly indignant Chinese."[101] In justifying China's requests for the cancellation of the treaties, Sze elaborated the recognized grounds on which international covenants and agreements could be revoked by unilateral declaration. First, Sze argued that "all international jurists concede that the rules governing the relations between sovereign States" are primarily founded upon the right to existence—the right of a state to protect its people in the enjoyment and maintenance of their material and cultural lives. Thus inequitable treaties between states might have binding force in strictly legal terms, "but never except as a result of force, fraud or mistake, for it does not need to be said that no government will voluntarily and knowingly sign away its essential rights."[102] Secondly, Sze invoked the doctrine of *rebus sic stantibus* suggesting that although the sanctity of a treaty must be scrupulously observed, greatly altered circumstances might from time to time call for the revision or denunciation of a specific treaty. Sze insisted that China reserved the right to unilaterally declare that it no longer held itself bound by international treaties when the conditions under which those treaties had been negotiated had changed dramatically.[103]

A significant test of these principles was not long in coming. In April 1926, the Foreign Ministry requested the Belgian government to comprehensively revise its expired treaty signed with China in 1865 and conclude a new treaty based on equality and reciprocity. In reply to China's note, the Belgian government insisted on a limited revision only, contending that the 1865 treaty did not give China the right of unilateral abrogation.[104] Invoking the doctrine of *rebus sic stantibus,* Wellington Koo, who, as one foreign columnist ob-

served, "has concentrated within himself almost all the nominal power remaining to the Peking Government," moved to take action against Belgium.[105] To the alarm of the Belgian government, in November 1926 a presidential mandate was issued canceling the Belgian treaty of 1865.[106] The
Belgian government brought the case before the Permanent Court of International Justice, but later withdrew its case and entered into negotiations
with China based on the principles of equality and reciprocity.[107]

CONCLUSION

In this chapter, I have sought to contribute to the study of China's international relations in the early twentieth century in two major areas. First, I have
argued that the Foreign Ministry of the Beijing government played a crucial
role in determining the management of foreign affairs at both provincial and
county level. By upholding the "sanctity" of treaties signed between China
and foreign countries, the Foreign Ministry maneuvered within the existing
treaty system with the aim of maintaining order in the regions and resisting
excessive foreign demands. Second, besides implementing international law
at the local level, the Foreign Ministry also worked at the international level
to bolster China's legal case for revising and abolishing the Unequal Treaties
by contesting the legal status of such treaties, as well as by invoking the *rebus sic stantibus* doctrine.

However, largely as a result of the diplomatic and legal campaign
mounted by first Republican China, the rhetorical tide was turning. In 1928,
Rodney Gilbert, a staunch defender of foreign treaty rights in China, observed that "the average newspaper reader, in or out of this country, proba-
bly feels by now that such terms as 'nationalism,' 'imperialism,' 'militarism'
or 'unequal treaties,' as applied to China, require no definition or explana-
tion."[108] Averse to radical propagandists of both the Soviet and Chinese
stamps, Gilbert sensed the advent of polemics of a different type in China in
the latter half of the 1920s. The wide circulation and unquestioned acceptance of new political catchphrases including the *Unequal Treaties* reflected a
rhetoricalization of the treaty issue, a development that has played a prominent role in Chinese politics, foreign relations, and media until the present
day.

NOTES

1. Useful treatments of the subject at the level of state-to-state diplomacy are Tang Ch'i-hua,
Beiyang "xiuyue waijiao" lunwen xuanji, and Lee Enhan, *Beifa hou de "geming waijiao."* In sharp
contrast to the work in English on the structure and dynamics of China's diplomacy after 1949,
Western scholarship on diplomacy in the first Republic is notable by its absence.
For serious scholarly accounts in English of Republican diplomacy, one must go back to the

classical studies such as the following: Dorothy Borg, *American Policy and the Chinese Revolution, 1925–1928* (New York: Macmillan, 1947); Robert T. Pollard, *China's Foreign Relations, 1917–1931* (New York: Macmillan, 1933); Claude A. Buss, "The Relationship of Tariff Autonomy to the Political Situation in China" (Ph.D. dissertation, University of Pennsylvania, 1927); Claude A. Buss, *War and Diplomacy in Eastern Asia* (New York: Macmillan, 1941); Werner Levi, *Modern China's Foreign Policy* (Minneapolis: University of Minnesota Press, 1953); Willoughby, *Foreign Rights.* William Kirby laments the paucity of Western literature on Republican international diplomacy. See William Kirby, "The Internationalization of China: Foreign Relations at Home and Abroad in the Republican Era," in *Reappraising Republican China,* ed. Frederic Wakeman Jr. and Richard Louis Edmonds (Oxford: Oxford University Press, 2000), 179–204.

2. The term is used by Frederick R. Dickinson, *War and National Reinvention: Japan in the Great War, 1914–1919* (Cambridge, Mass.: Harvard University Press, 1999), 8, 86.

3. The change of regime took place when Jiang Jieshi and the Guomindang Nationalists toppled the Beijing government in 1928, inaugurating the second Republic of China, based in Nanjing, which lasted until 1949.

4. Wu Chengzhang, *Waijiaobu yange jilue* [The History of the Foreign Ministry], reprint ed. (Taibei: Wenhai chubanshe, 1913, 1987); Chen Tiqiang, *Zhongguo waijiao xingzheng* [The administration of Chinese diplomacy] (Chongqing: Commercial Press, 1943); S. M. Meng, *The Tsungli Yamen: Its Organization and Functions* (Cambridge, Mass.: Harvard University Press, 1970); Richard Steven Horowitz, "Central Power and State Making: The Zongli Yamen and Self-Strengthening in China, 1860–1880" (Ph.D. dissertation, Harvard University, 1998).

5. The tenth day of the twelfth month of the tenth year of Xianfeng.

6. Jia Z. et al., *Chouban yiwu shimo (Xianfeng chao),* 8:2691–92.

7. Jia Z. et al., *Chouban yiwu shimo (Xianfeng chao),* 8:2714–19. In the end, the old buildings housing the headquarters of the Iron Coin Bureau in Dongtangzi Alley (located to the east of the Foreign Legations Quarter) to the east of the Forbidden City were chosen and opened for use after renovation in December 1861. Wu Fuhuan, *Qingji Zongli Yamen yanjiu* [A study of the Tsungli Yamen] (Taibei: Wenjin chubanshe, 1995), 18–19. The low ranking of the *Tsungli Yamen* in the Qing government was notable: until 1890, it was omitted from the *Jinshen Lu,* the so-called Red Book intended as a comprehensive directory of the institutions and personnel of both central and provincial government. See H. S. Brunnert and V. V. Hagelstrom, *Present-Day Political Organization of China,* trans. A. Beltcheko and E. E. Morgan (Shanghai: Kelly and Walsh, 1912), 104.

8. Masakata Banno, *China and the West: The Origins of the Tsungli Yamen* (Cambridge, Mass.: Harvard University Press, 1964), 228.

9. In one imperial edict the Qing, under pressure from the American, Japanese, and Spanish ministers, recognized that those *Tsungli Yamen* ministers holding concurrent posts "have been unable to dedicate themselves entirely to their duties. Therefore, it is necessary to set up sole and distinctive posts so that each may concentrate on his specific responsibilities." Zhu, *Guangxü chao donghua lu,* 4685.

10. MacMurray, *Treaties and Agreements,* 1:284. *Xinchou geguo heyue* [The Boxer Protocol of 1901], deposited at the Harvard-Yenching Library (Beijing: Waiwubu, 1901).

11. Qian Shifu, *Qingdai de waijiao jiguan* [The diplomatic establishment of the Qing dynasty] (Beijing: Sanlian shudian, 1959), 268–91.

12. Tsao Ju-lin, *Yisheng zhi huiyi* [Memoirs of Cao Rulin] (Hong Kong: Chunqiu zazhishe, 1966), 49–50.

13. W. W. Yen, *East-West Kaleidoscope, 1877–1944: An Autobiography* (New York: St. John's University Press, 1974), 53–55.

14. In 1884, Yuan Shikai (1859–1916) became the Manchu Imperial Resident at Seoul, Korea, until his expulsion with other Chinese at the time of the Sino-Japanese War (1894–1895). In 1898, he had assisted the Empress Dowager's suppression of the One-Hundred-Day Reform sponsored by Emperor Guangxü. In 1901, he succeeded the powerful Li Hongzhang as viceroy of

Zhili, a crucial post at the time. From 1903, Yuan presided over the formation of a modern Chinese army which reinforced his position in the Qing regime. With the abdication of the Qing emperor in February 1912, he was empowered to organize a constitutional government with the consent of revolutionary leaders such as Sun Yat-sen. In March 1912, Yuan took the oath as president in Beijing and in 1913 he was formally reelected as president of the Republic of China. See Henry George W. Woodhead, *The China Year Book* (Tientsin: Tientsin Press, 1912–1931), year 1916, 562–63; Jerome Ch'en, *Yuan Shih-K'ai*, 2nd ed. (Stanford, Calif.: Stanford University Press, 1972).

15. In 1928 GMD Nationalist forces occupied Beijing and the first Chinese constitutional experiment was over.

16. The seven heads of the Beijing government were: (1) Yuan Shikai, March 1912–June 1916; (2) Li Yuanhong, June 1916–July 1917 and June 1922–June 1923; (3) Feng Guozhang, August 1917–October 1918; (4) Xü Shichang, October 1918–June 1922; (5) Cao Kun, October 1923–November 1924; (6) Duan Qirui, November 1924–April 1926; (7) Zhang Zuolin, June 1927–June 1928. See Chen Xülu et al., *Zhongguo jindaishi cidian*, 797–803; Liu Shoulin et al., eds., *Minguo zhiguan nianbiao* [Tables of Republican officials by year] (Beijing: Zhonghua shujü, 1995], 3–129; Qian Shifu, ed., *Beiyang zhengfu zhiguan nianbiao* [Tables of officials in the Beiyang government by year] (Shanghai: Huadong shifandaxue chubanshe, 1991), 3–33; Hsi-sheng Ch'i, *Warlord Politics in China, 1916–1928* (Stanford, Calif.: Stanford University Press, 1976), 247–49; H. G. W. Woodhead, *The China Year Book.*

17. Works on the constitutionality and the culture of the Beijing government include: Andrew Nathan, *Chinese Democracy: Peking Politics, 1918–1923* (New York: Alfred A. Knopf, 1985); Andrew Nathan, "A Constitutional Republic: The Peking Government, 1916–1928," in *The Cambridge History of China*, ed. John King Fairbank, vol. 12, part 2 (Cambridge: Cambridge University Press, 1983); Andrew Nathan, "Some Trends in the Historiography of Republican China," *Republican China* 17, no. 1 (Nov. 1991), 117–32; Arthur Waldron, *From War to Nationalism: China's Turning Point, 1924–1925* (Cambridge: Cambridge University Press, 1995); James E. Sheridan, *China in Disintegration: The Republican Era in Chinese History, 1912–1949* (New York: Free Press, 1975); Lucian Pye, *Warlord Politics: Conflict and Coalition in the Modernization of Republican China* (New York: Praeger, 1971); Edward McCord, *The Power of the Gun: The Emergence of Modern Chinese Warlords* (Berkeley: University of California Press, 1993); Edward McCord, "Warlordism at Bay: Civil Alternative to Military Rule in Early Republican China," *Republican China* 17, no. 1 (November 1991), 38–70.

18. Other foreign ministers of the Beijing government were: Liang Ruhao (1912.9–1913.7); Sun Baoqi (1914.2–1916.4); Cao Rulin (1916.6–1917.5); Wu Tingfang (1917.5–7); Wang Daxie (1917.7–11); Tang Shaoyi (1924.11–1925.12); Hu Weide (1926.4–5); Cai Tinggan (1926.6–10); Wang Yintai (1927.6–1928.6).

19. These figures are from Guoqi Xü, "The Age of Innocence: The First World War and China's Quest for National Identity" (Ph.D. dissertation, Harvard University, 1999), appendix, 383.

20. See "Who's Who?" in Woodhead, *The China Year Book.*

21. See Akira Iriye, *After Imperialism: The Search for a New Order in the Far East, 1921–1931,* reprint ed. (Chicago: Imprint Publications, 1990), 12; Pye, *Warlord Politics,* 151–52; Guo Jianlin et al., "Beiyang zhengfu waijiao jindaihua luelun" [A brief account of the modernization of the diplomatic corps under the Beiyang government], *Xueshu yanjiu* 3 (1991): 73–77.

22. Pye, *Warlord Politics,* 152.

23. The *Tongwenguan* (College of Universal Learning) was a school for interpreters attached to the *Tsungli Yamen.*

24. Lo Kuang, *Lu Zhengxiang zhuan* [Biography of Lu Zhengxiang] (Taibei: Commercial Press, 1926); "Who's Who?" in Woodhead, *The China Year Book* (1926), 1186–87.

25. Wellington Koo, "The Wellington Koo Memoir," microfilm, New York, Columbia University, 1978, part 2, reel 1, under "The Foreign Office at Peking: The Reorganization of 1912."

26. In July 1915, the two departments of *Waizheng* and *Shuzheng* were merged into a single department of *Zhengwu* (Political Affairs). The *Tiaoyue Si* (Department of Treaties) and *Qingbao*

Jü (Intelligence Bureau) were added in 1921 and 1927, respectively. In 1927, the *Jiaoji Si* (Protocol Department) was abolished. See Guoshiguan gongzhi bianzuan weiyuanhui, ed., *Zhonghua minguoshi gongzhi zhi(chu gao)* [Record of public officials of the Republic of China], 1st draft (Taibei: Guoshiguan, 1990), 19–21. Yinzhu jü, *Zhiyuan lu* [Personnel directory] (Beijing: Yinzhu jü, 1912–1924).

27. For the duties of each position and department, see Yinzhu jü, *Zhiyuan lu* and Woodhead, *The China Year Book* (1913), 243–44.

28. Guoshiguan, *Zhonghua minguoshi gongzhi zhi* (*chu gao*), 234–35.

29. *Waijiao gongbao* [Foreign Affairs Bulletin], vols. 73 and 75, under "Foreign Ministry Official System" in "Faling," and "Revised Order for Diplomatic Consular Examinations," 1 and 1–8 respectively. These statutes directed that anyone seeking a position in the Foreign Ministry must take both the Foreign Ministry's preliminary examinations and the Diplomatic and Consular Service examinations. Individuals holding foreign degrees or an associate Chinese degree or above in political science, economics, law or foreign languages could submit a sample of translation work along with their C.V. to the selection committee. Those candidates who qualified would then be evaluated in an oral examination. The test subjects were composition in Chinese and one foreign language, and spoken foreign language skills. Finally, those passing the oral examination were required to take the Diplomatic and Consular Service Examinations, consisting of four sets of papers: Chinese and foreign languages (with a choice of either English, French, German, Russian, or Japanese); the constitution, international law, and diplomatic history; a third set in which candidates selected four out of ten fields including administrative law, criminal law, civil law, commercial law, political science, economics, and finance; and written and oral examinations on existing international treaties and regulations and diplomatic incidents.

30. "Waijiaoguan lingshiguan kaoshi zenlu kaojuan ji guize"[The diplomatic and consular examination papers and rules], for the year 1916, held in Zhongguo di'er lishi dang'an'guan (No. 2 Chinese Historical Archives), Archive No. 1039–218; "Renyuan lülibiao,"[Personnel resume], Archive No. 1039–222.

31. For biographical information on these four, see Howard L. Boorman, ed., *Biographical Dictionary of Republican China*, 5 vols. (New York: Columbia University Press, 1968); Guoshiguan, ed., *Guoshi nizhuan* [Biographies related to the history of the Republic of China], 3 vols. (Taibei: Guoshiguan, 1988).

32. Ch'ing Hua Ta Hsueh (Qinghua University), *Who's Who of American Returned Students* (Peking (Beijing): Tsing Hua College, 1917), 71.

33. Yen, *East-West Kaleidoscope*, foreword.

34. The main sources on Koo are the following: Koo, "The Wellington Koo Memoir"; Hui-lan Koo (Madame Wellington Koo), *Hui-lan Koo: An Autobiography* (New York: Dial Press, 1945) and *No Feast Lasts Forever* (New York: Quandrangle, 1975); Pao-chin Chu, *V. K. Wellington Koo: A Case Study of China's Diplomat and Diplomacy of Nationalism, 1912–1966* (Hong Kong: The Chinese University Press, 1981); William L. Tung, *V. K. Wellington Koo and China's Diplomacy* (New York: St. John's University, 1977); Stephen G. Craft, *V. K. Wellington Koo and the Emergence of Modern China* (Lexington: University Press of Kentucky, 2004).

35. Cheng-t'ing Wang, "Looking Backward and Looking Forward" (Sterling Memorial Library, Yale University); Boorman, *Biographical Dictionary*, 3:362–64; Guoshiguan, *Guoshi nizhuan*, 3:11–16; Liu Huanceng, "Wang Zhengting boshi bailing mingdan zhigan" [Commemorative thoughts on Dr. Wang Zhengting's 100th birthday], *Zhuanji wenxue* 42, no. 2 (1992): 10–20.

36. Jin Guangyao, "Waijiaoxi chutan," [A preliminary study of the Clique of Diplomacy] (paper presented at the international conference, "Beiyang shiqi de Zhongguo waijiao," [Chinese diplomacy during the Beiyang period], Fudan University, Shanghai, China, August 27–28, 2004). According to Jing, the term *Clique of Diplomacy* was first used in early 1922 in Chinese newspapers. The Clique comprised at least seven members: Wellington Koo, C. T. Wang, W. W. Yen, Wang Chonghui, Sao-ke Alfred Sze, and Luo Wengan, and possibly Qian Tai. (Conversation with Jin at the conference, August 27, 2004.)

37. A few examples will suffice to demonstrate the health of "the Wellington Koo research craze" *(Gu Weijun yanjiu re)* in contemporary China: Jin Guangyao, ed., *Gu Weijun yü Zhongguo waijiao* [Wellington Koo and Chinese Diplomacy] (Shanghai: Shanghai guji chubanshe, 2001); Jin Guangyao, *Gu Weijun zhuan* [Biography of Wellington Koo] (Shijiazhuang: Hebei renmin chubanshe, 1999); Shi Yuanhua, *Zhuming waijiaojia Gu Weijun* [The distinguished diplomat Wellington Koo] (Shanghai: Shanghai shehui kexueyuan, 1989); Wellington Koo, *Gu Weijun huiyilu [The Wellington Koo Memoirs]*, 13 vols., trans. Zhongguo shehui kexueyuan jindaishi yanjiusuo (Beijing: Zhonghua shujü, 1983). Other books on the foreign ministry group include Wanyan Shaoyuan, *Wang Zhengting zhuan* [Biography of C. T. Wang] (Shijiazhuang: Hebei renmin chubanshe, 1999); Chen Yan, *Yan Huiqing zhuan* [Biography of Yan Huiqing] (Shijiazhuang: Hebei renmin chubanshe, 1999); Shi Jianguo, *Lu Zhengxiang zhuan* [Biography of Lu Zhenxiang] (Shijiazhuang: Hebei renmin chubanshe, 1999); Zhang Liheng, *Wu Tingfang zhuan* [Biography of Wu Tingfang] (Shijiazhuang: Hebei renmin chubanshe, 1999).

38. The only relatively detailed English-language study of the institutional structure and state-building efforts of the *Waijiaobu* published to date is Julia C. Strauss's *Strong Institutions in Weak Polities: State Building in Republican China, 1927–1940* (Oxford: Clarendon Press, 1998). By applying a Weberian theory of bureaucratization and professionalism and contrasting it with the traditional Confucianist model, Strauss constructs a group portrait of the Examination Yuan, the Salt Inspectorate, the Ministry of Finance, and the Ministry of Foreign Affairs. The book, however, devotes only one chapter to the Foreign Ministry, 1927–1940. The only comprehensive scholarly work on this topic in Chinese is Chen Tiqiang's *Zhongguo waijiao xingzheng.*

39. December 3 of the tenth year of Xianfeng.

40. Jia Zhen et al., *Chouban yiwu shimo (Xianfen chao)*, 8:2676.

41. Immanuel C. Y. Hsü, *The Rise of Modern China*, 4th ed. (Oxford: Oxford University Press, 1990), 396–97.

42. Jiang Xianbin, "Shilun jindai de difang waijiao jiaoshe jiguan" [A preliminary study of local diplomatic bodies in the modern era], *Jiangxi shifan daxue xuebao* 33, no. 4 (November 2000): 52–56.

43. Chen, T., *Zhongguo waijiao xingzheng*, 102–6.

44. "Jiangsu jiaoshe gongshu zhiyuan lülibiao," [Resumes and positions in the Jiangsu Bureau of Negotiations], Year 1920, held in Zhongguo di'er lishi dang'an'guan, Archive No. 1039–26.

45. Waijiaobu, *Waijiaobu tiaoyue yanjiuhui baogao* [Reports of the Association for Treaty Studies of the Foreign Ministry] (Beijing: the Foreign Ministry, 1913).

46. Waijiaobu, *Waijiaobu tiaoyue yanjiuhui baogao*, 45–46. The Third Report of the Association for Treaty Studies, "Yingren zai Baoshan jianwu bukeng lingzhao ji Zhabei shizhengting zhengshou wairen fangchang juanxiang liang'an" [Two cases involving the refusal of British subjects to apply for new construction licenses, and the tax levied by the Zhabei city government on foreign property]. The Eleventh Report of the Treaty Studies Association, "di'er'ci baogao yingreng zai Baoshan jingnei jianzhu buzun difang zizhi zhangcheng an" [The second report on the flouting of local government construction regulations by British subjects].

47. Waijiaobu, *Waijiaobu tiaoyue yanjiuhui baogao*, 11. The Third Report of the Association for Treaty Studies.

48. Waijiaobu, *Waijiaobu tiaoyue yanjiuhui baogao*, 45. The Eleventh Report of the Association for Treaty Studies.

49. Waijiaobu, *Waijiaobu tiaoyue yanjiuhui baogao*, 41. The Tenth Report of the Association for Treaty Studies

50. Waijiaobu, comp., "Minjiao su'an jinke anzhao yuezhang banli wuyong lingding tiaowen zi" [Correspondence regarding law suits involving Christians and non-Christians should follow existing treaties and agreements, with no need to sign a further agreement], *Waijiao gongbao*, vol. 1 (1921).

51. Waijiaobu, comp., "Huayang susong zai xianshu chushen buzhun lüshi chuting wei ke yi dailiren zige chuting daisu yang zhuanchi zunzhao banli ling" [Order prohibiting foreign attorneys at the preliminary mixed trial in the county Bureau and permitting foreign agents in the mixed court], *Waijiao gongbao*, vol. 36 (May 3, 1924).

52. For the exercise of extraterritorial jurisdiction, see chapter 1.

53. Waijiaobu, comp., "Yantai Jiaoshe Yuan chengqing heshi guanyü huayang susong yiwen sandian qing heding jian fuhan" [Inquiries from the Yantai Jiaoshe yuan: on the reply concerning the three questions about the mixed legal case], *Waijiao gongbao*, vol. 63 (1926).

54. Wellington Koo, "The Status of Aliens in China" (Ph.D. dissertation, Columbia University, 1912).

55. Koo, "The Status of Aliens in China," 59.

56. Koo, "The Status of Aliens in China," 350.

57. Koo, "The Status of Aliens in China," 355.

58. Zhongguo di'er lishi dang'an'guan, Archive No. 1039–218. Although the archives date the test to 1916, Xü's essay mentions the end of the Great War and its implications for China. Possibly the test took place in early 1919. (Another sample test in Japanese, completed by Shen Mingqi, who scored 99 out 100, contained the same question and is dated 1919.)

59. Zhongguo di'er lishi dang'an'guan, Archive No. 1039–218.

60. Zhongguo di'er lishi dang'an'guan, Archive No. 1039–218.

61. *Waijiaobu ji zhuwai shilingguan zhiyuan lu* [Personnel directory of the Foreign Ministry and overseas embassies and consulates], Zhongguo di'er lishi dang'an'guan, Archive No. 1039–24.

62. Xü, "The Age of Innocence," 378.

63. Xü, "The Age of Innocence," 21.

64. Xü, 'The Age of Innocence," 115–40.

65. On January 18, 1915, Hioki Eki, the Japanese Minister at Beijing, privately handed President Yuan Shikai a document that became known as the "Twenty-one Demands." These demands, divided into five groups, urged China's recognition of Japan's assumption of the German position in Shandong; acceptance of Japan's special interests in southern Manchuria and eastern Mongolia in areas including politics, finance, defense, mining, railroad construction and coastal ports; acceptance of Japan's control of the Han'ye'ping Company which controlled China's major coal deposits; exclusion of other powers from territorial concessions and leased lands; and the demand that China should hire Japanese nationals as political, military, and financial advisors. The text of the original Japanese proposal is printed in *Beiyang zhengfu waijiaobu huangpishu: Zhongri jiaoshe shimo* [Yellow paper of the Foreign Ministry of the Beijing government: a comprehensive account of the Sino-Japanese negotiations], in Huang Jilian, ed., *Zhongri Er'shi'yi'tiao jiaoshe shiliao quanbian (1915–1923)* [The negotiations over the Sino-Japanese "Twenty-one Demands": Collected documents] (Hefei: Anhui daxue chubanshe, 2001), 20–22. Lacking commensurate military and economic power, the Chinese stalled for time and prolonged the negotiations. The Foreign Ministry, led by Lu Zhengxiang, refused to negotiate terms over items 4 and 5 of the Demands (see the Chinese revisions to the Japanese proposals and meeting minutes, in Huang Jilian, *Zhongri Er'shi'yi'tiao jiaoshe shiliao quanbian (1915–1923)*, 23–139). After receiving the Demands, President Yuan Shikai, who often became personally involved in foreign policy, studied the document painstakingly and in his own hand wrote out reasons for rejecting some of the demands (Lo K., *Lu Zhengxiang zhuan*, 102). On May 7, the Japanese government delivered an ultimatum to China demanding a satisfactory reply within forty-eight hours, threatening that "if no satisfactory reply is received before or at the designated time, the Imperial Government will take whatever steps they may deem necessary" (Lo K., *Lu Zhengxiang zhuan*, 140–44). After consulting with the British, Yuan Shikai and Lu Zhengxiang replied to Japan on May 8, 1915, accepting—with the exception of the articles in Group 5—all Japan's demands of January 18. Thus through the secret treaties signed by Lu Zhengxiang and Hioki on May 25, and the accompanying exchange of notes, "the Chinese Government agrees to give full assent to all matters upon which the Japanese Government may

hereafter agree with the German Government relating to the disposition of all rights, interests and concessions which Germany, by virtue of treaties or otherwise, possesses in relations to the Province of Shantung" (see King, *V. K. Wellington Koo's Foreign Policy*, 97–103). For Lu Zhengxiang, the forced signing of the secret treaties with Japan tormented him for the rest of his life (see Lo K., *Lu Zhengxiang zhuan*, 105).

66. Xü, "The Age of Innocence," 124.

67. Xü, "The Age of Innocence," introduction.

68. Dickinson, *War and National Reinvention*, 85, 92.

69. Charlotte Ku and Paul F. Diehl, eds., *International Law: Classic and Contemporary Readings*, 2nd ed. (Boulder, Colo.: Lynne Rienner Publishers, 2003), 48.

70. The full text of the Convention is available at http://www.un.org/law/ilc/texts/treaties.htm. (accessed September 29, 2004).

71. http://www.un.org/law/ilc/texts/treaties.htm. (accessed September 29, 2004).

72. For the confusion over the applicability of the 1969 Convention, see chapter 3. Peter Malanczuk, *Akehurst's Modern Introduction to International Law*, 7th ed. (New York: Routledge, 1997), 130.

73. Malanczuk, *Akehurst's Modern Introduction to International Law*, 139–41.

74. Mark W. Janis, *An Introduction to International Law*, 4th ed. (New York: Aspen Publishers, 2003), 37–38.

75. Malanczuk, *Akehurst's Modern Introduction to International Law*, 144.

76. Rebecca M. M. Wallace, *International Law*, 3rd ed. (London: Sweet & Maxwell, 1997), 241.

77. Janis, *An Introduction to International Law*, 38.

78. Malanczuk, *Akehurst's Modern Introduction to International Law*, 144.

79. Hans Kelsen, *Principles of International Law* (New York: Rinehart, 1952), 360.

80. Eugene Chen, later well-known as a "revolutionary diplomat," who was described by G. E. Morrison as "a firebrand but clear-headed." H. Lo, *The Correspondence of G. E. Morrison*, 2:716.

81. On the Chinese role at the Paris Peace Conference, see Koo, *The Wellington Koo Memoir*, part 2, "The Paris Peace Conference"; C. Wang, "Looking Backward and Looking Forward"; Stephen Bonsal, *Suitors and Suppliants: The Little Nations at Versailles* (New York: Prentice-Hall, Inc., 1946); King, *V. K. Wellington Koo's Foreign Policy*; Yen, *East-West Kaleidoscope*.

82. Under the Convention of March 6, 1898, between China and Germany, the Qing government granted Germany a lease of ninety-nine years over the Bay of Jiaozhou. In addition, Germany obtained the right to construct two railway lines to protect the Qingdao-Jinan Railway, and to develop mining properties along the railways.

83. The dispute over Shandong derived from the Great War. The Beijing government proclaimed its neutrality on August 14, 1914, shortly after the outbreak of hostilities. Two weeks later, Japan informed the Chinese government that Japan was at war with Germany and demanded the withdrawal of German troops and equipment from Chinese and Japanese waters and the handover to the Japanese government of the entire leased territory of Jiaozhou no later than September 15. The intent of these demands, in the words of the commander of the Japanese fleet, was to "destroy the root of the evil" and protect the interests of China. In early September 1914, about twenty thousand Japanese troops landed at Longkou, a port one hundred and fifty miles north of Qingdao. By the end of September, Japanese forces had occupied Jiaozhou Bay and Qingdao. See "A Dispatch from the Commander of the Japanese Fleet," John K. Davis (American Vice-Consul in Charge) of the American Consulate in Chefoo to J. V. A. MacMurray (the American Legation), September 7 and 16, 1914, in the National Archives Microfilm Publications, "Records of the Department of State Relating to Internal Affairs of China, 1910–1929," No. 329, Roll 7; "The Claim of China for Direct Restitution to Herself of the Leased Territory of Kiao-Chow, the Tsingtao-Chinan Railway and Other German Rights In Respect of Shantung Province," a memorandum submitted to the Peace Conference at Paris, February 1919, by Wellington Koo, in King, *V. K. Wellington Koo's Foreign Policy*. For the Chinese version,

see Cheng Daode, ed., *Zhonghua minguo waijiao ziliao xuanbian* [Selected Diplomatic Sources on the Republic of China] (Beijing: Beijing daxue chubanshe, 1985), 5–16.

84. Cheng D. et al., *Zhonghua minguo waijiao shiliao xuanbian*, 2–48.
85. Cheng D. et al., *Zhonghua minguo waijiao shiliao xuanbian*, 2–48.
86. Woodhead, *The China Year Book* (1921–1922), 726.
87. Cheng D. et al., *Zhonghua minguo waijiao shiliao xuanbian*, 2–48.
88. Cheng D. et al., *Zhonghua minguo waijiao shiliao xuanbian*, 45–47.
89. Mediated by Britain and the U.S., China, and Japan reached an agreement, on February 4, 1922—on the transfer of Shandong to China from Japan—outside the Washington Conference. Wu Canghai, *Shandong xuan'an jiejue zhi jingwei* [The entire of process concerning the resolution of the Shandong question] (Taibei: Taiwan Shangwu yinshuguan, 1987). For the full text of the Ten Points statement, see Westel W. Willoughby, *China at the Conference: A Report* (Baltimore, Md.: Johns Hopkins University Press, 1922), 32–35.
90. Wellington Koo, "Statement Regarding the Re-establishment of China's Tariff Autonomy," in King, *V. K. Wellington Koo's Foreign Policy*, 41.
91. Li Shaosheng, *Huashengdun huiyi zhi Zhongguo wenti* [The China question at the Washington Conference] (Taibei: Shuiniu chubanshe, 1973). See *Waijiabo gongbao*, 10 (1922): 21–40 for Chinese and English versions of the Treaty between the Nine Powers Relating to the Chinese Customs Tariff. The final resolutions were disappointing to China as the Powers left all the essential questions to a future Special Conference except the 2.5 percent surtax, which was also conditional on the ratification of the Treaty. The Treaty between the Nine Powers (the U.S., Belgium, Great Britain, China, France, Japan, the Netherlands, and Portugal) was signed in Washington, D.C., in February 1922.
92. American Society of International Law, ed., *Proceedings of the American Society of International Law at Its Twenty-First Annual Meeting (April 28–30, 1927)* (Washington, D.C.: American Society of International Law, 1927), 89.
93. American Society of International Law, *Proceedings of the American Society*, 90.
94. Hugo Grotius, *De Jure Belli Ac Pacis Libri Tres* [On the Law of War and Peace], trans. F. Kelsey (Washington, D.C.: Carnegie Endowment for International Peace, 1925), 2:394, 2:396–97, 2:804–5, 2:809; Nozari, *Unequal Treaties in International Law*, 117, 174.
95. Hungdah Chiu, "Comparison of the Nationalist and Communist Chinese Views of Unequal Treaties," in *China's Practice of International Law: Some Case Studies*, ed. Jerome Alan Cohen (Cambridge, Mass.: Harvard University Press, 1972), 240; Samuel Pufendorf, *De Jure Naturae et Gentium* [On the law of nature and nations], trans. C. H. Oldfather and W. A. Oldfather from the 1688 ed. (Washington, D.C.: Carnegie Endowment for International Peace, 1934), 2:1332.
96. For a summary of the legal writings on imposed treaties, see Stuart S. Malawer, *Imposed Treaties and International Law* (Buffalo, N.Y.: W. S. Hein, 1977); Emmerich de Vattel, *Le Droit de gens ou principes de la loi naturelle* [The law of nations or the principles of natural law], trans. Fenwick from the 1758 ed. (Washington, D.C.: Carnegie Endowment for International Peace, 1916), 356.
97. Nozari, *Unequal Treaties in International Law*, 89.
98. American Society of International Law, *Proceedings of the American Society*, 83–101.
99. American Society of International Law, *Proceedings of the American Society*, 87.
100. Bruce A. Elleman, *Wilson and China: A Revised History of the Shandong Question* (Armonk, N.Y.: M. E. Sharpe, 2002). Issues such as China's attitude toward "direct" and "indirect" restitution over Shandong are documented in Jin G., *Gu Weijun zhuan*, 69.
101. Sao-ke Alfred Sze, *Addresses by Sao-Ke Alfred Sze* (Baltimore, Md.: Johns Hopkins University Press, 1926), 105–31, "China's Unequal Treaties," address delivered at the Brooklyn Institute of Arts and Sciences, Brooklyn, New York, February 21, 1926.
102. Sze, *Addresses by Sao-ke Alfred Sze*, 120.
103. Sze, *Addresses by Sao-ke Alfred Sze*, 121.

104. Koo, *Gu Weijun huiyilu*, 1:355–60; Woodhead, *The China Year Book* (1928), 460.

105. *North-China Herald*, Nov. 13, 1926, 298.

106. Koo, *Gu Weijun huiyilu*, 1:357.

107. *Shi Bao* [The Eastern Times] (Shanghai), Nov. 4, 1926, 1–2, and Nov. 24, 1926, 1.

108. Rodney Gilbert, *The Unequal Treaties: China and the Foreigners* (London: John Murray, 1929), 1.

3

Disseminating the Rhetoric of *Bupingdeng Tiaoyue*, 1923–1927

This chapter focuses on an understudied phrase, *bupingdeng tiaoyue* (the Unequal Treaties)—a symbol invented mainly through the exploitation, by different historical agents, of its emotional and political connotations. Repairing this omission in the current lively discussion of political ceremonies and symbols in China's national awakening and identity-building, this chapter demonstrates how the Unequal Treaties were invested with a strongly symbolic role by analyzing the form, content, function, and impact of the Unequal Treaties rhetoric.[1] Moving away from earlier studies, I treat the discourse on the Unequal Treaties as a component in the construction of Chinese nationalism that yields multifold local and global meanings. First, I argue that the rhetoric of the Unequal Treaties constitutes a new and growing element in the stream of polemical attacks on imperialism and warlordism, especially in the 1920s. The emphatic characterization of China's recent humiliating past by both the GMD and CCP added a new vocabulary to the Chinese language. Both the GMD and CCP used the newly coined phrase *Unequal Treaties* to describe China's encounter with foreign nations in the preceding eighty years.

Second, the shared experience of both the Guomindang and the Communists with the Unequal Treaties reveals further details about a highly strained and precarious relationship in the United Front from 1924 to 1927.[2] An analysis of this relationship consequently requires us to consider, in our inquiry into Chinese nationalism, the complex divisions between the two parties as well as within them, and their further political implications. In other words, I attempt to locate the building of national identity in the discourse of the Unequal Treaties as mapped out by various forces in Chinese history. Using different interpretative and rhetorical strategies, the GMD and CCP both staked their claim to be true patriots by claiming credit for the termination of the Unequal Treaties.[3] The overlapping yet competing efforts of the two major political parties to construct Chinese national identity reflected the highly fluid nature of the first Republican politics.

Third, China's experience with the Unequal Treaties suggests that the spread and interpretation of international law can take place only on a particular nation's own terms. For ninety years, the unwavering interest in and repeated references to topics such as the Unequal Treaties and national humiliations have closely matched China's perceptions of its relations with the world from the perspective of international law.

THE USE OF THE PHRASE *UNEQUAL TREATIES*

The term *Unequal Treaties* originated in the political and cultural context of modern China. As we noted earlier, terminology relevant to the Unequal Treaties was used in the late nineteenth century. The vocabulary of the Unequal Treaties, however, did not originate with the May Fourth Movement, neither was it first used by the Communists. I have searched in vain for references to the phrase *Unequal Treaties* by prominent Chinese Communist leaders of the early 1920s. None of the prolific Communist writers such as Chen Duxiu (1880–1942), Li Daozhao (1889–1927), and Mao Zedong (1893–1976) made use of this expression before 1923.[4] Mao Zedong adopted the term following its original use by Sun Yat-sen, as we shall see below. The term *Unequal Treaties* first appears in Mao's writing in 1925 in his "Propaganda Outline for the Chinese Nationalist Party's Anti-Fengtian Warlords Campaign."[5] Taking over the position of head of the Propaganda Bureau in the United Front from Wang Jingwei (who replaced the GMD rightist faction's Dai Jitao in August 1924)—a post which he held from October 1925 until March 1926—Mao resolved to coordinate and reorganize party propaganda.[6] He issued a number of new slogans, including "Abolish the Unequal Treaties," (*qüxiao bupingdeng tiaoyue*) designed to awaken the masses.[7]

My surmise is that the Unequal Treaties entered the Chinese language in 1924, and was first used by Sun Yat-sen. Prior to this, *bupingdeng zhi tiaoyue* (treaty of inequality), a similar but not identical expression, was first used possibly in 1908 by Shao Yi.[8] It also appeared in the Guomindang's Declaration of January 1, 1923,[9] as well as in the Communists' "Guiding Principles of the Chinese Communist Party" issued in June 1923 and approved by the CCP Third Congress.[10] It is important to distinguish these very similar expressions from the first use of the actual phrase *Unequal Treaties*, since they never acquired the same rhetorical impact. In *Hu Hanmin xiansheng nianpu*, written by Jiang Yongjing and published in 1978, there is a reference to Hu's recollection of Sun's position on the Paris Peace Conference of 1919:

With the end of World War I, several members of the Guomindang attended the Paris Peace Conference. Mr. Sun said to them: "You should propose that the Unequal Treaties [*bupingdeng tiaoyue*] between China and the [Western] powers be abolished, that all alienated lands be returned, and that the independence of Korea be recognized. These [all] conform with the purpose of self-determination."[11]

Sun's alleged use of *bupingdeng tiaoyue* in 1919, however, derives from a second-hand account given by Hu Hanmin after 1924 when the term was already in use. It is best to regard Sun's 1919 reference as an allusion to the termination of the Unequal Treaties rather than as unequivocal evidence of the expression itself at this early date.[12]

In the Declaration of the Guomindang First National Congress on January 31, 1924, the cancellation of all Unequal Treaties was included in the Nationalist Party's political platform. Here Sun stated,

All Unequal Treaties (*yiqie bupingdeng tiaoyue*), including foreign concessions, consular jurisdiction, foreign management of customs services, and all foreign political rights exercised on China's soil, are detrimental to China's sovereignty. They all ought to be abolished so as to leave the way open for new treaties based on the spirit of bilateral equality and mutual respect for sovereignty.[13]

Although Sun's analysis contained nothing new compared with previous statements, this declaration appears to mark the emergence of one of the most widely used rhetorical terms in modern China. From his first use of *bupingdeng tiaoyue* to his death, Sun repeatedly emphasized that terminating the Unequal Treaties was central to the Nationalist Revolution. At the 1924 May First Labor Day celebrations, Sun gave a speech entitled, "The Harm Done by the Unequal Treaties to the Chinese Working Class," in which he claimed that "as a result of the Unequal Treaties, the status of Chinese workers, as the slaves of world powers, is the worst in the world."[14]

In his "Grand Peasant Alliance" speech, Sun went further by comparing all the Unequal Treaties to China's "self-selling indenture" (*maishen qi*): "Nationalism cannot prevail [in China] unless the 'self-selling indenture' is abolished."[15] A similar formulation occurred in Sun's speech, "Unite the Nation to Eradicate the 'Unequal Treaties,'" given on November 10, 1924, at the Workers' Association's farewell party.[16] In his interview with a Japanese journalist on November 24, 1924, Sun urged Japan to assist China in its efforts to abolish the Unequal Treaties:

Since the 1911 Revolution, China has been in chaos. China's disintegration is not the fault of the Chinese, but, instead, is caused exclusively by foreigners. Why? The answer lies in the "Unequal Treaties" between China and foreign countries. . . . In recent years, Westerners in China have gone even beyond the "Unequal Treaties" to abuse their treaty rights. . . . At present, China's abrogating of those treaties is dependent upon the sympathy of the Japanese people.[17]

Sun even proposed a Sino-Japanese alliance on economic and military matters in exchange for Japan's support. On December 1, Sun demanded the termination of the Unequal Treaties and the convening of the National Reconstruction Conference as the basis for reconciliation between the North and the South.[18]

Though making a clear connection between the Unequal Treaties and China's problems, including the country's internal chaos, Sun Yat-sen's use of the term *Unequal Treaties* was relatively restrained and supported by rational argument. However, the rhetorical range of the expression, as well as its tone, changed explosively after 1923 as a result of a string of political events. The phrase *bupingdeng tiaoyue* rapidly took on confrontational and class connotations and was linked closely with such concepts as *threat*, *slavery*, and the *misery* inflicted upon China by imperialism and its agent (*daili*) militarism (*junfa zhuyi*). China's attainment of international equality was to be identified with the party that could provide the road map for the nation's future through consistent recourse to the Unequal Treaties story. The rhetoric of the Unequal Treaties brought intense public pressure to bear on warlords and imperialists alike. As we shall see, the GMD and CCP had invented a shared legacy of powerful political polemic.

DISSEMINATING THE RHETORIC OF THE UNEQUAL TREATIES AS A FORM OF NATIONALISM

Spurred by the Sino-Soviet Treaty, the Unequal Treaties Cancellation Movement, (hereafter abbreviated to the Treaty Cancellation Movement), initiated by over fifty intellectual organizations in Beijing, developed rapidly in the summer of 1924.[19] In July, intellectuals in Beijing formed the Grand Anti-Imperialist Alliance, followed by Shanghai in August. On July 18, faculty and staff of eight universities in Beijing jointly issued the Declaration on Treaty Cancellation, which demanded the restructuring of international relations: "All the citizens of imperialist countries should have all unequal conventions and agreements revoked."[20] The Grand Anti-imperialist Alliance proposed September 3–9 as Anti-imperialist Movement Week, and organized mass rallies in all the major cities which placed the blame for all China's troubles and backwardness on foreigners.[21] China's independence and prosperity hinged on the abrogation of the Unequal Treaties.[22] An article in *Xiangdao zhoubao* declared that "unless all international treaties of inequality (*bupingdeng zhi tiaoyue*) are revoked, there is no hope of independence for oppressed nations."[23] The Treaty Cancellation Movement associated itself with a number of memorial days linked to the various unequal treaties signed between China and foreign countries. In an essay entitled "The Treaty Cancellation Movement and the September Seventh Commemoration,"[24] the anonymous author viewed the unequal treaties as interlocking sets of shackles so that piecemeal revision was ruled out. "If we do things completely in line with existing treaty regulations, then generation after generation of our children will be enslaved for ever." The author called for the masses of all classes, on the September Seventh Memorial Day, "to rally against imperialism, to examine our organizational strength, and to make imperialism tremble. Our final goal is to turn the national humiliation day of September Seventh into a Chinese national independence day."[25]

Although the fact has been largely ignored in existing research, both the GMD and CCP were vocal in airing opposition to their common enemies, imperialism and warlordism: the two targets of their polemic on the Unequal Treaties.[26] In spite of the frequently open bickering within the Nationalist Revolution over issues such as the distinction between revolutionaries and counterrevolutionaries, their commitment to the Unequal Treaties issue did reveal, at some levels at least, a coordinated unity of opinion between the two groups. Referring to the gamut of propaganda employed by the GMD and the CCP, Fitzgerald notes that, after Mao took the helm of the Propaganda Bureau, "both parties were in agreement on the need for unity and discipline—indeed, even on the means of its enforcement."[27] The two parties certainly played on the issue of the Unequal Treaties in order to isolate their common foes—warlords and imperialists. In public pronouncements, in an effort to reinforce their claim to political legitimacy, both claimed a patriotic, even messianic, role in keeping China out of perilous waters.

In the wake of the Gold Franc Controversy of 1925,[28] both parties directed scathing criticism at the Beijing government's diplomatic handling of the treaty issue in rhetorical language loaded with emotive phrases, striking verbs, accusatory nouns, and vivid metaphors. In the CCP–run *Xiangdao zhoubao*, the Gold Franc Incident was presented as an orchestrated conspiracy by Japanese, British, French, and American imperialists, joint oppressors of China.[29]

In its third declaration on the Gold Franc Controversy in summer 1925, the Guomindang declared that

> throughout history, our country's diplomacy has been manipulated by imperialism. Because of this, our party's policies on foreign relations aim at the renunciation of the Unequal Treaties. The settlement of the Gold Franc case will be no different from all previous diplomatic arrangements—does China have any hope of eliminating imperialist oppression?![30]

In 1925, the Unequal Treaties once again came into focus in the new anti-imperialist wave. The series of events that took place that year prompted the emergence of a polemic that focused attention on the Unequal Treaties as the protective shield which helped the Japanese and British get away with their brutal behavior in the May Thirtieth Incident of 1925.[31] In an essay titled "Expedite Research on the Unequal Treaties," one writer maintained that "this tragedy [the May Thirtieth Incident] is the natural consequence of the

'Unequal Treaties.'"[32] He continued, "Without fixed tariffs as their amulet (*hushenfu*), Japanese cotton mills [in China] could never be prosperous. [By the same token,] it would no longer be impossible for Chinese industries to develop, and Chinese workers would not be begging at the Japanese pirates' (*wonu*) door."[33] "Without the concession provision," the author went on, "would the British dare to run amuck like this? Without consular jurisdiction, would we need to worry that the British murderers would fail to pay for life with life?" Finally, the author concluded, "If we want to prevent such a tragedy from happening again, we have to embark on the fundamental task—the cancellation of the 'Unequal Treaties.'"[34]

In discussing forms of mythic expression, Murray Edelman has pointed to two characteristic themes that myths employ in order to engage the emotions of large numbers of people. One theme is the "evocation of an out-group," defined as "malevolent" and "plotting to commit harmful acts." The other is the belief that a benevolent political force or leader is offering to "save people from danger."[35] In the discourse of the Unequal Treaties, we see this powerful mythic strategy at work. For example, public petitions frequently linked foreign powers and the warlord Beijing government with images of oppressors and villains, responsible for all China's torments. In these petitions, Edleman's second theme is also visible: the Guomindang and the Communists consistently portrayed themselves as the saviors of China. Many more examples can be found. In June 1925, the Duan Qirui warlord government in Beijing sent the foreign powers a note urging revision of the treaties, albeit restrained in tone. In the note, the Beijing government expressed its hope that "the friendly Powers would give sympathetic consideration to the well-known aspirations of the Chinese people."[36] In response, the Guomindang issued its second "Declaration on Abolishing the Unequal Treaties," which called for the immediate and unilateral abrogation of all Unequal Treaties. In striking contrast to Beijing's revisionist approach to "atrocious imperialists," the declaration stated that "abolition and a request for revision [of the Unequal Treaties] are two entirely different things. Our national citizenry will not be deluded by the Beijing Provisional Government's treacherous act." It concluded: "What Beijing is doing is like 'asking a tiger for its skin [*yühu moupi*].'"[37]

Referring only rarely to past treaties as the Unequal Treaties, the Beijing government promoted a peaceful negotiating approach to readjust treaty relations with contracting countries. Deriding their common enemy, the Beijing government, as the running dogs of imperialism, the GMD and CCP on the other hand demanded the unconditional termination of all unequal treaties. With regard to the Beijing-sponsored Special Tariff Conference, the GMD Humen Branch, in its Declaration on the Tariff Conference of 1925, proclaimed that

> our party branch believes that, while in the short run this conference curries favor with the public, in the long run it will undoubtedly bring damage to China.

Why do we say this? Because the conference is being held right after the imperialists' massacre of our people in the Shanghai, Hankou . . . and Guangdong areas, and it is designed to dissipate the hostile atmosphere [directed against imperialism in China]. . . . The Chinese representatives [the Beijing government officials] at the conference have neither decent nor firm proposals. So, if there are no delegates of our party attending this conference, how can they [the Chinese representatives] fail to be trapped by vicious imperialists?[38]

In 1926, the military conflict between warlords Wu Peifu-Zhang Zuolin and Feng Yuxiang forced the Tariff Conference to close without reaching any agreement. Opposing its reopening, the GMD, in one of its circular telegraphic messages, began by denying the legitimacy of the incumbent Beijing government:

Fellow Countrymen! As you know, at present Beijing has absolutely no government which can represent China. Those who currently claim to be the government of China are nothing but the dirty politicians of the warlords' running dogs. In disguise as the Chinese government, they are conducting traitorous deals.[39]

It then charged that foreign imperialists were in league with the warlords and planning to reconvene the Tariff Conference in order to relieve the warlords in their straitened circumstances. Calling for all fellow countrymen to rebel against the Tariff Conference, the declaration ended with the slogans "Down with the Tariff Conference! Down with the warlords! Long Live the Nationalist Revolution!"[40] Imperative verbs, emotive nouns, and strident phrases were to resonate to similar effect in later Guomindang and Communist party formulations.[41] Several GMD party branches issued similar statements attacking the warlords and imperialism. A declaration issued by the GMD Suixi (Guangdong) branch reads as follows:

In order to save China and improve the People's livelihood, our Party advocates the abolition of the "Unequal Treaties" and the restoration of tariff autonomy. We absolutely refuse to allow additional terms and revised conditions [to be imposed on us by imperialists]. . . . However, under the shield of his master, the British imperialists, the traitorous warlord Wu Peifu has resurrected his control over the Beijing Government, and his dying embers are glowing again. Recently, Warlord Wu has designated his running dogs, Wellington Koo and W. W. Yen, to lobby for the re-opening of the Tariff Conference. . . . We hope all of our people can rise up to strongly oppose [the resumption of the Tariff Conference], and join our national revolution. Down with Bandit Wu and all other reactionary warlords![42]

In Chinese politics then, unconditional treaty termination became the dividing line between revolution and counterrevolution, and between good and bad. In the polemical exhortations that filled the air, new concepts and analogies were frequently introduced. In Jiang Jieshi's speech "To Accomplish the Revolution, First Down with Imperialism," for instance, Jiang referred to imperialists as the puppet "wirepuller" (*qianxian ren*) of the warlords, and a "monster" (*guaiwu*) with a "snake's body and the appearance of beauty."[43]

In January 1926 in his "Reports on Propaganda," Mao Zedong referred to the success of Sun Yat-sen's twin slogans—"National Reconstruction Conference" and "Abrogating the Unequal Treaties." Through the dissemination of verbal and written propaganda by both the GMD and CCP, these revolutionary slogans had penetrated deep into the hearts of the masses.[44] Like Mao, many writers found evidence of popular acceptance of the stance taken by both parties on the Beijing government's unilateral termination of the 1865 Sino-Belgian Treaty, a move that should have been a populist triumph for the government. One article in a Communist newspaper commented, "As an imperialist running dog and pettifogger of the Zhi Clique warlord, Wellington Koo's attitude in the negotiations was rather ambiguous. Koo's announcement of the expiration of the Sino-Belgian Treaty was made under pressure from the general populace."[45] The Guangzhou Republican Daily frequently ran headlines such as "All Unequal Treaties Should Be Abolished" and "Rewrite the Treaties with Equal and Reciprocal Respect for Sovereignty." Articles on the treaties were couched in strong language saturated with abusive terms.

In July 1926, the Guomindang and Communists launched the Northern Expedition, declaring their determination to eliminate the warlords and to swiftly abrogate the Unequal Treaties, although no real practical measures were offered. In opposition to the North's policy of gradualism and diplomacy by negotiation, Jiang Jieshi was uncompromising in his public declaration of November 1926 that "the people of China would never be satisfied with a mere revision of the treaties."[46] In the same month, in an interview with Bruno Schwartz of the *Hankow Herald*, Jiang reaffirmed that the nationalist revolution would not end until all foreign privileges were repudiated and the Unequal Treaties abolished.[47]

The tendency to attribute all national ills since the Qing to the evils of the treaties continued to strengthen in China throughout 1926. "The 'Unequal Treaties' are the self-selling indenture imposed upon us by the Manchu government," one commentator wrote. "They are shackles on us. Relinquishing such treaties is our only way out."[48] In December 1926, after taking over Wuhan, the Nationalist Expedition forces had a rock on Mt. Turtle carved with seven characters, *Feichu bupingdeng tiaoyue* (Abolish the Unequal Treaties), each word measuring 14.99 meters wide and 13.32 meters long. The inscription was intended to "make it clear to all what were Sun Yat-sen's unfulfilled wishes, which the Nationalists were bent on realizing in the shortest possible time."[49] In 1926, Hu Shi, who is often described as "the father of the Chinese renaissance" and who considered the Canton government "the best, most honest and most efficient administration in the whole of China," attributed the success of the Guomindang to its Leninist political organization and modern nationalist ideals borrowed from Soviet Russia. Hu Shi questioned why the "Old Diplomacy of the Old Powers" was still blind to the fact that foreign special privileges and rights were widely perceived "as monumental testimonies to imperialist aggression and Chinese humiliation."[50]

THE POLEMIC OF THE UNEQUAL TREATIES:
A COMPARISON OF THREE MODES OF DISCOURSE

The first third of the twentieth century, as Prasenjit Duara observes, was the time "when the narrative of history and a new vocabulary associated with it—such as feudalism, self-consciousness, superstition, and revolution—entered the Chinese language."[51] The phrase *Unequal Treaties* was one such narrative vehicle invented by the Guomindang, along with the Communists, to express China's long-smoldering rage and frustration. Three types of discourse on the Unequal Treaties can be distinguished here—moral, legal, and rhetorical. The moral discourse embodies the construal of the treaty establishment by late Qing literati. Their interpretation was used as a basis for moral persuasion, for an appeal to the foreign powers in China to recognize the unfairness of the unequal treaties. This moral discourse led the Qing regime to initiate a number of legal reforms. The terms used in the moral argument—such as *gongping, bugong, ziding guanshui, shibao, xilü, ding zeli*, and *tiaoyue gaizheng*—are classical Chinese, and thus were not intended to help the general public understand the issues involved. Similarly, the legal discourse excludes the participation of ordinary Chinese insofar as treaty issues were deemed the exclusive domain of the first Republican diplomats. In fact, both Wellington Koo and W. W. Yen, on different occasions, expressed intense irritation with the notion of "People's Diplomacy." Koo once commented that "to aim at 100 percent success—which is always the slogan of 'People's Diplomacy'—can never bring success, and only spoils the negotiations."[52] However, unlike the moral discourse, the legal one stresses the lack of legal validity of imposed treaties.

The rhetorical discourse differs from the first two in a number of ways. First, this mode of discourse adopts vernacular Chinese terms that are easily intelligible and hold a strong emotive charge. To the general public, words such as *daili, zougou* (running dogs), *maishen qi, nuli shenfen* (slave status), *hushenfu, guaiwu*, and *jiasuo* (shackles) were much easier to understand than expressions such as *e'wai faquan* (also, *zhiwai faquan*), and *xilü* previously in use. The public pronouncements of the Guomindang and the Communists were colloquial and emotional, and very often took the form of slogans. Examples include *feichu bupingdeng tiaoyue* (abolish the Unequal Treaties), *dadao diguo zhuyi* (down with imperialism) and *dadao junfa* (down with war-lordism). This form of language proved much more appealing than the rational, argumentative phraseology used by the Beijing government. Identifying peasants and laborers as revolutionary forces against both foreign and domestic foes, Jiang was keenly aware of his target audience: "The object of our last re-organization of the Kuomintang," Jiang stated at the Third National Labor Conference in Canton in May 1926, "was to admit all the farmers and the laborers of the country in order to achieve the final success of our nationalist revolutionary movement."[53]

The rhetorical mode of discourse involved a dual process of "dulling" and "awakening" that was deliberately manipulated by party propagandists. On the one hand, the "chronic repetition" associating the Unequal Treaties with imperialism and militarism was, in Edelman's words, carried out like "a ritual, dulling the critical faculties" and facilitating an uncritical response among the audience.[54] On the other hand, popular outrage against the whole idea of the Unequal Treaties was channeled to produce a "controlled awakening," a means to produce a "party-inspired consciousness" among the masses.

A further point relates to the theoretical persuasiveness of the rhetorical strategy in the China of the 1920s. Soviet Russia, along with the Third International—the Comintern—not only laid down the basic revolutionary strategies for the CCP, but also provided the GMD with a modern party ideology. The emergence of a number of new concepts and expressions including imperialism, warlordism, colonialism, semicolonialism, and semi-feudalism, had direct links with the Russian Bolshevik theory of world revolution. Lenin urged that China be liberated from the shackles of Western exploitation and become a part of the world Communist revolution.[55] In order to achieve independence and freedom, the semicolonial and backward countries must, according to Lenin, "oust the imperialist powers and smash its own ruling class which compromises with those powers."[56] Lenin's theories of a worldwide revolution, nationalist movement, and united front provided sound explanations of and political solutions to the problems facing China.[57] In his eulogy of the Russian leader, Sun called Lenin a "National Friend and People's Mentor."[58] In Jiang Jieshi's words, the appeal of the Soviet Bolsheviks to China, "where a sub-colonial state had resulted from a series of unequal treaties imposed upon her," lay in their promise of "a short cut to Utopia by a world revolution of the masses [against imperialism and capitalism]."[59] The formula was simple: the source of China's misery was the Unequal Treaties, imperialism, and warlordism, and the remedies were apparent—abolish the Unequal Treaties, do away with imperialism, and do away with warlordism.

Prior to their rift in April 1927, the GMD and CCP jointly created a common vocabulary referring to the Unequal Treaties. However, this does not mean that their discourses were identical. First, the divergence between the two parties' rhetoric lay in the CCP's wholesale adoption and application of the lexicon of class struggle to the Chinese situation and in a view of world history with a predilection for workers and peasants. The CCP enthusiastically fused its vision for China with the discourse of class struggle. In Chen Duxiu's words, "What the current situation really demands is the creation of a truly independent Chinese Republic, by means of a political campaign." In the era of the Nationalist Revolution, Chen continued, the political campaign against overbearing warlords and imperialists ought to be waged through the joint efforts of two otherwise weak groupings, the proletariat and capitalist classes [the CCP and the GMD] in China.[60] Failure to acknowledge the importance of class struggle would only compromise the nationalist cause. While encouraging all classes of Chinese to repeat slogans such as "Abolish the Unequal Treaties!" and "Long Live the Final Victory of Yat-senism!" Tong Bingrong distinguished several different groups, including the West Hill Faction, within the GMD. He ascribed the development of such divisions in the GMD to sabotage by counterrevolutionaries.[61] In his commemoration of Sun Yat-sen, Xiao Chunü criticized those elites who were misled by their idealist notions so that they failed to recognize class struggle as the cardinal principle of revolution. In a similar vein, Xiao defined nationalism as the struggle of oppressed nations against the minority, imperialist, ruling class in foreign countries.[62]

Another difference can be found in the CCP's conscious emphasis on the function of political propaganda: "In the Chinese Nationalist Revolution, a noticeable phenomenon is the absence of consistent, well-planned, organized propaganda operated by a political party."[63] The essay by Sun Duo from which this quotation is drawn directs criticism at nationalist revolutionaries, including Sun Yat-sen's loyal followers, for their heavy emphasis on the military aspect of the revolution at the expense of the dissemination of nationalism. On June 3, 1926, *Xiangdao zhoubao* published a special issue headed "Shanghai Citizens Commemorate the May Thirtieth Movement." Reflecting on activities in Shanghai on the first anniversary of the May Thirtieth Movement, Chen frowned on the rather subdued and tepid atmosphere of remembrance evident among university professors, merchant leaders, and the GMD rightists. Chen was candid about his grievances: "The GMD rightists didn't even come to the mass memorial rally held at the public stadium. On the contrary, they went along with some fake labor unions and counterrevolutionaries and held a separate memorial service in the Huining Merchant Association Hall in Xieqiao." However, Chen softened his tone in the interests of unity:

> The reason I nagged about these [issues] is to point out the weaknesses of each class in the hope that we can all rectify old ideas and attitudes. We are all one family rather than enemies, regardless of whether we are radicals or moderates. Our enemies are imperialism and the warlords. We ought to distinguish

between our foes and our own members. Those who belong to our side must cooperate, and should never work with our enemies to turn against our own people.[64]

Other CCP ideologues also insisted strongly on the importance of class consciousness: "If a Communist party member has not the slightest sense of class and is only willing to participate in the Nationalist Revolution with no desire to serve the interests of workers and peasants, then we should spare no effort to give him to the Nationalist party [the GMD]."[65] In *Xiangdao zhoubao*, Communist writers stepped up their attacks on the GMD's handling of the Unequal Treaties question. On the second anniversary of Sun Yat-sen's death, Chen Duxiu vented his frustration at the lack of progress on the issue: "Abolishing the Unequal Treaties along with the convening of the National Reconstruction Conference is the gist of Mr. Zhongshan's [Sun Yat-sen] will. Ever since the death of Mr. Zhongshan, although his will was read aloud at every single gathering, nobody, in his heart, remembers the essence of his wishes, not to mention their implementation. . . . The notion of the absolute protection of foreigners has replaced the slogan of terminating the Unequal Treaties."[66] The mounting criticism of the GMD rightists, along with the rightist tendency within the Nationalist Revolution, that appeared in *Xiangdao zhoubao* presaged the bloody split of April 1927.[67]

A third point of difference lay in the fact that, in the CCP's discourse on the Unequal Treaties, China's experience was often portrayed as part of a global humiliation shared by other nations in a similar situation. An article in *Xiangdao zhoubao* expressed it thus: "Spearheaded by military force to impose unequal treaties [upon others], and followed by political and economic penetration, [the West forced] weak nations to become vassals and enslaved their people. These are the very brutal and cunning means imperialism employs to invade backward countries. . . . Over the past eighty years of painful diplomatic history, China, bound in the fetters of the Unequal Treaties, has descended to the condition of a semi-colony."[68] On September 7, 1925, in response to the May Thirtieth Incident, the Shanghai Anti-imperialist Grand Union was formed. At its celebration party, organizers put up red posters with black-ink slogans including "Unite, All Oppressed Nations!" among the more familiar exhortations such as "Abrogation of the Unequal Treaties," "Down with Imperialism," and "Relinquish Extraterritoriality." According to *Shishi xinbao*, the CCP leader Yun Daiying, in the course of an hour-long speech, moved his audience with eloquent references to the long international history of inequitable treaty settlements. Yun concluded his speech with the words: "The Chinese anti-imperialist movement should assist the anti-imperialist movement in other countries, and they in their turn should assist the Chinese anti-imperialist movement."[69]

Fourth, despite efforts to maintain some appearance of unity, the rhetorical strategies adopted prior to April 1927 were characterized more by discord than harmony. In summarizing the May Thirtieth Movement, the CCP leader, Qü Qiubai expressed his opposition to infighting within the anti-imperialist national liberation movement, in particular over the questions of abrogation of the Unequal Treaties, tariff autonomy, recognition of labor unions, and increased wages. The barriers to a Chinese revolution, Qü argued, were the usual suspects—British and Japanese imperialism as well as "traitorous warlords," in particular the Feng Clique, who had orchestrated the massacres in Shanghai, Wuhan, Qingdao, Tianjin, and elsewhere. However, in the aftermath of the May Thirtieth Incident, Qü continued, catty big bourgeois, the Shanghai Chamber of Commerce, and some GMD leaders like Dai Jitao had colluded to torpedo the terms of negotiation more favorable to workers on strike. The seventeen items on the agenda included the abolition of extraterritoriality and the demand for the complete withdrawal of British and Japanese naval and army forces stationed in Shanghai issued by the Shanghai Workers, Merchants, and the Students Association on June 8, 1925. Qü argued that Dai Jitao's tactic of "Returning Japan to the Orient"—whereby China should form an alliance with Japan to isolate Britain within the anti-imperialist movement—had done more harm than good and, in combination with the tariff issues discussed above, had led Japanese factory workers to sign unfavorable agreements.[70]

The rhetorical contest over the Unequal Treaties conducted in the two major newspapers, *Guangzhou minguo ribao* and *Minguo ribao* (Shanghai), run by the CCP and GMD, respectively, pointed to strained relationships within the Nationalist Revolution camp. Many of the essays that appeared in *Guangzhou minguo ribao* were heavily influenced by the Communists' radical class interpretation of global revolution, whereas *Minguo ribao,* dominated by conservative Nationalist factions,[71] was more level-headed and commercially driven. *Guangzhou minguo ribao* missed no opportunity to articulate its position on treaty-related issues, and its coverage was systematic, controversial, and confrontational. In April 1926, the Foreign Ministry of the Beijing government advised the Belgian government to replace the expired 1865 treaty with a new treaty based on equality and reciprocity. In November 1926, invoking the doctrine of *rebus sic stantibus*, the Beijing government, to the shock of the Belgian government, unilaterally ended the Belgian Treaty.[72] Dismissing any possible contribution from the Beijing government in this affair, *Guangzhou minguo ribao* devoted substantial column space to the active role played by the people and particularly Chinese expatriates in Belgium, Netherlands, and other European countries. In Guangzhou, the GMD and CCP formed the Committee for the Relinquishing of Expired Treaties (*qüxiao qiman tiaoyue yundonghui*), devolving upon Shang Wenli the leadership of its propaganda bureau. On November 4, 1926, the propaganda bureau convened its first meeting to discuss the draft telegrams to be dispatched to all newspapers in Shanghai, Tianjin, Hankou, and Beijing, and to peasants', merchants', and students' organizations. At this meeting, consensus was reached on methods of communication:

> First, the Declaration shall be handled by Zeng Juejun. Second, print the entire texts, in poster form, of the Sino-Belgian, the Sino-Japanese, and the Sino-French treaties. Third, circulate special issues. Fourth, ask *Minguo ribao* and *Guomin xin-wen* to publish news and articles on the Treaty Cancellation Movement. Fifth, arrange for the publication of illustrated magazines by the propaganda units in the Central Servicemen's Bureau and in the Central Political Bureau. Sixth, greet news reporters. Seventh, telegrams to Chinese overseas to be dispatched by Zhu Hengqiu. Eighth, letters to the oppressed classes and weak nations of the world shall be drafted by Mei Shuzeng. Ninth, organized by Shang Liwen, translations of all statements and telegrams by this Committee [for the Relinquishing of Expired Treaties] into French, English, and German shall be published in pamphlet form. Tenth, statements to the Belgian masses and government are to be handled by Shang Liwen. Eleventh, the division of labor will be arranged at the next meeting.[73]

By contrast, in *Minguo ribao* (Shanghai), almost lost between the hair oil advertisement alerting consumers to fake products and a report on a beauty contest in California, a tiny column quoted Sun Yat-sen's unfulfilled wishes regarding the Unequal Treaties: "Now, the whole way of life in our country is in the hands of foreigners. The more treaties are signed, the more damage they cause, because the rights granted by treaties are always unequal. . . . So we must fight!"[74] Even in the aftermath of the May Thirtieth Incident, *Minguo ribao* continued to run prominent cigarette advertisements side by side with impassioned copy mourning the dead and expressing anger. A particularly ludicrous example occurred when a cigarette advertisement was inserted alongside a special editorial announcement that all entertainment columns would be suspended in honor of those who had died in the May Thirtieth Incident. It carried the caption, "One Capstan, and all that pent-up tension will melt away and you will never be anxious again."[75]

AMBIGUITIES OF THE UNEQUAL TREATIES

Despite its wide use, the term *Unequal Treaties* remains legally undefined and ambiguous in real-life contexts. In modern Chinese dictionaries, the Unequal Treaties refers to treaties detrimental to other countries' sovereignty and territorial integrity. "It has been a tool used in imperialist and hegemonist penetration and expansion."[76] Another definition is provided by diplomat and historian Qian Tai: "Generally, treaties between states are based on mutual benefit and equality; if only one party undertakes an obligation and the other party does not have a corresponding [obligation], the inequality is obvious."[77] In Qian's view, the absence of reciprocity between nation states determines the nature of treaties concluded between them. Mao Zedong took the argument a step further. Referring in 1945 to the conclusion of the new "equal" treaties between the Guomindang government and foreign countries, Mao contended that even bilaterality and mutuality do not guarantee true equality:

> The Chinese people welcome the decision of a number of foreign countries to revoke the Unequal Treaties with China and to take steps to sign new equal treaties. However, the conclusion of the new equal treaties, in our opinion, does not mean that China has, in reality, gained a true equal footing. True equal status can be obtained only by the Chinese people's own efforts rather than by being endowed by foreign governments. The way [to reach such a goal] lies in making China a new democratic nation, politically, economically, and culturally. Otherwise there will be only sham independence and equality.[78]

Furthermore, the precise number of Unequal Treaties signed between China and foreign countries is unclear, as summarized in the introduction. The main source of reference on the treaty issue used by mainland scholars is the three-volume *Zhongwai jiuyuezhang huibian*, containing the texts of 1182 documents. This work is compiled by Wang Tieya, who did not, however, define *Unequal Treaties*.[79] Nor is any figure given for the number of the Unequal Treaties in *Zhongguo duiwai tiaoyue cidian*, an expansion of Wang's standard reference tool, which lists 1,356 treaties.[80]

However, the very vagueness of the phrase *Unequal Treaties* helps explain the unquestioning acceptance of the cultural and political construct embodied by the notion of the treaties. The Unequal Treaties have become a symbol invested with a host of meanings extending well beyond the implications of the first treaty encounter between China and Britain in 1842.[81] I would argue that the ideological conceptions of political groupings, and the historical interpretation of China's encounter with the West jointly created by the CCP and GMD in their revolutionary polemic against imperialism and warlordism, have survived in popular consciousness to this day. The question of the Unequal Treaties is consequently a matter not only of historical, academic, and diplomatic debate, but also of current political and cultural interest.

CONCLUSION

On the basis of the above discussion, a number of observations can be made. First, the discourse of the Unequal Treaties carried on in the 1920s provides insight into the changing nature of the relationship between the GMD and the CCP in the making of modern China. Challenging the conventional view, Wang Qisheng stresses the vigorous and preeminent role played by the CCP in the first United Front.[82] He concludes that commonly used categories of *ronggong* (inclusion of the Communists) and *liangong* (unite with the Communists) are too narrow to capture the nuances in the development of the relationship between the two parties from 1924 to 1927. In 1923, the Communists with only 432 members were far outnumbered by the Guomindang, which allegedly had over 200,000 members.[83] In the shared discourse of the Unequal Treaties, the Communists, as a small yet young and potent political force, took a leading role, injecting the concepts of world and proletariat revolution into their party's propaganda campaign. The circulation of *Xiangdao zhoukan*, the Communists' main journal, reached a claimed circulation of fifty thousand, a notch above other newspapers including the Communist-influenced *Guangzhou guomin ribao* (twelve thousand copies). The GMD had no party newspapers that could compete with the combined strength of the CCP–backed *Xiangdao zhoukan*, *Xin qingnian*, *Zhongguo qingnian* (Chinese Youth), *Qianfeng* (Vanguard), and *Juewu* (Awakening, supplement to the Shanghai *Guomin ribao*). Other indicators of the CCP's advantageous position in the propaganda war was the prolific output by a rather small group of Communist theorists, including Chen Duxiu, Qü Qiubai, and Xiao Chunü, who simply overwhelmed their GMD rival Dai Jitao. The number of articles—albeit an incomplete total—reprinted in *Selected Essays of Chen Duxiu*, written by Chen between January 1924 and April 1927, is 438[84]—an achievement no one in the GMD, after the death of Sun, could match.

Secondly, elements of the content, style, rhetoric, and polemic of the discourse of the Unequal Treaties have been integrated into the common inheritance of Chinese-ness. Significant legacies of the century-long history of the Unequal Treaties and their accompanying national humiliations are the twin contradictory images of China as a victim of Western imperialism and as a vanquisher who rises from the ashes like a phoenix, determined to terminate foreign rights.

Both the Guomindang and the Communists tapped into the same vocabularies and specifics of the Unequal Treaties for their own political ends. In 1943, labeling the treaties as the "yoke" (*shufu*) and "national humiliation" (*guochi*) that "prevented our [the GMD] efforts to build a nation," Jiang Jieshi acclaimed the removal of the Unequal Treaties as "a new epoch" (*xin jiyuan*) and "the most important page" in Chinese history.[85] Fifty-four years later, at the ceremony celebrating Hong Kong's return to China in 1997, Chinese President Jiang Zemin described the handover as "the redemption (*xuechi*) from one hundred years of national humiliation (*bainian guochi*)," and attributed this success to the Chinese people under the leadership of the Communists.[86] Hong Kong's reversion to China, Jiang continued, had been perceived in every corner of the nation as a great landmark in China's century-long pursuit of equality in the world order of nation states.[87] At the same time, across the Taiwan Strait, the National Palace Museum, in association with the Ministry of Foreign Affairs, the Academia Historica, and the Government Information Office, had organized an exhibition entitled "Humiliation and Revival: From the Treaty of Nanking to the Japanese Surrender."[88] According to the organizers, the exhibition was arranged around two themes: "humiliation" documented the Qing dynasty's repeated diplomatic defeats beginning with the Treaty of Nanjing in 1842, whereas "revival" recorded the efforts to abolish inequitable treaties since the founding of the Republic of China in 1912. Just prior to the return of Macau to China in December 1999, a second exhibition, entitled "The Twists of Destiny: A Special Exhibition of Historical Documents on Macau," was held by the same organizers with the same aims.[89] These events are reminders of the shared experience in the construction of China's identity in the first third of the twentieth century—an achievement for which neither the GMD nor the CCP can claim sole credit.

Thirdly, the perplexing discourse of the Unequal Treaties in China also has its global relevance. For instance, on September 12, 1983, the *New York Times* published a letter from Stuart S. Malawer, a law professor at the George Mason University, in response to the assertion made by Sol M. Linowitz, chief U.S. negotiator of the Panama Canal Treaty. Linowitz had suggested, with reference to the Sino-British negotiations of the future of Hong Kong, that prior to the drafting of the UN Charter in 1945 all unequal treaties should be considered illegal.[90] In his letter, Malawer comments that "Ambassador Sol M. Linowitz proposes a reasonable suggestion concerning use of the Panama Canal Treaties as a precedent in renegotiating the status of Hong Kong. However, his statements that the claim of 'unequal treaties' by both Panama and China invalidates their respective agreements [of 1903 and of 1898, respectively] are grossly misleading and need to be refuted." Malawer is correct in stating that the newly developed international law as specified in the Vienna Convention on the Law of Treaties does not apply to treaties concluded before the coming into force of the 1969 Convention.

In sum, both the content and form of the Unequal Treaties discourse were widely utilized in the mid 1920s and can be best understood as part of the endeavor to bring about mass mobilization and attain political legitimacy by competing and collaborating political forces. In *Awakening China: Politics, Culture, and Class in the Nationalist Revolution*, John Fitzgerald connects nationalism with the political culture of mass awakening.[91] Fitzgerald details the rather complicated relationship, sometimes manifested in chaotic squabbles and sometimes in partnership (or in tutorship) between Sun Yat-sen, Mao Zedong, Dai Jitao, and Ye Chucang, in the making of party-state ideologies.[92] From a different perspective, Steve A. Smith links nationalism with the labor movement by noting that the massive labor protests and labor organizations that sprang up between 1925 and 1927 were "an expression of militant nationalism rather than of class consciousness." Therefore, "class," Smith observes, "formed a fault line around which competing conceptions of the nation crystallized."[93] I depart from both these views and argue that China's struggle for national identity is alternatively reflected in the discourse of the Unequal Treaties. The nub of this discourse lies in the broad political narrative of national humiliation and eventual salvation. In the years 1923–1927 the discourse of the Unequal Treaties came to define both the realities of China's most recent past and those who were to be hailed as its messianic patriots. The rhetoric used in the debate about the Unequal Treaties can thus be seen as instrumental in the nation-building process.

The discourse of the Unequal Treaties—moving from rambling imperial expressions, to diplomatic exegesis, to organized party rhetoric, then to the competing polemic of the GMD and CCP in making their contributions to expunging one hundred years of humiliation (1842–1943)—exhibits the pattern of Chinese nationalism, in contrast to other countries' handling of the same issue, in particular Japan and Turkey.[94] The discourse therefore became a Chinese repository of techniques for achieving national salvation and national strength.

NOTES

1. Key works in the most recent English historiography are Henrietta Harrison, *The Making of the Republican Citizen: Political Ceremonies and Symbols in China, 1911–1929*, reprint ed. (Oxford: Oxford University Press, 2002); Terry Bodenhorn, ed., *Defining Modernity: Guomindang Rhetorics of a New China, 1920–1970* (Ann Arbor: University of Michigan Press, 2003); Henrietta Harrison, *Inventing the Nation: China* (London: Arnold, 2001); John Fitzgerald, *Awakening China: Politics, Culture, Class in the Nationalist Revolution* (Stanford, Calif.: Stanford University Press, 1996); Stephen Anthony Smith, *Like Cattle and Horses: Nationalism and Labor in Shanghai, 1895–1927* (Durham, N.C.: Duke University Press, 2002); Kai-wing Chow, ed., *Constructing Nationhood in Modern East Asia* (Ann Arbor: University of Michigan Press, 2001); Paul A. Cohen, "Remembering and Forgetting National Humiliation in Twentieth-Century China," *Twentieth-Century China* 27, no. 2 (April 2002): 1–39.

2. Disagreeing with Lee Enhan, Edmund S. K. Fung distinguishes radical and moderate phases in the GMD's dealing with the Unequal Treaties between 1924–1927 and 1928–1931 by stressing the inner dynamics in Nationalist foreign relations. He argues that China's internal problems had a greater bearing on the Nationalist Party's limited achievements (on the treaty issue) than did external (foreign) resistance. Edmund S. K. Fung, "The Chinese Nationalists and the Unequal Treaties 1924–1931," *Modern Asia Studies* 21, no. 4 (1987): 793–819; Lee, *Beifa hou de geming waijiao*. For a detailed discussion of the negotiations over the abrogation of British and American extraterritoriality in China, see K. C. Chan, "The Abrogation of British Extraterritoriality in China 1942–1943: A Study of Anglo-American-Chinese Relations," *Modern Asian Studies* 2, no. 2 (1977): 257–91.

3. Hungdah Chiu's "Comparison of the Nationalist and Communist Chinese Views of Unequal Treaties" expands the legal dimension of the development of the concept of the Unequal Treaties in China. Nonetheless, consideration of the overlapping roles of the GMD and CCP and the rhetoricalization of the concept of the Unequal Treaties is omitted in his study. See Chiu, "Comparison of the Nationalist and Communist Chinese Views," 239–67. Also see Hungdah Chiu, "China's Struggle against the 'Unequal Treaties,' 1927–1946," in *Chinese Yearbook of International Law and Affairs* (Baltimore, Md.: Occasional Paper/Reprints Series in Contemporary Asian Studies, Inc., 1985), 5:1–28.

4. For Chen Duxiu's and Li Daozhao's commentaries on the Paris Peace Conference and May Fourth Movement, see Ding Shouhe et al., eds., *Zhongguo jindai qimeng yundong sichao* [Modern Chinese enlightenment thought], vol. 2 (Beijing: Shehui kexue wenxian chubanshe, 1999).

5. *"Zhongguo guomindang zhi fanfeng zhanzheng xuanchuan dagang"* [Propaganda Outline for the Chinese Nationalist Party's Anti-Fengtian Warlords Campaign]. See Mao Zedong, *Mao Zedong ji* [Collected works of Mao Zedong], vol. 1 (1917–1927) (n.p.: Yishan tushu, 1976), 101–7.

6. *Guangzhou minguo ribao* [Guangzhou republican daily], October 6, 1925.

7. In this outline, Mao formulated nine slogans in all including "Dadao yingmeiri diguo zhuyi" [Down with British, American and Japanese Imperialism], "Dadao yiqie yinmou zhengpai" [Down with all plotting political factions], and "Qüxiao bupingdeng tiaoyue" [Abolish the Unequal Treaties]. Mao Z., *Mao Zedong ji*, 1:101–7.

8. See introduction.

9. Qin Xiaoyi, ed., *Guofu quanji* [The complete works of the founding father] (Taibei: Jindai zhongguo chubanshe, 1989), 2:111.

10. The Chinese equivalence is *Zhongguo gongchandang danggang cao'an*. Zhongyang dang'an'guan, ed., *Zhonggong zhongyang wenjian xuanji* [Selected documents of the Central Committee of the Chinese Communist Party] (Beijing: Zhonggong zhongyang dangxiao chubanshe, 1989), 1:141.

11. Jiang Yongjing, *Hu Hanmin xiansheng nianpu* [A chronicle of the life of Mr. Hu Hanmin] (Taibei: Zhongguo guomindang dangshi weiyuanhui, 1978), 232.

12. Cheng Taisheng, *Hu Hanmin de zhengzhi sixiang* [The political thought of Hu Hanmin] (Taibei: Liming wenhua shiye gufen youxian gongsi, 1980), chapter 4, particularly 102–5.

13. Qin, *Guofu quanji*, 2:138.

14. "Zhongguo gongren suoshou bupingdeng tiaoyue zhihai" [The harm done by the Unequal Treaties to the Chinese working class], Qin, *Guofu quanji*, 3:462–67.

15. "Nongmin da lianhe" [The grand peasant alliance], Qin, *Guofa quanji*, 3:482–87.

16. Qin, *Guofa quanji*, 3:516–25.

17. Cheng D. et al., *Zhonghua minguo waijiaoshi ziliao xuanbian*, 1:292–93.

18. "Northern Trip Declaration," November 10, 1924, in *Zhonghua minguo waijiaoshi ziliao xuanbian, 1919–1931*, ed. Cheng D. et al., 1:288–92, 1:296–99.

19. The treaty was signed by Wellington Koo and L. M. Karakhan in May 1924. In Article 12, Soviet Russia agreed to renounce all special rights and privileges acquired by the Tsarist Government under all previous treaties. The study by Bruce A. Elleman reveals Soviet Russia's treacherous posture on its extraterritorial rights in China. In practice, the Soviet Union still retained extraterritorial rights until 1960, by turning legal ambiguities to their advantage and signing a series of secret treaties with China in 1929, 1939, 1945, and 1950. Bruce A. Elleman, "The End of Extraterritoriality in China: The Case of the Soviet Union, 1917–1960," *Republican China* 21, no. 2 (April 1996): 65–89.

20. "Beijing baxiao lianxihui feiyue xuanyan "[Declaration on treaty cancellation by the union of the eight universities in Beijing] *Xiangdao zhoubao* [Guide Weekly] 76 (July 30, 1924).

21. Shang Hai et al, eds., *Minguoshi da cidian* [Dictionary of the history of the Republic of China] (Beijing: Zhongguo guangbo dianshi chubanshe, 1991), 80; Pollard, *China's Foreign Relations*, 289.

22. *China Weekly Review* 29 (August 2, 1924): 291; Pollard, *China's Foreign Relations*, 289.

23. Wei Zhi, "Feiyue yundong" [The Treaty Cancellation Movement], *Xiangdao zhoubao* 76 (July 30, 1924).

24. September Seventh, considered a "day of humiliation" in China, is the day when the Boxer Protocol was signed.

25. Long Chi, "Feiyue yundong yü jiuqi jinian" [Treaty cancellation and the September Seventh commemoration], *Xiangdao zhoubao* 170 (September 10, 1926).

26. Chiu, "Comparison of the Nationalist and Communist Chinese Views," 239–403.

27. Fitzgerald, *Awakening China: Politics, Culture*, 237.

28. On the condition that every signatory ratified the treaty, the Nine-Power Treaty of February 1922 authorized the convening of a special conference on tariffs to address China's concern

over its low fixed tariffs. However, the divergence of opinion on the annual payment of the Boxer indemnities between China and France, known as the Gold Franc Controversy, became an excuse for the French government to suspend its ratification of the Washington treaties. Because of currency devaluation after World War I, the French government demanded the Beijing government should pay the remainder of the Boxer indemnities in gold franc, instead of franc. The gold franc at the time had a higher exchange rate than the franc. The Gold Franc Controversy was settled by Chinese concessions under the Duan Qirui administration. Lai Xinxia et al., *Beiyang junfa* [The Beiyang warlords] (Tianjin: Nankai daxue chubanshe, 2000), 2:868–74; Shang et al., *Minguoshi da cidian*, 72. For a pro-French interpretation, see Woodhead, *The China Year Book* (1924–1925), 837–49. For a detailed description and analysis of China's losses in figures, see Wang Shu-hwai, *Gengzi peikuan*, 365–426.

29. "Guochi jinianri xigao quanguo tongbao" [A letter to all compatriots on National Humiliation Day], *Xiangdang zhoukan* 64 (May 7, 1924).

30. Zhongguo di'er lishi dang'an'guan, ed., *Zhonghua mingguoshi dang'an ziliao huibian* [Collected archival sources for the history of the Republic of China], vol. 4 (Nanjing: Jiangsu guji chubanshe, 1979), 1554 (in part 2).

31. In early 1925, workers at a Japanese cotton mill in Shanghai went on strike. On May 15, Gu Zhenghong, one of the labor representatives who went to negotiate with the management, was killed in a melee. The foreign controlled Shanghai Municipal Council failed to prosecute the Japanese who opened fire, but arrested some workers for disturbance. This resulted in a series of mass demonstrations and protests. On May 30, 1925, students and laborers participated in memorial services in honor of Gu. The crowds proceeded to parade in the International Settlement. The British police started shooting killing thirteen demonstrators and wounded many more. The May Thirtieth Incident triggered off nationwide strikes and boycotts organized against British and Japanese goods and factories. "May Thirtieth Incident," Encyclopedia Britannica Premium Service, http://www.britannica.com/eb/article?eu=52852 (accessed July 19, 2004).

32. Xing Heng, "Suqi yanjiu bupingdeng tiaoyue" [Expedite research on the unequal treaties], *Liuxue tekan* [Bleeding special issue], *Ziqiang* [Self-strengthening], no. 2 (June 9, 1925). Reprinted by and ed. *Shenbao* and Qinghua xueshenghui [*Shenbao* and Qinghua Student Association], *Wusha tongshi* [The bitter history of May Thirtieth] (Taibei: Wenhai chubanshe, 1966–1987), 174–75.

33. Xing, "Suqi yanjiu bupingdeng tiaoyue." The author meant that without the low fixed tariffs, it would be impossible for Japanese to set up their factories in China, and Chinese would not need to seek employment from Japanese firms.

34. Xing, "Suqi yanjiu bupingdeng tiaoyue." For similar views, see Meng Sen's article in *Wusha tongshi*, ed. *Shenbao* and Qinghua xueshenghui, 179–82. Taiwanese scholar Li Jianmin has produced a thorough study of the anti-British propaganda movement that arose in the aftermath of the May Thirtieth Incident, focusing on propaganda organizations, approaches, activities, content and impact. See Li Jianmin, *Wusha hou de fanying yundong* [The Anti-British movement following the May Thirtieth Incident, 1925–1926] (Taibei: Institute of Modern History, Academia Sinica, 1986), chapter 2.

35. Murray Edelman, *Politics as Symbolic Action* (New York: Academic Press, 1971), 76–80. The theoretical framework presented in Edelman's *The Symbolic Use of Politics* (Urbana: University of Illinois Press, 1964) and *Politics as Symbolic Action* has proved useful in conceptualizing the rhetoric of the Unequal Treaties. For works on mass mobilization and the role of political parties in the use of symbolic power, see James R. Townsend, *Political Participation in Communist China* (Berkeley: University of California Press, 1967); Alan P. L. Liu, *Mass Politics in the People's Republic of China: State and Society in Contemporary China* (Boulder, Colo.: Westview Press, 1996); Jeffrey N. Wasserstrom and Elizabeth J. Perry, eds., *Popular Protest and Political Culture in Modern China: Learning from 1989* (Boulder, Colo.: Westview Press, 1991).

36. Woodhead, *The China Year Book* (1926), 934–35.

37. Zhongguo Guomingdang zhongyangweiyuanhui dangshi weiyuanhui, *Geming wenxian* [Revolutionary documents] (Taibei: Zhongguo Guomingdang zhongyangweiyuanhui dangshi weiyuanhui, 1978), 69:140–42.

38. Zhongguo di'er lishi dang'an'guan, *Zhonghua mingguoshi dang'an ziliao huibian*, 4:1608 (in part 2).

39. Zhongguo Guomingdang zhongyangweiyuanhui dangshi weiyuanhui, *Geming wenxian*, 69:177–79.

40. Zhongguo Guomingdang zhongyangweiyuanhui dangshi weiyuanhui, *Geming wenxian*, 69:177–79.

41. For an analysis of the language adopted by the CCP as a form of power, see Michael Schoenhals, *Doing Things with Words in Chinese Politics: Five Studies* (Berkeley: University of California Press, 1992).

42. Zhongguo di'er lishi dang'an'guan, *Zhonghua minguoshi dang'an ziliao huibian*, 4:1610–11 (in part 2).

43. Jiang Jieshi, "Wancheng geming, bixian dadao diguo zhuyi" [To accomplish the revolution, first down with imperialism] August 1925. See Jia Botao, ed., *Jiang Zhongzheng xiansheng yanshuo ji* [Collected speeches of Mr. Jiang Jieshi] (Shanghai: Shanghai sanmin chubanshe, 1925), 96–112.

44. Mao Z., *Mao Zedong ji*, vol. 1 (1917–1927), 141–51.

45. Xuan, "Zheng fei biyue de mianmian guan" [A comprehensive examination of the abrogation of the Belgian Treaty] *Xiangdao zhoubao* 178 (November 15, 1926).

46. Pollard, *China's Foreign Relations*, 295.

47. *The North-China Herald*, November 27, 1926, 387; Nicholas R. Clifford, *Spoilt Children of Empire: Westerners in Shanghai and the Chinese Revolution of the 1920s* (Hanover, N.H.: Middlebury College Press, 1991), 165.

48. Cheng Weijia, "Feichu bupingdeng tiaoyue wenti" [The question of the abolition of the Unequal Treaties], *Dongfang zhazhi* [The Eastern Miscellany] 23, no. 12 (December 25, 1926): 5–23.

49. The original Chinese measurements of the carved stone inscriptions are 3 *zhang* and 5 *chi* wide, and 4 *zhang* long per character. (1 *zhang*=3.33 meters, 1 *chi*=1 meter). See Waiyü jiaoxue yü yanjiu chubanshe, ed., *Xiandai hanying cidian* [A Modern Chinese-English Dictionary], 5th reprint (Beijing: Waiyü jiaoxue yü yanjiu chubanshe, 1991), 112, 1120; *Guangzhou minguo ribao*, December 30, 1926.

50. Hu Shi, "The Chinese Situation Today," *The North-China Daily News*, December 24, 1926.

51. Duara, *Rescuing History from the Nation*, 5.

52. Koo, "The Wellington Koo Memoir," reel 1, "Diplomats and Diplomacy."

53. *The North-China Herald*, May 22, 1926, 334.

54. Edelman, *The Symbolic Use of Politics*, 121, 124.

55. Allen S. Whiting, *Soviet Policies in China, 1917–1924*, 2nd ed. (New York: Columbia University Press, 1957), 11–23.

56. Zhongguo shehui kexueyuan, trans., *Gongchan guoji youguan zhongguo geming de wenxian, 1919–1928* [The Comintern documents on the Chinese revolution, 1919–1928], vol. 1, the Communist International Second Congress, July 19–August 7, 1920 (Beijing: Zhongguo shehuikexue chubanshe, 1980), 15–32.

57. C. Martin Wilbur and Julie Lien-ying How, *Missionaries of Revolution: Soviet Advisers and Nationalist China, 1920–1927* (Cambridge, Mass.: Harvard University Press, 1989), introduction; R. A. Ulyanovsky, ed., *The Comintern and the East: The Struggle for the Leninist Strategy and Tactics in National Liberation Movements* (Moscow: Progress Publishers, 1979), preface.

58. Guandong shehui kexueyuan, ed., *Sun Zhongshan quanji* [Collected works of Sun Zhongshan] (Beijing: Zhonghua shujü, 1986), 9:509.

59. Kai-shek Chiang, *Soviet Russia in China: A Summing-up at Seventy* (New York: Farrar, Straus & Cudahy, Inc., 1957), 5.

60. Chen Duxiu, "Zaoguo lun" [On the creation of the nation-state], *Xiangdao zhoubao* 2 (September 20, 1922). On the issue of uniting two classes, Gao Junyü held divergent views. See "Du Duxiu jun zaoguolun de yiwen" [Some questions on Mr. Duxiu's essay on the creation of the nation-state], *Xiangdao zhoubao* 4 (October 4, 1922).

61. Tong Bingrong, "Zhongshan xiansheng shishi hou de Guomindang" [The Nationalist Party after the death of Mr. Zhongshan], *Guangzhou minguo ribao*, March 20, 1926.

62. Chunü, "Jinian zongli ying wuwang Zongli de geming fanglue" [For those who commemorate the Premier, don't forget the Premier's revolutionary strategies], *Guangzhou minguo ribao Sun Zongli zhounian jinianhao* [Commemorative issue on the Premier's first anniversary, Guangzhou minguo ribao], March 12, 1926, 6.

63. Sun Duo, "Guomin yundong gemingjun he geming xuanchuan" [Revolutionary Army and revolutionary propaganda in the Nationalist Movement], *Xiangdao zhoubao* 9 (November 8, 1922).

64. Chen Duxiu, "Duiyü Shanghai Wusha jinian yundong zhi ganxiang" [Reaction to the May Thirtieth commemorative activities in Shanghai], *Shanghai shimin jinian Wusha yongdong tekan* [Special issue on the May Thirtieth commemorative activities among Shanghai citizens], *Xiangdao zhoukan* 156 (June 3, 1926).

65. Zhang Guotao, "Yifeng gongkai de xin zhi guomindang quanti dangyuan" [An open letter to all Guomindang party members], *Xiangdao Zhoubao* 139 (December 20, 1925).

66. Chen Duxiu, "Sun Zhongshan xiansheng shishi er zhounian zhong zhi beifen" [Anguish on the second anniversary of Mr. Sun Zhongshan's death], *Xiangdao Zhoubao* 191 (March 12, 1927).

67. See Shu Zhi, "Muqian geming youqing de weixian" [The danger of the Rightist tendency in the current revolution]; Du Xiu, "Guomingdang dangnei jiufen yü Zhongguo geming" [The GMD's internal strife and the Chinese revolution], *Xiangdao zhoubao* 190 (March 6, 1927); Du Xiu, "Ping Jiang Jieshi sanyue qiri zhi yanjiang" [On Jiang Jieshi's March 7 speech], *Xiangdao zhoubao* 190 (March 18, 1927).

68. Long Chi, "Feiyue yundong yü jiuqi jinian" [The Treaty Cancellation Movement and Remembering September Seventh], *Xiangdao zhoubao* 170 (September 10, 1926).

69. "Shanghai fan diguo zhuyi datongmeng chengli dahui" [The celebration party of the Shanghai Anti-imperialist Grand Union], *Shishi xinbao* (September 8, 1925), in *Wusha yundong shiliao* [Sources on the May Thirtieth Movement], ed. Shanghai shehui kexue lishi yanjiusuo (Shanghai: Shanghai renmin chubanshe, 1986), 2:747–49.

70. Qiu Bai, "Wusha yundong zhong zhi guomin geming yü jieji douzheng" [The Nationalist Revolution and class struggle in the May Thirtieth Movement], *Xiangdao zhoubao* 129 (September 11, 1925). See also Qü Qiubai, "Guomin huiyi yü Wusha yundong: Zhongguo gemingshi shang de yijiu er'wu" [The National Reconstruction Conference and the May Thirtieth Movement: 1925 in Chinese revolutionary history], *Xin qingnian*[New Youth], no. 3 (March 25, 1926). For the content of the 17-clause terms of negotiation, see *Minguo ribao*, June 8, 1925, in *Wusha yundong shiliao*, ed. Shanghai shehui kexue lishi yanjiusuo, 2:280–82. See also 251–67 and 583–84 for details of, and the debate over, the 13-clause terms of negotiation proposed separately by the Shanghai Chamber of Commerce on June 12, 1925.

71. For parochial and ideological cleavages between the Shanghai and Guangzhou offices of the CCP and GMD, see Fitzgerald, *Awakening China*, chapter 6, "One Party, One Voice: The Nationalist Propaganda Bureau." However, internal fractures, especially within the CCP, were far more complicated than Fitzgerald suggests. From time to time, editorials in the CCP–influenced *Guangzhou minguo ribao* expressed dissatisfaction with what they labeled "unfounded criticism" of the GMD rightists by the CCP's *Xiangdao zhoubao*. See Fu Mu, "Gao piping Guomingdang de tongzhi" [To those comrades who are critical of the GMD], *Guangzhou minguo ribao* (November 3 and 4, 1924).

72. Koo, *Gu Weijun huiyilu*, 1:355–60.

73. *Guangzhou minguo ribao*, November 4, 1926.

74. *Minguo ribao* (Shanghai), April 26, 1925.

75. *Minguo ribao* (Shanghai), June 3, 1925. For comparison, see *Guangzhou guomin ribao*, June 29, 1925.

76. Cihai bianji weiyuanhui, ed., *Cihai* [Chinese Encyclopedia], 2nd ed. (Shanghai: Shanghai cishu chubanshe, 1983), 1331.

77. Qian Tai, *Zhongguo bupingdeng tiaoyue zhi yuanqi jiqi feichu zhi jingguo* [The origins and abrogation of the Chinese Unequal Treaties] (Taibei: Guofang yanjiusui, 1961). Hungdah Chiu's translation is adopted here. Chiu, "Comparison of the Nationalist and Communist Chinese Views," 249.

78. Mao Zedong, "Lun lianhe zhengfu" [On the United Government], in *Zhonggong zhongyang wenjian xuanji*, ed. Zhongyang dang'an'guan, 15:406.

79. Wang Tieya, *Zhongwai jiu yuezhang huibian*. Most mainland historians now accept that not all the instruments collected in Wang's work can be classified as unequal treaties. See Deng Zhenglai, ed., *Wang Tieya xueshu wenhua suibi* [Wang Tieya's academic and cultural essays] (Beijing: Zhongguo qingnian chubanshe, 1999), 33.

80. Zhu Huan and Wang Hengwei, eds., *Zhongguo duiwai tiaoyue cidian* [Dictionary of treaties between China and foreign countries] (Changchun: Jilin jiaoyü chubanshe, 1994).

81. On this point I have been inspired by James Hevia's article on the changing meaning of the Oberlin arch. "Monument and Memory: The Oberlin College Boxer Memorial as a Contested Site," manuscript.

82. Wang Qisheng, "Cong 'ronggong' dao 'rongguo': 1924–1927 nian guogong dangji guanxi zai kaocha" [From "Inclusion of the Communists" to "Inclusion of the Guomindang"— reexamining the 1924–1927 GMD–CCP relationship], *Jindaishi yanjiu* 4 (2001): 37–85.

83. "Zhongguo gongchandang ge shiqi dangyuan renshu tongji shuzi" [Statistics of CCP membership at different periods], Zhongguo shehui kexueyuan and Zhongguo gongchandang dangshi xuehui; "Wei zhonghua zhi jueqi: jinian Zhongguo Gongchandang chenli bashi zhounian" [For the rise of China: in memory of the 80th anniversary of the CCP], http://www .cass.net.cn/zhuanti (accessed October 20, 2004). For the numerical strength of the GMD, see Wang Qisheng, "Cong 'ronggong' dao 'rongguo': 1924–1927 nian guogong dangji guanxi zai kaocha."

84. Wang Q., "Cong 'ronggong' dao 'rongguo'"; Sanlian shudian, ed., *Chen Duxiu wenzhang xuanbian* [Selected essays of Chen Duxiu] (Beijing: Sanlian shudian, 1984).

85. Jiang Jieshi, *Zhongguo zhi mingyun* [China's Destiny] (Chongqing: Zhengzhong shujü, 1943), 118; Chiang Kai-shek (Jiang Jieshi), *China's Destiny*, trans. Wang Chonghui (New York: MacMillan, 1947), introduction.

86. Jiang Zemin's speech at the celebration ceremony in Beijing, *Renmin ribao*, July 2, 1997.

87. Jiang Zemin's speech on Hong Kong's handover, *Remin ribao* [The People's Daily], July 2, 1997; Townsend, "Chinese Nationalism," 97–130.

88. http://www.npm.gov.tw/exhibition (accessed February 10, 2003).

89. http://www.npm.gov.tw/exhibition/mac9912/ehtm/emac9912.htm (accessed February 28, 2004).

90. Sol M. Linowitz, winner of the Presidential Medal of Freedom in 1998, is a former U.S. ambassador to the Organization of American States (1966–1969), a conegotiator of the Panama Canal treaties and, later, President Carter's ambassador-at-large for Middle East negotiations (1979–1981). See Darryl Geddes, "Trustee Emeritus Sol Linowitz Given Top Civilian Honor," *Cornell Chronicle* 20, no. 18 (January 22, 1998).

91. Fitzgerald, *Awakening China*. In chapter 6, "One Party, One Voice," Fitzgerald narrates the story of competing political styles and personnel change in revolutionary organizations, as well as Mao Zedong's measures to standardize propaganda operations in the Nationalist Propaganda Bureau.

92. Ye Chucang was the editor of the Shanghai *Minguo ribao*. For a sketch of the history of the Shanghai *Minguo ribao* (1916–1947), see Wang H. and Zhu H., *Zhongguo baokan cidian*, 72–73;

Zhang Xianwen et al., eds., *Zhonghua minguo da cidian* [Dictionary of the Republic of China] (Nanjing: Jiangsu guji chubanshe, 2001), 617.

93. Smith, *Like Cattle and Horses*, 2, 190.

94. For works on Japan's experience with the Unequal Treaties, see Louis G. Perez, *Japan Comes of Age: Mutsu Munemitsu and the Revision of the Unequal Treaties* (Cranbury, N.J.: Associated University Press, 1999); I. H. Nish, "Japan Reverses the Unequal Treaties: The Anglo-Japanese Commercial Treaties of 1894," *Journal of Oriental Studies* VXIII, no. 2 (1975): 137–45; Shinya Murase, "The Most-Favored–Nation Treatment in Japan's Treaty Practice during the Period 1854–1905," *The American Journal of International Law* 70, no. 2 (1976): 273–97; Michael R. Auslin, *Negotiating with Imperialism: The Unequal Treaties and the Culture of Japanese Diplomacy* (Cambridge, Mass.: Harvard University Press, 2004).

4

Redeeming a Century of National Ignominy: Nationalism and Party Rivalry over the Unequal Treaties, 1928–1947

This chapter argues that after the break-up of the GMD–CCP alliance in 1927, how to interpret the Unequal Treaties remained a hotly contested area in the two parties' struggle for power and legitimacy.[1] A careful examination of CCP and GMD documents related to the Unequal Treaties between 1928 and 1937 suggests that the Communists, as an outlawed and persecuted party in the late 1920s and early 1930s, did not cede the "high patriotic ground" of national independence to the incumbent Nationalist government, and vice versa.[2] The representation of the Unequal Treaties by both the GMD and the Communists during their anti-Japanese United Front from 1937 to 1945 displayed—in its reference both to the past and the present—an emphasis on unity, coalition, and contested claims to political authority and national history.

The issue of who carries the mandate of Heaven to represent the Chinese people and their future manifested itself in the different interpreations and changing arguments presented by the two rivals over three sets of treaties— the 1943 Sino-British Treaty for the Abolition of Extraterritoriality and Related Rights in China, along with the Treaty between the Republic of China and the U.S. for the Relinquishment of Extraterritorial Rights in China and the Regulation of Related Matters; the 1945 Treaty of Friendship and Alliance between the Republic of China and the U.S.S.R.; and the 1946 Sino-American Treaty of Friendship, Commerce, and Navigation.[3] Over the years, competing forces within China had highlighted the problematic nature of these treaties. In particular, changing memories and judgments about the treaties functioned as a vital resource for both the GMD and CCP in developing their grand strategies for winning China. Claims for legitimacy and authority were asserted and reasserted through the repeated labeling and relabeling of the Unequal Treaties in party and state controlled historiography.

COMPETITION OVER THE UNEQUAL TREATIES, 1928–1937: VITAL OR IN ECLIPSE?

In this section, I argue that from 1928 to 1937 partisan discourse about the Unequal Treaties, far from fading, remained alive and contributed to inter-party clashes, although not on the same scale or in the same manner as in the pre-1928 and the post-1945 periods. Although the ten years between 1930 and 1940 saw no breakthrough in the struggle for the abolition of extraterritoriality, the Unequal Treaties did not disappear from the sphere of public discourse. On the contrary, the intellectual and popular interest in, and publications on, the Unequal Treaties flourished during this period. For the GMD, the Unequal Treaties remained a live issue in the party discussions on foreign policy. For the Communists, though, as Jerome Ch'en notes, this "was a time of disaster, trial and tribulation" that brought them close to extinction,[4] the sources reveal that in spite of the failure to maintain its underground urban work, and the forced strategic relocation (Long March) from its Soviet bases in the mountainous Jiangxi and Fujian provinces, the party worked to keep the issue of the Unequal Treaties alive, at least in its political rhetoric. References to the Unequal Treaties made by the CCP at this period suggest that the Communists had by no means scrapped nationalism and patriotism and left these causes to be championed by the Nationalists.

Rather than being forgotten, the rhetorical use of the term *Unequal Treaties* was evolving. First, the issue of the Unequal Treaties was given a central place on the agenda of the Jiang Jieshi GMD government inaugurated in Nanjing on April 18, 1927, one week after Jiang's purge of the Communists. As it consolidated its power, the GMD also pursued the issue of the Unequal Treaties with new vigor. In a statement made on June 15, 1928, the Nanjing government announced that China was at last unified and that the civil wars were over. The Nationalist government had begun its reconstruction work amid the ruins left by military operations and the time was ripe for taking immediate steps "in accordance with legitimate and diplomatic procedures, to negotiate new treaties with friendly countries on the basis of equality and mutual respect."[5] Among the foreign powers, it was the U.S. that took the lead in consenting to sign a new treaty with the Nationalists. On June 11, despite the fact that the U.S. had not yet formally recognized the new government, Frank B. Kellogg, the American secretary of state, agreed to discuss the questions of tariffs with Wu Chaoshu, the GMD minister to Washington. After a few days of meetings between John Van Antwerp MacMurray and T. V. Soong, a new treaty was agreed on July 25, 1928. The new treaty, which constituted a de facto recognition of the GMD government, contains only two articles. On the condition that the U.S. would continue to enjoy most-favored-nation status, the U.S. recognized China's right of tariff autonomy.[6] Other countries that signed similar treaties with the Nanjing government included Germany (August 1928), Norway (November 1928), the Netherlands (November 1928), Sweden (December 1928), Britain (December 1928), France (December 1928), and Japan (May 1930).

As for the issue of extraterritoriality,[7] during the first few years of its existence the GMD government made resolute attempts to bring all foreigners in China under Chinese jurisdiction. On December 28, 1929, the GMD went so far as to revoke foreign exterritorial rights unilaterally with effect from January 1, 1930—something that would have subjected all foreign residents to Chinese law.[8] However, two days later, Foreign Minister Wang Zhengting (C. T. Wang) made a statement toning down this stern measure and indicating that the Nanjing government would negotiate exceptions with any country that might have problems meeting the requirements of the new law, within a given time frame.[9] In 1931, the new national crisis triggered by the Mukden Incident put an end to the protracted negotiations between the GMD, Britain, the U.S., and Japan.[10] On December 29, 1931, the GMD government announced the suspension of its order revoking exterritorial rights issued two years before.[11]

Besides the high priority given to the Unequal Treaties issue by the GMD regime, a second major factor in the revival of the polemic associated with the Unequal Treaties, in pronouncements emanating from both parties, was the frequent linking of the Unequal Treaties with the terms for shame and humiliation. However, the tone of the debate had changed. The incumbent GMD government labeled the CCP as troublemakers and rebels who made the most of an opportunity to stir up the masses. In contrast to the restrained expression of its differences on the Unequal Treaties prior to 1927,[12] in this period the Communists' verbal assaults on the Nationalists were focused, explicit, and aggressive. Each party used the Jinan Incident of May 3, 1928, to highlight its role as the guarantor of a better China by offering interpretations of events reflecting its own interests and perspectives.

In May 1928, as GMD troops approached Shandong Province on their Northern Expedition aimed at unifying China, the new Japanese prime minister and foreign minister, Tanaka Giichi, dispatched troops to Shandong on the pretext of protecting Japanese civilians. On May 3, Japanese soldiers fired on Nationalist troops and civilians. In self-defense, the GMD forces launched limited counterattacks, but did not engage the Japanese forces further. The Japanese retaliated, bombing residential areas and invading the GMD's foreign affairs bureau, causing thousands of military, diplomatic, and civilian casualties.[13] The Nanjing government reacted by labeling the "May Third Massacre" a galling act of shame and humiliation (*qichi daru*), denouncing the Japanese action as a premeditated violation of international law and Chinese sovereignty committed by the Tanaka warlords. In its May

Third guidelines for propagandists, the Nationalist Party advised its supporters to exercise restraint and preserve order so as to prevent the Communist "bandits" from making trouble and taking advantaging of anti-Japanese sentiment. GMD propaganda included the slogans: "We shall fight under GMD leadership" and "We ask the Northern Expedition Army to take over Beijing, to unify China, and to urge Japan to cancel all unequal treaties."[14]

The CCP, in the meantime, commented on the outbreak of the Jinan Incident and on the GMD's reaction, which, in the Communist view, underlay the "internal" conflict of interests within the camp of the Japanese imperialists and the Jiang government. The CCP, on the one hand, condemned Jiang as the new tool of imperialism while, on the other, admiting that the camp of the imperialists and the national bourgeoisie class, represented by the Jiang government, was not homogenous.[15]

The employment of such provocative language—that is, to openly label the other rival as either a new imperialist pawn or a rebel troublemaker—leads on to a second point. The frequent appearance of the phrase *Unequal Treaties* in the CCP's public pronouncements after 1927 indicates that the Communists continued to cling to the Communist International's (Comintern) global ideology—class struggle, theories of imperialism, and proletariat revolutions—both in their search for strategies and in the way they defined their enemies.[16] In a resolution on the abortive Guangzhou (Canton) Insurgency of December 1927, passed by the CCP's Central Provisional Poliburo on January 3, 1928, the CCP emphasized its alliance with the Soviet Union and world proletariats by branding the Nationalists as traitors both to the Chinese revolution (*beipan zhongguo geming*) and to the Han (*hanjian*). Treating all imperialists as a monolithic bloc, the Communists insisted that the immediate renunciation of the Unequal Treaties and China's withdrawal from the "imperialist" League of Nations be made a part of China's foreign policy in the national revolution.[17] In its emotionally charged "Declaration on the Current Situation" dated September 20, 1928, the CCP stated that the new warlords of the GMD "are all the same kind of bloodsuckers, traitors, and butchers as the warlords Zhang Zuolin, Wu Peifu, Sun Chuanfang and Zhang Zongchang in the White Terror." The statement continued: "Having laid aside the Jianan Massacre till today, and using the so-called 'treaty revision' to divert attention, [the GMD government] is in fact conducting treacherous secret diplomacy."[18] The CCP ended the declaration with a barrage of florid slogans such as "Abolish all Unequal Treaties automatically and oppose all treacherous treaties fawning on foreign powers."[19]

As a small, weak party sheltering under the banner of the Comintern after its split with the Nationalists in April 1927, the CCP depended on the notions of class struggle and imperialism both in defining its own position and formulating blanket attacks on its enemies, both internal and external—the Guomindang, the national bourgeoisie class, and American, British, and

Japanese imperialism.[20] The CCP had nothing to lose by antagonizing its enemies and discrediting the form of nationalism and patriotism represented by the GMD government. "Ever since the founding of the Nanjing government, has a single day passed when it has not attempted to sell our country out? The treaties they have signed with imperialists are a complete acceptance of imperialist privileges."[21]

A third and final point should be made here. In the 1930s the term *Unequal Treaties* was often tied to dire warnings of national subjugation and racial extinction (*wangguo miezhong dahuo*), and was linked with the notions of life and death juncture, (*shengsi guantou*) war resistance, saving the country, and the national united front. The intensified incursions of the Japanese gave the Communists, largely immobilized by the GMD's encirclement campaign, a new opportunity to increase its profile on the national stage through the Unequal Treaties issue. In doing so, the CCP linked its policy firmly with national survival and independence, thus transforming itself from a party of fugitives and bandits on the verge of annihilation to a competitor and partner in defining a new framework for national salvation and nation-building.

On September 20, 1931, two days after the Mukden Incident, the CCP's Red Army issued a resolution appealing to all Chinese workers, farmers, and soldiers to resist the Japanese "robbers." In derogatory language, the Communists described the Manchurian Incident and the Nationalists' policies of nonresistance and the diplomacy of forbearance as the very embodiment of the Guomindang's record of shameless submission and national betrayal (*chumai minzu liyi*). The CCP formulated a set of slogans such as "Resist the Japanese imperialists' occupation of the Three Northeastern Provinces!" and "Unilaterally abolish all the Unequal Treaties!"[22] The slogan "Abolish all the Unequal Treaties signed by imperialists and the Chinese landlord-bourgeoisie government" was introduced into the Foreign Affairs Manifesto of the Chinese Soviet Republic's Provisional Government formed on November 7, 1931, at its base in Ruijin, Jiangxi.[23]

As the war with Japan dragged on, the CCP changed its policy of fighting two enemies at the same time—Jiang, "the traitor of the Han," (*hanjian maiguozei*) and imperialist Japan—to one of pressurizing the GMD to join the Communist-initiated second United Front of 1937. This shift in the CCP's wartime strategy was signalled in the three conditions proposed by Mao Zedong, as chairman of the Chinese Soviet Provisional Central Government, on January 17, 1933, in casting about for allies in the struggle against Japan. The coalition envisaged by Mao was inclusive and broad:

> Contingent upon the following terms, the Chinese Workers' and Peasants' Red Army is prepared to sign military agreements with any armed forces to fight jointly against the Japanese imperialist encroachment. The conditions are: First, cease attacks immediately on the Chinese Soviet area. Second, promptly

guarantee the democratic rights of the general population. Third, immediately arm the existing volunteer forces, organized by the masses, to defend China and strive for China's independence, unification and territorial integrity.[24]

Despite several attempts, Mao's desire to have a share of the leadership in saving China and preserving China's sovereignty was not to be realized until after the Xi'an Incident of December 12–25, 1936.[25] Abrogating all treaties with Japan and reclaiming all the territories leased by the Japanese were given the highest priority in Mao Zedong's Ten Policies to Save the Nation proclaimed on August 25, 1937.[26] In Mao's view, such policies, along with Sun Yat-sen's Three Principles of the People , constituted the cardinal basis for the Anti-Japanese National United Front which was intended to unite all the forces opposed to the Japanese—the GMD, all parties, factions, and social classes, as well as all military personnel, in short, the whole of the Chinese people.[27]

In summary, as a de facto fugitive from the incumbent Nanjing GMD establishment, the CCP, even at the nadir of their fortunes in the ten years of 1927–1937, escalated its verbal offensive to undermine the GMD's leadership in nation building and national independence. Although both the GMD and CCP, in essence, saw the abolition of the Unequal Treaties as the key to saving China and gaining national independence, the GMD came to tread on the heels of its defeated enemy, the warlord Beijing government (1912–1928), in the matter of the Unequal Treaties, by adopting the same tactics, that is, to dissolve the Unequal Treaties through diplomatic negotiations. This approach made the GMD a vulnerable target—as the previous Beijing government had experienced—in the propaganda war with the rebel party CCP. Explicitly labeling the GMD as the traitors of the Han and the new imperliast agent replacing the warlord Beijing government, the CCP located its slogans within the Marxist and Lenist rhetorical framework of class struggle and world imperialism.

In the 1930s, the CCP wasted no time in defining the Japanese invasion as the crossroads of life and death for the Chinese race. The turn of tide in the CCP ideological war featured the CCP as a viable political force working for national liberation, independence, democracy, and the advancement of the nation on the national scence. As the Communists became better positioned to bargain, challenge, and ultimately undermine the policies of the Nationalists, as well as to question their interpretation of history, the Unequal Treaties once again acquired new meanings in the power struggles of the 1940s.

THE NEW AND EQUAL TREATIES
(*PINGDENG XINYUE*) OF 1943: WHOSE SUCCESS?

One of the key changes in the political landscape of the 1940s was the increasing visibility of the Unequal Treaties in rival forums monopolized by the Nationalist Party and the Communists. Settled in a wartime coalition with each other, both the GMD and the CCP were all the keener to advance their own interpretation of the Unequal Treaties, endeavoring to highlight their central role in leading the nation toward independence. The narration of the national history from 1842 to 1943 became a contest about who actually led the Chinese nation to the "success" of abolishing extraterritoriality, the last emblem of the "treaty century," in 1943.

On January 11, 1943, the Sino-American Treaty for the Relinquishment of Extraterritorial Rights in China and the Regulation of Related Matters was signed in Washington by Wei Daoming, Chinese ambassador to the U.S., and Cordell Hull, the secretary of state of the U.S. The core provision of this eight-clause treaty is found in Article 1: "Nationals of the United States of America in such territory [the territory of the Republic of China] shall be subject to the jurisdiction of the Government of the Republic of China in accordance with the principles of international law and practice."[28] On the same day, in Chongqing, T. V. Soong, Chinese foreign minister, and Horace J. Seymour, British ambassador to China, signed the Sino-British Treaty for the Abolition of Extraterritoriality and Related Rights in China.[29] The day following the signing, the Nationalist government published *A Letter to All Servicemen and the Masses*, claiming the credit for the fact that "we, the Chinese nation, after fifty years of bloody revolution and five and a half years of sacrifice in the War of Resistance, have finally transformed the hundred years' history of sorrow surrounding the Unequal Treaties into a glorious record of the termination of the Unequal Treaties."[30]

Two days after the signing of the new treaties, *Zhongyang ribao*, the official Guomindang newspaper in Chongqing, featured a celebratory editorial headed "Whose success?" and heaped praise on Jiang Jieshi:

> Although the Unequal Treaties are now indistinguishable from a stack of waste paper, thinking of the past one hundred years in which our nation lived in shackles, our jubilation has no bounds. . . . Notwithstanding how much the world has changed in the past century, if it were not for our party and for Premier [Sun Yat-sun] and Generalissimo [Jiang Jieshi], the Unequal Treaties would still have been in force. . . . The cancellation of the Unequal Treaties has been earned by all soldiers and civilians, under the leadership of Chairman Jiang, with their flesh and blood and even with their lives. Today we rejoice in the signing of the new treaties, and the clearest slogan [we can use] is simply to congratulate Chairman Jiang on the success of his revolutionary nation-building.[31]

A further editorial in *Zhongyang ribao* remarked that the signing of the new treaties opened a brand new page in modern Chinese history, one that marked the most glorious chapter in Chinese revolutionary history. "Who wrote this new page, and who achieved this most glorious record?" the editorial asked. Again, Jiang was credited with having assumed the leadership of all the national martyrs (*xianlie zhishi*) and countless patriotic compatriots over the past fifty years.[32]

The monopoly of credit claimed by the GMD for the abolition of the Unequal Treaties produced a strong reaction from the CCP. Two weeks after the promulgation of the new treaties, the CCP produced a resolution on celebrating the cancellation of the old treaties.[33] In restrained tones, this short document contained three major points. First, it presented a linear model of modern Chinese history, depicting China as gradually degenerating first into a semicolony and then a full colony, setting this against a counter-history of the Chinese people's heroic struggle for national independence and liberation. Second, the resolution stressed the cardinal contribution made by the united front initiated by the CCP to the rise in China's international status and to the abolition of the Unequal Treaties. Third, it pointed out that, ever since its birth, the CCP had been at the forefront of the national liberation struggle.

On January 30, the CCP mustered its manpower and resources in preparation for the February 4 celebration party in Yan'an. In contrast to the emphasis given to the event by the GMD, the Yan'an celebration connected the signing of the new treaties with the CCP's leadership in the Sino-Japanese War, fulfillment of the 1943 production plan for the Communists' border bases, condemnation of "the scum of the nation" (*minzu bailei*), such as Wang Jingwei, and celebration of the victories of the Soviet Red Army and the Allies in Africa.[34] Following this, *Jiefang ribao* devoted four issues, from February 4 to 7, 1943, to the subject of the Unequal Treaties. The CCP's most prominent leaders, theorists, historians, and writers including He Long, Gao Gang, Tian Jiaying, Ai Siqi, Chen Boda, Ai Qing, and Zhou Yang, all contributed pieces to these special issues.

This historical contest exerted a profound influence on later mainland Chinese and Taiwanese historiography. For Taiwanese scholars, the signing of the 1943 treaties marked the end of the Treaty Abolition Movement (*feiyue yundong*). Historian Chang Yü-fa refers to the new treaties as the "fruits" of "our state's" persistent resistance against Japan.[35] Taking stock of its record on the abolition of the Unequal Treaties during the 1940s, the Nationalist government assessed the signing of the "new and equal treaties" as the zenith of its diplomatic achievements during the Sino-Japanese war.[36] Any contribution made by the Communists was completely eclipsed by their rivals in Lin Quan's 1124-page compilation, *Sources on the Abrogation of the Unequal Treaties during the Period of the Anti-Japanese War*.[37]

On the other hand, since the opening up of China to the world in 1978, mainland Chinese study of the Nanjing government's handling of the Unequal Treaties has gradually become more flexible and resulted in a more nuanced and in-depth treatment of the domestic and global power struggles of the 1940s. For instance, scholars have drawn attention to Japan's strategy in decoying both the Wang Jingwei and the Nanjing governments into signing a secret agreement to retract the Unequal Treaties in order to "help China become liberated step by step from its East Asian semi-colonial status."[38] However, even the most recent historiography still makes reference to the disputed question of who brought "glory" to Chinese history:

> Under the leadership of the Chinese Communist Party, the Chinese people persevered during the 8-year War of Resistance, and eventually won. All the Unequal Treaties imposed on China by the Japanese imperialists were thus revoked. . . . Without the CCP's efforts, without the CCP as the firm rock standing midstream (*zhongliu dizhu*), China's independence and liberation would have been impossible.[39]

In sum, in this section, through the celebration of the conclusion of the 1943 treaties marking the relingquishment of foreign consular judicial rights in China, the Communists challenged the GMD version of modern Chinese history, especially on the question of claiming credit for the redemption of "a century of national ignominy." Despite the varied implications of the 1943 treaties, the Guomindang and the Communists stood together in condemning the Unequal Treaties as an unequivocal symbol of foreign aggression and threat, and in seeing their abrogation as the result of the struggle of the Chinese people. Their consensus broke down, however, when it came to deciding the legitimate leader and real redeemer of China's humiliations. The polemic surrounding the 1943 treaties indicates that each of the two rival parties used different interpretations of the Unequal Treaties in order to develop their own version of China's one hundred years of humiliation. There was one main aspect that set the CCP controlled historiography apart from the GMD's version of the one hundred years of national ignominy. The CCP projected a linear model of modern Chinese history, depicting China as gradually degenerating first into a semicolony and then a full colony, setting this against a counterhistory of the Chinese people's heroic struggle, led by the CCP ever since its birth, for national independence and liberation.

THE TREATY OF FRIENDSHIP AND ALLIANCE BETWEEN THE REPUBLIC OF CHINA AND THE U.S.S.R. (1945)

Party rivalry over who should control the interpretation of recent Chinese history was also displayed in the controversy over the two treaties signed in 1945 and 1946. Furthermore, this controversy was central to the CCP's invention of the narrative about how the party played a decisive role in creating a strong, new China, which would stand up as an equal or even a superior in the world community.

This part of the chapter focuses on one of the two treaties, the Treaty of Friendship and Alliance between the Republic of China and the Soviet Union, signed on August 14, 1945 (coming into force on August 21, 1945), by the GMD foreign minister, Wang Shijie, and the Soviet minister for foreign affairs V. M. Molotov.[40] The other treaty, the 1946 Treaty of Friendship, Commerce and Navigation between China and the U.S., will be covered in the next section.

The terms of the 1945 treaty were set at thirty years. Under pressure from the U.S. and Britain, who sought an early end to the war in the Asian theater, the Guomindang government grudgingly signed such a treaty, the content of which had mostly been determined at the Yalta Conference. In February 1945, in exchange for allowing the immediate entry of Russian troops into China's Three Northeastern Provinces to confront Japanese forces, the U.S. and Britain made secret agreements with Stalin that compromised Chinese sovereignty. These secret deals remained unknown to the public until 1955 when the Department of State of the U. S. declassified documents relating to the Yalta Conference.[41]

The secret agreement concluded between the U.S., Britain, and the U.S.S.R. was not disclosed to the Chinese government until June 15, four months after the Yalta Conference had ended.[42] The 1955 published records on the Yalta Conference reveal the political nature of the Yalta secret agreements relating to China without the concurrence of the Chinese government, the essence of which was that Joseph Stalin made Franklin Roosevelt agree to his political conditions in order for Russia to enter the war against Japan:

> After the formal Conference meeting in the afternoon [of February 10, 1945] between the President [Roosevelt], the Prime Minister [Churchill], Marshal Stalin and their associates, Marshal Stalin came to me [W. A. Harriman] to explain the further changes he had in mind for the Agreement. He said that he was entirely willing to have Dairen [Dalian] a free port under international control, but that Port Arthur was different, it was to be a Russian naval base and therefore Russia required a lease.
>
> The President agreed to Marshal Stalin's revised proposal regarding the ports as above.[43]

Apart from the above, it was agreed that decisions about other issues, such as when and where to inform the Chinese side of the secret deal, should be left at the discretion of the Russians:

> The President asked Marshal Stalin whether he (Stalin) wished to take these matters up with T. V. Soong when he came to Moscow or whether Stalin wished the President to take them up with the Generalissimo [Jiang Jieshi].
>
> Marshal Stalin replied that as he was an interested party he would prefer to have the President do it.
>
> The President then asked when the subject should be discussed with the Generalissimo having in mind the question of secrecy.
>
> Marshal Stalin said he would let the President know when he was prepared to have this done.[44]

The unequal nature of the 1945 treaty is apparent from four sets of documents annexed to it. First, there is the exchange of notes between Wang Shijie, minister for foreign affairs, and V. M. Molotov, the people's commissar for foreign affairs, dated August 14, 1945. This exchange concerns China's binding recognition of the independence of Outer Mongolia, which had long been seen by China as an integral part of Chinese territory. Second, in the agreement between the Republic of China and the U.S.S.R. concerning the Chinese Changchun Railway, both sides agreed that:

> After the Japanese armed forces are driven out of the Three Eastern Provinces of China, the main trunk line of the Chinese Eastern Railway and the South Manchurian Railway from Manchuli to Suifenho and from Harbin to Dairen and Port Arthur united into one railway under the name "Chinese Changchun Railway," shall be in joint ownership of the U.S.S.R and of the Republic of China and shall be operated by them jointly.[45]

The third set of documents is known as the Agreement on Port Arthur; it made Port Arthur an exclusive naval base to "be used only by Chinese and Soviet military and commercial vessels." The jurisdiction of the Port Arthur naval base would fall under the Sino-Russian military commission, whose chairman "shall be appointed by the Soviet side."[46] Fourth, the Agreement on Dairen stipulated that the harbor-master in the port at Dairen (Dalian) must be a Soviet national, even though the port administration belonged to China. Further, China agreed to "lease to the U.S.S.R. free of charge half of all port installations and equipment." This arrangement resembled that of leased territories under the Unequal Treaty system which had been annulled in 1943.

Wang Shijie was later to argue that, in the absence of Chinese delegates, any decisions relating to China made at the Yalta Conference were not legally binding on China. However, Wang also admitted that, "owing to the complicated circumstances and evolving realities [of the situation], I was compelled to accept the [Yalta] agreement, and to bear the pain of putting my signature on the Sino-Russian Friendship and Alliance Treaty." According to Wang, the GMD had three main motives in accepting the secret Yalta agreements. First, China was unwilling to run the risk of isolating itself by alienating the U.S., China's most powerful ally. Second, the GMD government was hoping to improve relations with the U.S.S.R. so that Russia would moderate its support of the CCP and its "rebellious behavior."[47] In the 1945 treaty, the Jiang government was recognized as "the Central Government of China," and designated as the sole recipient of Russian moral and material support.[48] Third, Wang stated that the Russian Red Army had already entered Manchuria on August 8 because Russia feared that Japan might surrender too quickly in response to the first atomic bomb dropped on Hiroshima on August 6, before the U.S.S.R. could enter the war in Manchuria. Given these circumstances, Wang argued that if the Nationalist government had refused to accept the Yalta deal, then the GMD would have had no way of regaining "red" Manchuria without using force to expel the Red Army and prevent the CCP and Russia from forming alliances of their own.[49]

The Nationalist government's decision to sign the 1945 Sino-Russian treaty was clearly motivated by political considerations (i.e., the desire to have a greater say in the postwar settlement in Manchuria and to annihilate the Communist Party) rather than by concerns about national sovereignty. And the GMD's questioning of the legality of the 1945 treaty between 1949 and 1955 was no less politically motivated than its signing. In 1949, much to the vexation of the GMD, the CCP won control of mainland China and publicly announced its "lean-to-one-side" policy of joining the Soviet bloc.[50] In response, Jiang Tingfu, the Guomindang representative at the United Nations, took legal action to bring Russia to "court" in an attempt to annul the 1945 treaty.[51]

The 1945 Sino-Russia treaty, troublesome as it was to the Guomindang government, has been labeled by Taiwanese scholars as "the heaviest loss" inflicted on China during the eight-year War of Resistance.[52] Taiwanese writer Li Ao refers to the 1945 treaty as a "typically traitorous treaty," arguing that, by means of it, the U.S.S.R. restored to itself all the colonial privileges and rights enjoyed by Tsarist Russia prior to the Russo-Japanese War. Worst of all, Li continues, because of the 1945 treaty China lost Outer Mongolia, an area of 58,000 square miles, forty-four times larger than Taiwan.[53]

If the Guomindang agitated to have the treaty thrown out or ameliorated in the early 1950s, so did the the Communists of the People's Republic of China, who were bound by the 1945 treaty signed by the GMD Republic of China.

It seems that Mao at times made use of proxies to air his private dissatisfaction with the 1945 treaty. For example, in a letter to Stalin dated July 4, 1949, Mao's deputy Liu Shaoqi praised the treaty while vaguely suggesting that the CCP could either continue to recognize the existing treaty or sign a new treaty in the spirit of the old, to adapt it to new circumstances.[54] The CCP, however, refrained from public criticism of the gross inequalities embodied in the 1945 treaty and, indeed, never characterized it as violating Chinese sovereignty. On the contrary, according to the CCP historian Peng Ming, given the historical circumstances, the 1945 treaty was in the interests of the Chinese people and was an expression of Sino-Soviet friendship.[55] China was therefore the main beneficiary. In an interview with a British journalist, Mao remarked that, along with other covenants, the treaty was supported by the Chinese and Russian peoples and was beneficial to world peace and particularly to peace in the Far East.[56] Public comments such as these cemented the favorable verdict on the Treaty of Friendship and Alliance between the Republic of China and the U.S.S.R. reflected in mainland historiography for over thirty years.

Since the opening up of China in 1978, the 1945 treaty has become the subject of serious scholarship. Criticism of the treaty has gained strength, and particularly in the last ten years a consensus view of it has emerged as an unequal treaty driven by Russian chauvinism and national self-interest.[57] Some scholars have recognized that the issue of the CCP was the U.S.S.R.'s trump card in its bargaining with the Nationalist Party over the terms of the treaty and in maintaining the Yalta order in place in Asia.[58] Some commentators blame the U.S. for selling out China, while others criticize Jiang Jieshi for subjecting national sovereignty to party interests in order to obtain the U.S.S.R.'s neutrality in the conflict with the Chinese Communist Party.[59]

In a number of studies published since the 1990s, Yang Kuisong of the Institute of Modern History in the Chinese Academy of Social Sciences has provided insights into the many complex factors, such as state interests and national sentiment, which prompted Mao Zedong to enter into negotiations with the Soviet Union in 1950 to rescind some of the more unfavorable terms of the 1945 treaty.[60] The result was the 1950 Sino-Soviet Treaty of Friendship, Alliance, and Mutual Assistance, whereby Stalin agreed to withdraw Russian forces from Port Arthur and transfer the Changchun Railway to China. In exchange, China had to agree to set up Sino-Soviet joint stock companies for the mining of oil and nonferrous metals in Xinjiang, and to continue to recognize the independence of Outer Mongolia.[61]

The positive and negative impact of the 1945 Sino-Soviet treaty on the postwar CCP has been carefully evaluated in recent years. As mainland historian Liu Xifa of Jilin University notes, it prevented the U.S. from intervening in northeastern China and deterred GMD troops from entering the Northeast, something which gave the CCP the chance to forestall its rival in the postwar competition for control of this strategically important area. Both Mao and Jiang fully understood the value of the Three Northeastern Provinces in winning control of China after the Japanese surrender. In the Agreement Regarding Relations between the Chinese Administration and the Commander-in-Chief of the Soviet Forces after the Entry of Soviet Troops into the Three Eastern Provinces of China, for instance, Article 5 stipulates that "as soon as any part of the liberated territory ceases to be a zone of immediate military operations, the Chinese National Government will assume full authority in the direction of public affairs and will render the Commander-in-Chief of the Soviet forces every assistance and support through its civil and military authorities."[62] Viewing Manchuria as its "sphere of influence" as determined at the Yalta Conference, the Soviet Union expressed its annoyance at the GMD for using American warships to transfer its troops. Fearing American influence in Manchuria, in October 1945 the Russians refused permission to land in Port Arthur and Dalian to Nationalist forces transported from remote southwestern China on American warships. When Jiang's army was permitted to enter Yingkou and Hulu Dao, they found themselves besieged by CCP forces which had spent the war years in Manchuria. Finally, the Nationalist troops were forced to reroute to Qinhuang Dao and enter the Three Northeastern Provinces overland. As a result of the lack of Soviet cooperation, the GMD lost four to five valuable weeks in the race to take over Japanese-occupied territory. This gave the CCP a crucial edge as it rushed its cadres and troops to Manchuria to develop base areas.[63] On June 25, 1947, the Guomindang Foreign Ministry reported that Port Arthur and Dalian were still not under the control of the Nationalist government, and demanded that the Soviet Union fulfill its treaty obligations.[64]

The 1945 Treaty of Friendship and Alliance between China and the Soviet Union received a closer examination in the late mainland historian Wang Yongxiang's monograph published in Taiwan. Recognizing the importance of the treaty in cementing the Sino-Russian collaboration to bring WWII in Asia to a close, Wang called the treaty "shackles imposed upon the Chinese people" by the Yalta secret agreement. The treaty can be characterized as "unequal" as it took away Mongolia from China and restored the old tsarist privileges and rights in the Northeastern China. In other words, Wang put the blame on international power politics rather than on the GMD government.[65]

Placing the Chinese experience in an international context, Jian Chen argues that, to some extent at least, the rivalry between the CCP and the GMD in the 1940s defined the nature of Soviet-American competition in Asia and thus formalized "a Cold War environment in East Asia, as well as in the world."[66] The Communist Party's tolerant position on the 1945 treaty from the 1940s to the early 1970s lends support to Chen's findings that "cooperation, or the willingness to cooperate, was the dominant aspect of CCP–Soviet relations in 1949."[67] This had the effect of compromising relations with the U.S. so that "it was next to impossible for the two sides [the CCP and the U.S.] to establish a normal working relationship, let alone for them to reach an accommodation."[68] Despite all the disagreements with Stalin, Mao Zedong was unable to abandon his anti-imperialist rhetoric and as a consequence remained estranged from the U.S.[69]

The reason behind the GMD's signing of and annulment of the 1945 treaty, as well as the CCP's complicated attitudes towards it, was that both the Guomindang and the Communists professed loyalty to the ideal of a united and strong China at the same time as they fought each other about who should be in charge of the new China that would appear as an equal or as a superior state on the world stage. And again the conflict manifested itself in the rhetoric surrounding the Unequal Treaties.

THE 1946 TREATY OF FRIENDSHIP, COMMERCE, AND NAVIGATION BETWEEN THE REPUBLIC OF CHINA AND THE U.S.

The intense public discourse and the evolving narrative about the Sino-American 1946 Treaty of Friendship, Commerce, and Navigation manifest a similar pattern of concerns about how to use the nation's past to suit the needs of the present. Party-controlled historiography on the subject of the Unequal Treaties was further developed as part of the effort to assert party leadship in the struggle for national independence.

On November 4, 1946, the Treaty of Friendship, Commerce, and Navigation between the Republic of China and the U.S., was signed by Wang Shijie and Wang Huacheng for the GMD government, and J. Leighton Stuart and Robert Lacy Smyth for the U.S. In a situation of increasing hostility between the Guomindang and the Communist Party, such a treaty became an instant target for the CCP. The Communists switched from the restrained sophistication that had characterized the discussions over the 1943 and 1945 treaties to direct and belligerent confrontation.

Containing thirty clauses, the 1946 treaty has been considered a lengthy commercial treaty.[70] One can find the legal legitimacy of negotiating such a treaty in the 1943 Sino-American treaty, under which the U.S. gave up its extraterritorial right in China. Thus, the 1946 treaty represented an endeavor to redefine the economic relationship between China and the U. S. in the aftermath of WWII. In general, the treaty reframes the scope of interaction between Americans and Chinese particularly in the sphere of commerce, the equal treatment of Chinese and American nationals, and the most-favored-nation treatment.

First, both American and Chinese citizens were permitted to reside, travel and engage in activities of all sorts on each other's land. Second, the most-favored-nation treatment was confirmed in articles throughout the treaty, as in the case of Article 2, paragraph 3:

> The nationals of either High Contracting Party shall not in any case, in the enjoyment of the rights and privileges provided by paragraphs 1 and 2 of this Article, receive treatment with respect to such rights and privileges less favorable than the treatment which is or may hereafter be accorded to the nationals of any third country.[71]

Third, equal treatment of Chinese and American citizens, with regard to acquisition of movable and immovable property, tariff, surcharges, and international taxation, was accorded, as a result of China's compromise, in articles such as Article 3, paragraph 3:

> The High Contracting Parties, adhering generally to the principle of national treatment with respect to the matters enumerated in this paragraph, agree that corporations and associations of either High Contracting Party shall be permitted, throughout the whole extent of the territories of the other High Contracting Party, in conformity with the applicable laws and regulations, if any, which are or may hereafter be enforced by the duly constituted authorities, to engage in and carry on commercial, manufacturing, processing, financial, scientific, educational, religious and philanthropic activities; to acquire hold, erect or lease,

and occupy appropriate buildings, and to lease appropriate lands, for commercial, manufacturing, processing, financial, scientific, educational, religious and
philanthropic purposes.[72]

Strongly positioned after the Sino-Japanese War, the CCP immediately
equated the signing of the 1946 treaty with the loss of China's autonomy in
all respects. *Jiefang ribao* condemned the treaty as "the most shameful and
treacherous treaty in history. It is a significant witness to the turning of China
into a satellite country of America by the Jiang regime. It is a new national
humiliation of the Chinese race."[73] On January 20, 1947, the CCP Shan'-
gan'ning government designated November 4 as a *Guochi jinianri* (National
Day of Shame), asserting that such a treaty opened the entire territory of
China to American merchants and effectively sold off the country to the U.S.
"from heaven to earth."[74]

On February 1, 1947, the CCP Central Committee made an announcement
and was ready to take up arms.[75] This announcement opens with a direct
statement that the Chinese Political Consultative Conference, formed on January 10, 1946, by all major parties and groups based on the CCP-GMD peace
talk on October 10, 1945, was the supreme political organ in China, recognized by all of the people and the world powers. Then, it went on to attack
the legitimacy of the GMD government's unilateral negotiations with foreign governments, since the GMD had not obtained the consent of the Chinese Political Consultative Conference. The other point the statement made
was about the credibility of the GMD's foreign policy, which "was entirely
against the people's will," "which had led to and would continue to lead to
crises of civil war, degradation, loss of sovereignty and national shame, col-
onization, and turbulence."[76] The announcement concluded that in order to
get the motherland "out of the hot water" and to safeguard national rights
and the dignity of the Political Consultative Conference, the CCP would reject all treaties and agreements signed by the GMD government.

On October 10, 1947, with two more years of a three-year Civil War, the
CCP's victory over Jiang already being in sight, the CCP announced the
Manifesto of the Chinese People's Liberation Army, drafted by Mao Zedong.
Article 8 urges the people to "reject the Quisling diplomacy of the authori-
tarian Jiang Jieshi government, annul all treacherous treaties . . . sign equal
and reciprocal treaties of commerce and friendship with foreign countries."[77]

Apart from the savage denunciation from the CCP, some Chinese lumi-
naries, such as Ma Yinchu, were also critical of some inequitable provisions
of the 1946 treaty. The strong reaction against the 1946 treaty in China did
not go unnoticed in American academia. In the defense of the treaty given
by M. E. Orlean, this reaction in China, however, was simply brushed aside
as fanatical, irrational, and incomprehensible. Blind to the obvious political
context in which the treaty was made, as well as the political implications being read into the Sino-American Commercial and Navigational Treaty of

1946, Orlean insisted that "the new treaty should thus have occasioned no surprise since it was intended merely as a routine instrument for facilitating commercial relations between the two countries."[78] Orlean's position rested upon the American "search for sales in the refound markets of China in the 1940's," which was accompanied by its quest for order in the US–China economic relations.[79] The other point Orlean made was that the stipulations of the treaty were consistent with the Nanjing government's stated economic policy on international cooperation; therefore, the treaty was "in no sense forced on China by deliberate American pressure."[80]

Archival sources reveal that the Chinese Ministry of Economy and Finance, which was involved in the preparation and negotiation of the treaty, recognized the political meanings that the treaty might be given. The Ministry of Economy and Finance—noting that "what we ask from the United States is more than what the United States is asking from us"—concluded that the whole situation must be taken into consideration so as not to try to save a little only to lose a lot.[81] The Ministry of Economy and of Finance was in favor of setting limits to the most-favored-nation treatment, as well as the equal treatment of U.S. nationals in China granted to the U.S., but to no avail. The following provision also caused much controversy at the time:

> Vessels of either High Contracting Party shall be permitted to discharge portions of cargoes at any ports, places or waters of the other High Contracting Party which are or may hereafter be open to foreign commerce and navigation, and to proceed with the remaining portions of such cargoes to any other such ports, places or waters, without paying other or higher tonnage dues or port charges in such cases than would be paid by national vessels in like circumstances, and they shall be permitted to load in like manner, in the same voyage outward, at the various ports, places and waters which are or may hereafter be open to foreign commerce and navigation.[82]

The critical verdict on the 1946 Sino-American treaty went unopposed by mainland commentators until 1978, but renewed interest in the past decade in the study of the Unequal Treaties and their history has resulted in the emergence of divergent views on this treaty. On the one hand, there are those scholars who continue the critical line censuring the principles of reciprocity and equality expressed in the 1946 treaty as a mere formality, given that the semifeudal and semicolonial China at the time had virtually no capacity to implement such provisions—for example, by investing in the American market, or by making use of the treaty right to sail vessels and warships into American sea ports and on American inland waters. Some critics have even labeled the treaty a "new Twenty-One Demands."[83]

Then there are those scholars who adopt a different and more neutral perspective. Thus the 1946 treaty has been subject to a critical reevaluation in a dynamic debate between Zheng Zemin and Zhang Zhenkun, both members of the Institute of Modern History of the Chinese Academy of Social Sciences.[84] In ₛ's opinion, terms like *favorable* (*youli*) or *unfavorable* (*buli*) provide a more ₁se way of characterizing the treaty than do terms like *equal* and *unequal*. ₁us, while Zhang rejects the categorization of the 1946 Treaty of Friendship, ₂ommerce, and Navigation as "unequal," he nevertheless holds that it was "unfavorable" to China.[85] And, from a different angle again, Ren Donglai places the 1946 Sino-American commercial treaty in the broader framework of the Sino-American alliance against Japan from 1937 to 1948. Ren notes that this alliance, particularly ·after the Japanese surrender in 1945, was between the Jiang Jieshi government and America against the Chinese Communists. He suggests that the basis of the Sino-American alliance diplomacy was China's lobbying for aid and the American provision of political, military, and economic aid to China.[86] Ren holds the opinion that the 1946 treaty was subject to party struggle. To Jiang Jieshi, opening the China market to American businesses was in return for obtaining U.S. assistance in its anti-CCP campaigns; to the U.S., the 1946 Sino-American treaty, ratified by the U.S. Senate in November 1948, provided an opportunity to monopolize the China market and eventually integrate China into the United States–controlled global economy as well as the anti-Soviet camp.

Finally, some Taiwanese scholars, such as Tu Heng-chih, see the treaty as based on the principles of complete equality and friendship, and regard it as a paradigmatic example of bilateral commercial treaties of equitable character signed between China and foreign countries.[87] In Tu's view, the demise of the Unequal Treaties was brought about by two main factors: the joint efforts of the government (GMD) and the people, and improvements in the international legal order.[88] Wu Lin-chun of National Hualien Teachers College in Taiwan argues that,

> from the perspective of the historical development of the one hundred years of Unequal Treaties, the significance of the 1946 Sino-American treaty lies in its confirmation of the "abandonment" of those privileges which the United States had agreed upon in the "new and equal treaty" [of 1943] which replaced the commercial treaties of the Unequal Treaties system.[89]

Wu, therefore, concludes that it would be unfair to label the 1946 treaty as "a new unequal treaty," solely on the ground that the Chinese economic situation at the time virtually prevented China from enjoying the equal and mutal benefits of the treaty.

CONCLUSION

This chapter examines the verbal contest, during the 1930s and 1940s, between the CCP and the GMD over the issue of the Unequal Treaties, and represents an attempt to connect party authority and legitimacy with the question of nationalism. Within the context of the competition for political mandate in representing the "people's will" between the GMD and CCP, the contest over the Unequal Treaties in the twenty years between 1928 and 1947 throws light on the complex issue of how the two parties tried to reconcile the effort to secure party support with a professed faith in a unified, strong, and independent China. In such a process of reconciliation, the Chinese Communist Party was particularly aggressive in molding popular conceptions of political groupings (e.g., warlords, imperialists, patriots, and traitors) and promulgating the linear model of modern Chinese history using the notions of semifeudalism and semicolonialism to interpret the Sino-Western encounters since 1840.[90] Scholars have variously attributed the 1949 Communist victory to the Yenan (Yan'an) Way, peasant nationalism, and anti-Japanese military resistance.[91] An analysis of party pronouncements on the Unequal Treaties, however, allows us to approach the question of the second United Front and the CCP's 1949 victory from a different angle.[92]

NOTES

1. For the pre-1927 polemics about the phrase used by the CCP and the GMD, see Dong Wang, "The Discourse of the Unequal Treaties in Modern China," *Pacific Affairs* 76, no. 3 (2003): 399–425. In 1924, the Guomindang (GMD) and the Communists (CCP) formed a coalition, known as the first United Front, to work together in the anti-imperialist and anti-warlord Nationalist Revolution. The first United Front came to an end in April 1927 when Jiang Jieshi, the leader of the GMD, staged a bloody purge of Communists in the areas under his control. The CCP was forced to flee to the rural areas of Jiangxi and Fujian where they established independent authorities known as "soviets."

2. Hunt, *The Genesis of Chinese Communist Foreign Policy*, 113.

3. The Chinese spelling of those three sets of treaties are: Zhongying guanyü qüxiao Yingguo zai hua zhiwai faquan jiqi youguan tequan tiaoyue, 1943; Zhongmei qüxiao Meiguo zaihua zhiwai faquan ji chuli youguan wenti tiaoyue, 1943; Zhongsu youhao tongmeng tiaoyue, 1945; Zhongmei youhao tongshang hanghai tiaoyue, 1946.

4. Jerome Ch'en, "The Communist Movement," 13:168.

5. "Guomin zhengfu feichu jiuyue xuanyan" [The Nationalist government's manifesto on the nullification of the treaties], in *Zhonghua minguo dang'an ziliao huibian* [Collected archival sources on the history of the Republic of China], ed. Di'er lishi dang'an'guan, vol. 5 (Nanjing: Jiangsu guji chubanshe, 1991), 33–34 (in part 1); Wu Chaoshu, *The Nationalist Program for China* (New Haven, Conn.: Yale University Press, 1929), 103; Wang Zhengting, *Guomin zhengfu jin sannian lai waijiao jingguo jiyao* [A summary of the foreign relations of the Nationalist government for the past three years, 1926–1929], reprint ed. (Taibei: Wenhai chubanshe, publication date unknown), 37–38.

6. The non-discrimination clause of the new treaty guaranteed the U.S. virtually the same treatment received by other countries. See Foreign Affairs Ministry, *Zhongwai tiaoyue jibian, 1927-1957* [Treaties between the Republic of China and foreign states, 1927–1957] (Taibei: Ministry of Foreign Affairs, 1958), 648–49; Wang Shijie, *Zhongguo bupingdeng tiaoyue zhi feichu* [The abolition of the Chinese Unequal Treaties] (Taibei: Jiang Zongtong dui Zhongguo ji shijie zhi gongxian congshu bianzuan weiyuanhui, 1967), 150–201.

7. For a comprehensive study of the origins and history of extraterritoriality, and its evolution and implications in China, see Sun Xiaolou and Zhao Yinian, *Lingshi caipanquan wenti* [The question of extraterritoriality] (Shanghai: Shangwu yinshuguan, 1937).

min zhengfu teling" [The special order of the Nationalist government], Di'er lishi ,uan, ed., *Zhonghua minguo dang'an ziliao huibian*, 5:52 (in part 1).

Waijiao bu guanyü feiyue de xuanyan" [Foreign Ministry statement on the abolition of eaties], Di'er lishi dang'an guan, *Zhonghua minguo dang'an ziliao huibian*, 5:52–53 (in part 1).

.he same statement, Wang also explained the December 28 order as a measure to eliminate .ny details that might cause misunderstanding and to improve Sino-foreign relations. Shi Yuan-hua, *Zhonghua minguo waijiao shi* [The diplomacy of the Republic of China] (Shanghai: Shanghai renmin chubanshe, 1994), 350–52.

10. On the night of September 18, 1931, the Japanese Kwantung Army blew up a portion of the Japanese-controlled South Manchurian Railway, an act used as a pretext to attack GMD troops. The so-called Mukden Incident marked the beginning of Japanese aggression in China that did not end until 1945, and also signalled the beginning of WWII in Asia. Shinkichi Etō, "China's International Relations 1911–1931," 13:74–115 (in part 2).

11. "Guomin zhengfu wei huanxing guanxia zaihua wairen shishi tiaoli de xunling" [Order of the Nationalist government on the suspension of regulations governing foreigners in China], in *Zhonghua minguo dang'an ziliao huibian*, Di'er lishi dang'an guan, 5:68 (in part 1).

12. D. Wang, "The Discourse of the Unequal Treaties in Modern China."

13. "Guomin gemingjun zong silingbu sanmouchu Jinan can'an jilu" [Record of the Jinan Massacre by the Staff Office of the Headquarters of the Nationalist Revolutionary Army], in *Zhonghua minguo dang'an ziliao huibian*, Di'er lishi dang'an guan, 5:274–306 (in part 1). It should be noted that there are discrepancies between the GMD account of events and that provided by Shinkichi Etō. Etō, "China's International Relations."

14. "Guomindang zhongchanghui yiding zhi 'Wu San' Can'an biaoyü" [Slogans on the Jinan Massacre proposed by the Guomindang Central Standing Committee], in *Zhonghua minguo dang'an ziliao huibian* ed. Di'er lishi dang'an guan, 5: 269–70 (in part 1).

15. "Zhongyang tonggao di sishiba hao: Wu San Cai'an hou de fandi douzheng" [Circular No. 48 of the Central Committee: The Anti-imperialist struggle following the May Third Massacre], in *Zhonggong zhongyang wenjian xuanji*, ed. Zhongyang dang'an'guan, vol. 4 (May 9, 1928), 195. It is unknown where this circular was orginally issued, because the compilers of *Zhonggong zhongyang wenjian xuanji* only note that the circular was first published in *Zhongyang zhengzhi tongxun* [Political newsletter of the Central Committee], no. 29.

16. The Communist International (Comintern) was established by the Soviet Bolsheviks in 1919 and dissolved in 1943.

17. "Guangzhou baodong zhi yiyi yü jiaoxuan" [The significance and lessons of the Guangzhou Insurgency]. See Zhongyang dang'an'guan, *Zhonggong zhongyang wenjian xuanji*, vol. 4 (1928), 43.

18. "Zhongguo gongchandang du shijü xuanyan" [The CCP Declaration on the current situation], in *Zhonggong zhongyang wenjian xuanji* 4 (September 20, 1928), Zhongyang dang'an'guan, 604–12.

19. Zhongyang dang'an'guan, *Zhonggong zhongyang wenjian xuanji*, 4:611.

20. Michael Hunt characterizes the CCP's worldview in the 1920s–1930s as "the May fourth outlook," which consists of "a picture of China beleaguered by imperialism," "the belief in a special relationship with the U.S.S.R.," and "a belief in the unity of the weak and oppressed." Hunt, *The Genesis of Chinese Communist Foreign Policy*, 83–121.

21. "Zhonggong zhongyang gongqingtuan zhongyang wei fandui junfa zhanzheng xuanyan" [The declaration of The CCP Central Committee and the Chinese Youth League Central Committee on the warlord conflicts], in *Zhonggong zhongyang wenjian xuanji*, ed. Zhongyang dang'an'guan, vol. 5 (May 28, 1929): 99. This declaration originally appeared in *Bu'er saiweike* [The Bulsheviks] 2, no. 6 (April 1, 1929).

22. "Zhongguo gongchangdang wei riben diguozhuyi qiangbao zhanling gongsansheng shijian xuanyan" [The CCP Declaration on the Japanese occupation of the Northeastern Provinces], Zhongyang dang'an'guan, ed., *Zhonggong zhongyang wenjian xuanji* 7 (September 20, 1931): 399. This declaration originally appeared in *Hongqi zhoukan* [The red flag weekly], no. 19 (October 1931).

23. "Zhonghua suwei'ai gongheguo linshi zhengfu duiwai xuanyan" [The Foreign Affairs Manifesto of the Chinese Soviet Republic's Provisional Government], in *Zhonggong zhongyang wenjian xuanji* 7 (November 7, 1931), Zhongyang dang'an'guan, 802–3.

24. "Zhonghua suwei'ai linshi zhengfu gongnong hongjun geming junshi weiyuanhui xuanyan—wei fandui Riben diguozhuyi qinru huabei yuan zai sange tiaojie xia yü quanguo ge junhui gongtong kangri" [The declaration of the Chinese Soviet Provisional Central Government and the Workers' and Peasants' Red Army Revolutionary Committee: three conditions for jointly resisting Japanese aggression in North China with all armed forces], in *Zhonggong zhongyang wenjian xuanji* 9 (January 17, 1933), Zhongyang dang'an'guan, 457–58. This declaration first appeared in *Hongse zhonghua* [The red China], no. 48, in Jiangxi, in the name of Mao Zedong, Xiang Ying, Zhang Guotao, and Zhu De.

25. The Xi'an Incident refers to the seizure of Jiang Jieshi by General Zhang Xueliang who opposed Jiang's policy of continuing to fight the CCP rather than co-operating in resisting Japan. Jiang was released after agreeing to form an alliance with the Communists against Japan.

26. The policies adopted by the Second United Front originated in the following CCP statements, declarations, and telegraphic circulars:

(1) "Zhonghua suwei'ai linshi zhengfu gongnong hongjun geming junshi weiyuanhui xuanyan—wei fandui riben diguozhuyi qinru huabei yuan zai sange tiaojie xia yü quanguo ge junhui gongtong kangri" [The declaration of the Chinese Soviet Provisional Central Government and the Workers' and Peasants' Red Army Revolutionary Committee: three conditions for jointly resisting Japanese aggression in North China with all armed forces], in *Zhonggong zhongyang wenjian xuanji* 9 (January 17, 1933), Zhongyang dang'an'guan, 457–58.

(2) August 1, 1935, August First Declaration (also known as "Wei kangri jiuguo gao quanti tongbao shu" [A letter to all compatriots on the Anti-Japanese war]), in "Zhongguo gongchandang zai kangri zhanzhen shiqi de renwu" [The CCP's tasks during the Anti-Japanese War], note 3, in *Mao Zedong xuanji* [Selected works of Mao Zedong], vol. 1 (May 3, 1937) (Beijing: Renmin chubanshe, 1952).

(3) December 25, 1935, "Guanyü muqian de zhengzhi xinshi yü dang de renwu jueyi" [Resolution on the current political situation and the party's tasks], note 4, in *Mao Zedong xuanji*, vol. 1 (May 3, 1937).

(4) May 3, 1936, "Tingzhan yihe yizhi kangri tongdian" [Cease-fire talks, joint anti-Japanese resistance circular], in *Mao Zedong xuanji*, vol. 1 (August 25, 1936); letter to the GMD, in "Guanyü Jiang Jieshi shengming de shengming" [Comment on the statement of Jiang Jieshi], note 6, in *Mao Zedong xuanji*, vol. 1 (December 28, 1936); *Mao Zedong xuanji*, vol. 1 (May 3, 1937).

(5) September 17, 1936, "Guanyü kangri jiuwang yongdong de xin xingshi yü dangde renwu jueyi" [Resolution on the new situation and the democratic republic during the anti-Japanese and national salvation movement], in "Zhongguo gongchandang zai kangri zhanzhen shiqi de renwu" [The tasks of the CCP during the Anti-Japanese War], note 7, in *Mao Zedong xuanji*, vol. 1 (May 3, 1937).

(6) December 28, 1936, "Guanyü Jiang Jieshi shengming de shengming" [Comment on the statement of Jiang Jieshi], note 6, in *Mao Zedong xuanji*, vol. 1 (May 3, 1937).

(7) February 10, 1937, telegram to the GMD, in "Zhongguo gongchandang zai kangri zhanzhen shiqi de renwu" [The tasks of the CCP during the Anti-Japanese War], note 9, in *Mao Zedong xuanji*, vol. 1 (May 3, 1937).

Mao Zedong designated September 22 and 23, 1937, when the formation of the GMD and CCP alliance was officially announced in the media, as the official start of the Second United Front. See Mao Zedong, "Guogong hezuo chengli hou de poqie renwu" [Pressing tasks after the establishment of the CCP–GMD United Front], in *Mao Zedong xuanji*, vol. 2 (September 29, 1937), 352. For a summary of the various perspectives on this issue, see the bibliographical essay by Xue Yü, "Kangri minzu tongyi zhanxian yü di'er'ci guogong hezuo" [The Anti-Japanese National United Front and the CCP–GMD Second United Front], in *Kangri zhanzhengshi yanjiu shuping* [Review of Research on the Anti-Japanese War], ed. Guo Dehong (Beijing: Zhonggong dangshi chubanshe, 1995), 179–215.

27. "Wei dongyuan yiqie liliang zhengqü kangzhan shengli er douzheng" [Mobilize all forces and struggle for victory in the anti-Japanese War victory], in *Mao Zedong xuanji*, vol. 2 (August 25, 1937), 341.

28. Foreign Affairs Ministry, *Zhongwai tiaoyue jibian*, 660.

29. Foreign Affairs Ministry, *Zhongwai tiaoyue jibian*, 589–94.

30. Jiang Jieshi, "Zhongmei Zhongying pingdeng xinyue gaocheng gao quanguo junmin shu" [A letter to all servicemen and the masses to mark the conclusion of the new equal treaties between China and the U.S., and between China and Britain] (January 12, 1943), in *Xian zongtong Jianggong sixiang yanlun zongji* [Collected thoughts and speeches of the late President Jiang], ed. Zhongguo guomindang zhongyang weiyuanhui (Taibei: Zhongguo guomindang zhongyang weiyuan hui, 1984), 32:4–7.

31. "Shui de chenggong?" [Whose success?], *Zhongyang ribao* [Central Daily] and *Saodang bao* [Sweeping newspaper], joint ed. (January 14, 1943); Xiandai yingyü zhuanxiu xuexiao (The dean's office of the Modern English Training School), ed., *Zhongmei Zhongying xinyue wenxian* [Anglo-Chinese edition of the new Sino-British and Sino-American Treaties and other related materials] (Chongqing: Tiandi chubanshe, 1943), 55–58.

32. "Wushi nian lai fendou de chengguo" [The fruits of the fifty-year struggle], *Zhongyang ribao* (January 16, 1943).

33. "Guanyü qingzhu Zhongmei Zhongying jian feichu bupingdeng tiaoyue jueding" [Resolution on the celebration of the abrogation of the Unequal Treaties between China and the U.S., and between China and Britain] (January 25, 1943), in *Zhonggong Zhongyang wenjian xuanji*, ed. Zhongyang dang'an'guan, 14:17–19.

34. "Benshi gejie choubei qingzhu feiyue dahui" [Preparation for the party to celebrate the abolition of the treaties among all occupational groups in the city], *Jiefang ribao* (January 31, 1943).

35. Chang Yü-fa (Zhang Yüfa), *Zhongguo xiandai shi* [Modern Chinese history], 9th ed. (Taibei: Donghua shujü, 1997), 2:655.

36. Foreign Affairs Ministry, *Zhongwai tiaoyue jibian*, preface.

37. Lin Q., *Kangzhan shiqi feichu bupingdeng tiaoyue shiliao.*

38. Wang Jianlang, *Kangzhan chuqi de yuandong guoji guanxi* [The international relations of the Far East in the initial phase of the anti-Japanese War] (Taibei: Dongda tushu gongsi, 1996), 223–24; *Rihua mimi xieyi* [The Japanese-Chinese secret agreement], in *Riben diguo zhuyi duiwai qinlue shiliao xuanbian, 1931–1945* [Selected historical sources on the aggression of the Japanese imperialists], ed. Fudan daxue lishixi (Shanghai: Shanghai renmin chubanshe, 1975).

39. Kuang Heping, "Zhongguo gongchandang yü bupingdeng tiaoyue de feichu" [The Chinese Communist Party and the nullification of the Unequal Treaties], *Nankai xuebao* 4 (2001): 7–12.

40. Foreign Affairs Ministry, *Zhongwai tiaoyue jibian*, 505–24. This treaty and related documents were declared null and void by the GMD government in Taiwan on February 25, 1953, in response to the hostile environment engendered by the Cold War in Asia.

41. U.S. Department of State, *Foreign Relations of the United States: Diplomatic Papers: The Conferences of Malta and Yalta, 1945* (Washington, D.C.: U.S. Government Printing Office, 1955); Waijiaobu qingbaosi, trans., *Ya'er'da huiyi mimi wenjian: youguan Zhongguo ji yuandong bufen* [Secret documents of the Yalta Conference relating to China and the Far East] (Taibei: Lifayuan waijiao weiyuanhui, 1955); Wang Yongxiang, *Ya'er'da miyue yü Zhongsu Risu guanxi* [The secret agreements of the Yalta Conference and Sino-Soviet and Japanese-Soviet relations] (Taibei: Dongda tushu gongsi, 2003).

42. Wang Shijie, "Zhongsu youhao tongmeng tiaoyue zhi dijie yü feizhi" [The signing of the Treaty of Friendship and Alliance between the Republic of China and the U.S.S.R.], in *Wang Shijie xiansheng lunzhu xuanji* [Selected works of Mr. Wang Shijie] (Taibei: Yütai gongsi, 1980), 349.

43. U.S. Department of State, *Foreign Relations of the United States*, 895.

44. U.S. Department of State, *Foreign Relations of the United States*, 895.

45. Foreign Affairs Ministry, *Zhongwai tiaoyue jibian*, 512.

46. Foreign Affairs Ministry, *Zhongwai tiaoyue jibian*, 512.

47. Wang Shijie, "Zhongsu youhao tongmeng tiaoyue zhi dijie yü feizhi" [The signing of the Treaty of Friendship and Alliance between the Republic of China and the U.S.S.R.], in *Wang Shijie xiansheng lunzhu xuanji*, 349–50.

48. Foreign Affairs Ministry, *Zhongwai tiaoyue jibian*, 508.

49. Wang Shijie, *Wang Shijie xiansheng lunzhu xuanji*, 349–50; Xue Xiantian, *Zhongsu guojia guanxishi ziliao huibian (1945–1949)* [Collection of documents on the Sino-Soviet relations] (Beijing: Shehui kexue wenxian chubanshe, 1996).

50. Mineo Nakajima, "Foreign Relations: From the Korean War to the Bandung Line," in *The Cambridge History of China*, ed. Roderick MacFarquhar and John K. Fairbank (Cambridge: Cambridge University Press, 1987), 14:259–89.

51. Wang Shijie, *Zhongguo bupingdeng tiaoyue zhi feichu*, chapter 7.

52. Chang Y., *Zhongguo xiandai shi*, 2:656.

53. Wang Zurong and Li Ao, *Jiang Jieshi pingzhuan* [Biography of Jiang Jieshi] (Beijing: Zhongguo youyi chuban gongsi, 2000), 509.

54. Liu Shaoqi, "Daibiao zhonggong zhongyang gei liangong (bu) zhongyang Si Dalin de baogao" [Report to the Soviet Central Committee chairman Stalin on behalf of the CCP Central Committee], in *Jianguo yilai Liu Shaoqi wengao* [The Liu Shaoqi paper since the founding of the People's Republic of China](Beijing: Zhongyang wenxian chubanshe, 1998), 15–16.

55. Peng Ming, *Zhongsu renmin youyi jianshi* [A brief history of the friendship of Sino-Soviet peoples] (Beijing: Zhongguo qingnian chubanshe, 1995), 111.

56. "Mao Zedong dui Ying jizhe Gan Bei'er shi'er xiang wenti zhi dafu" [Chairman Mao's responses to twelve questions put by British journalist Gan Bei'er (Chinese spelling)], in *Zhongsu renmin youyi jianshi*, ed. Peng Ming, 112, 114.

57. Li Zhixue, "Cong qüru tuoxie dao duli zizhu: Zhongsu youhao tongmeng tiaoyue yü zhongsu youhao tongmeng huzhu tiaoyue bijiao yanjiu" [From humiliating compromise to independence: A comparative study of the Treaty of Friendship and Alliance between the Republic of China and the U.S.S.R., and the Treaty of Friendship, Alliance, and Mutual Assistance], *Xuexi yü tansuo* 3 (2002):126–30.

58. Liu Xifa, "Zhongsu youhao tongmeng tiaoyue pingxi" [An analysis of the Treaty of Friendship and Alliance between the Republic of China and the U.S.S.R.], *Shehui kexue zhanxian* 3 (1996): 210–16; Liu Li, "Zhongsu youhao tongmeng tiaoyue de qianding jiqi dui guogong liangdang guanxi de yingxiang" [The signing of the Treaty of Friendship and Alliance between the Republic of China and the U.S.S.R. and its impact on the relationship between the CCP and the GMD], *Shiji qiao* 4 (2000): 29–30. For a more balanced account of Sino-Soviet relations during the Sino-Japanese war, see Wang Zhen, *Dongdang zhong de tongmeng: Kangzhan shiqi Zhongsu guanxi* [Allies in uncertainty: The Sino-Soviet relation in the Anti-Japanese War] (Guilin: Guangxi shida chubanshe, 1993).

59. Yang Gongsu, *Zhonghua minguo waijiao jianshi* [A brief diplomatic history of the Republic of China] (Beijing: Shangwu yinshuguan, 1997), 280–84; Zhu and Wang, *Zhongguo duiwai tiaoyue xidian*, 55 (in preface).

60. Yang Kuisong, "Zhongsu guojia liyi yü minzu qinggan de zuichu pengzhuang: yi Zhongsu youhao tongmeng huzhu tiaoyue de qianding wei beijing" [The initial encounter of state interests and national sentiment between China and the Soviet Union: The signing of Sino-Soviet Treaty of Friendship, Alliance, and Mutual Assistance], *Lishi yanjiu*, no. 6 (2001): 103–19.

61. It is worth noting that the public announcement of the 1950 Sino (People's Republic of China)–Soviet Treaty of Friendship, Alliance, and Mutual Assistance drew immediate condemnation from the Guomindang on Taiwan. Tapping into the same vocabulary that the CCP had previously used to smear the GMD Nanjing regime, commentaries like the following (published in Taiwan in 1950) were common: "judging the terms of the [1950] treaty itself, one can easily tell that the CCP connived with the Soviet to sell out the [Chinese] nation." Chen Buxiu and Lin Jian, eds., *Zhongsu miyue* [The secret agreement between the People's Republic of China and the Soviet Union] (Taibei: Taipingyang xinwenshe, 1950), 15. The 1950 treaty, the commentary continues, discloses "the Soviet Union's overweening and aggressive ambition" and "binds the CCP to forfeit Cina's future." Some in Taiwan speculated that the announced 1950 treaty was only a cover for an outright traitrous secret agreement signed by the Communist China with the Soviet Union.

62. Zhongguo lishi di'er dang'an'guan, ed., *Zhonghua minguo dang'an ziliao huibian*, 5:698 (in part 3).

63. On the GMD's failure in the race to implement a military and civilian administration in Manchuria, see Suzanne Pepper, "The KMT-CCP Conflict 1945–1949," 723–29 (in part 2).

64. Zhongguo lishi di'er dang'an'guan, ed., *Zhonghau minguo dang'an ziliao huibian*, vol. 5, 706–8 (in part 3).

65. Wang Yongxiang, *Ya'er'da miyue yü Zhongsu Risu guanxi*, 113.

66. Jian Chen, *Mao's China and the Cold War* (Chapel Hill: University of North Carolina Press, 2001), 37.

67. Chen, *Mao's China and the Cold War*, 44.

68. Chen, *Mao's China and the Cold War*, 38.

69. The CCP's brief probes into the question of possible future alliances with the U.S. are documented in both public announcements and Mao's private communications with Deng Xiaoping, Liu Bocheng, Chen Yi, and Huang Hua between April and August 1949. "Ruguo Meiying duanjue tong Guomindang de guanxi ke kaolü he tamen jianli waijiao guanxi" [If the U.S. and Britain cut off their ties with the GMD, the CCP can consider establishing diplomatic relations with them], April 28, 1949, Mao's handwritten telegram to Deng Xiaoping, Liu Bocheng, and Chen Yi, etc.; "Huang Hua tong Situ Leideng tanhua ying zhuyi de jige wenti [Several questions for Huang Hua to think about in his conversation with Suart], Mao's response, in a handwritten telegram, to the City Committee of Nanjing, May 10, 1949; Zhonghua renmin gongheguo waijiaobu and Zhonggong zhongyang wenxian yanjiushi, eds., *Mao Zedong waijiao wenxuan* [Selected works of Mao Zedong] (Beijing: Zhongyang wenxian chubanshe, 1994), 83, 87.

70. For the negotiation of the 1946 treaty, see Ren Donglai, *Zhengchao buxiu de huoban: meiyuan yü zhongmei kangri tongmeng* [Quarrelling partners: American aid and the Sino-American anti-Japan alliance] (Guilin: Guangxi shifan daxue chubanshe, 1995), 202–10.

71. The Sino-American Commercial and Navigation Treaty of 1946, Article 2, in *Zhongwai tiaoyue jibian*, ed. Foreign Affairs Ministry, 690.

72. The Sino-American Commercial and Navigation Treaty of 1946, Article 3, in *Zhongwai tiaoyue jibian*, ed. Foreign Affairs Ministry, 691.

73. "Ping Jiangmei shangyue" [Commentary on the commercial treaty between Jiang and the U.S.], *Jiefang ribao* (November 1946).

74. Zhu and Wang, *Zhongguo duiwai tiaoyue xidian*, 1.

75. "Guanyü bu chengren Jiang zhengfu yiqie maiguo xieding de shengming" [Statement on the non-recognition of all traitorous agreements signed by the Jiang government], in *Zhonggong zhongyang wenjian xuanji*, ed. Zhongyang dang'an'guan, 16:401–2; *Jiefang ribao* (February 4, 1947).

76. *Jiefang ribao* (February 4, 1947).

77. "Zhongguo renmin jiefangjun xuanyan" [The manifesto of the Chinese People's Liberation Army], in *Mao Zedong waijiao wenxuan*, ed. Zhonghua renmin gongheguo waijiaobu and Zhonggong zhongyang wenxian yanjiushi, 63.

78. M. E. Orlean, "The Sino-American Commercial Treaty of 1946," *The Far East Quarterly* 7, no. 4 (1948): 354–67.

79. Jerry Israel, "The Economic Dimension of Sino-American Relations (1931–1949): Profits and Predictability," in *Perspectives in American Diplomacy: Essays on Europe, Latin American, China, and the Cold War*, ed. Jules Davids (New York: Arno Press, 1976), 267–68.

80. Israel, "The Economic Dimension of Sino-American Relations," 361.

81. "Jingjibu dui Zhongmei shangyue cao'an yijianshu" [Reaction of the Ministry of Economics to the draft of the Sino-American Commercial Treaty], in "Zhongmei shangyue tanpan guocheng wenjian" [Documents on the negotiation of the Sino-American Commercial Treaty], Guomin zhengfu waijiaobu dang'an [The Foreign Ministry Archives of the Nationalist Government], Zhongguo di'er lishi dang'an'guan [No. 2 Chinese Historical Archives], Archive No. 3034–18; Ren Donglai, *Zhengchao buxiu de huoban: meiyuan yü zhongmei kangri tongmeng*, 203–10.

82. The Sino-American Commercial and Navigation Treaty of 1946, Article 14, in *Zhongwai tiaoyue jibian*, ed. Foreign Affairs Ministry, 709–10.

83. Zhu and Wang, *Zhongguo duiwai tiaoyue cidian*, 56 (in preface); Tao Wenzhao, *Zhongmei guoxi shi, 1911–1950* [History of Sino-American relations, 1911–1950] (Chongqing: Chongqing chubanshe, 1993), 32–33; Zeng Zhi, "Meiguo yü Nanjing zhengfu de guanshui zizhu" [The U.S. and the tariff autonomy of the Nanjing government], in *Meiguo yü jinxiandai Zhongguo* [The U.S. and modern China], ed. Tao Wenzhao and Liang Biying (Beijing: Zhongguo shehui kexue chubanshe, 1996), 243–61.

84. Zheng Zemin, "Guanyü bupingdeng tiaoyue de ruogan wenti: yü Zhang Zhenkun xiansheng shangque" [Some questions on the Unequal Treaties: A discussion with Mr. Zhang Zhenkun], *Jindaishi yanjiu* 1 (2000): 215–37; Zhang Zhenkun, "Zaishuo 'Er'shi'yi tiao' bushi tiaoyue" [One more time: Twenty-one Demands are not a treaty], *Jindaishi yanjiu* 1 (2002): 238–52.

85. Zhang Z., "Zaishuo 'er'shi'yi tiao' bushi tiaoyue," 248.

86. Ren, *Zhengchao buxiu de huoban*, 218–19, 235.

87. Tu Heng-chih, *Zhongwai tiaoyue guanxi zhi bianqian* [The evolution of the Sino-foreign treaty relations] (Taibei: Zhonghua wenhua fuxing yundong tuixing weiyuanhui, 1981), 270–78.

88. Tu, *Zhongwai tiaoyue guanxi zhi bianqian*, 1–4.

89. Wu Lin-chun, "1946 nian Zhongmei shangyue de lishi yiyi" [The historical significance of the 1946 Sino-American Commercial Treaty], *Guoli zhengzhi daxue lishi xuebao* 21 (May 2004): 42–66.

90. In contrast to the CCP linear model of modern Chinese history, Wang Gungwu has highlighted war, trade, science and governance as major issues in the Sino-Anglo encounters since 1800. Wang G., *Anglo-Chinese Encounters since 1800*.

91. Mark Selden, *China in Revolution: The Yenan Way Revisited* (Armonk, N.Y.: M. E. Sharpe, 1995); Chalmers A. Johnson, *Peasant Nationalism and Communist Power* (Stanford, Calif.: Stanford University Press, 1962); Odoric Y. K. Wou, *Mobilizing the Masses: Building Revolution in Henan* (Stanford, Calif.: Stanford University Press, 1994). The Yenan Way, a term first coined by Mark Selden, embraces the complex political, military, economic and social programs implemented by the Communists in the border areas of Northern China during the Sino-Japanese War. Selden extends the decisive influence of the Yenan Way in the Chinese revolution to the global anti-colonial and post-colonial movements. See also Yang Wu, "CCP Military Resistance During the Sino-Japanese War: The Case of Beiyue and Jidong," *Twentieth-Century China* 29, no. 1 (2003): 65–104. Through case studies of Beiyue, Hebei, and Jidong, Jin'Cha'Ji, the two CCP–controlled areas subject to the heaviest Japanese offensives, Yang Wu challenges the views of both Johnson and Wou. While confirming that anti-Japanese military resistance was an important factor in the CCP's success, Wu argues that such resistance did not automatically result in peasant support for the CCP because the peasants were more terrorized than antagonized by the brutality of the Japanese, and because significant popular support for the CCP did not materialize until late 1944 when Japanese defeat was certain (see especially pp. 89–90).

92. More points are made in the conclusion.

5

Universalizing International Law and the Chinese Study of the Unequal Treaties: The Paradox of Equality and Inequality

On June 29, 1929, at a time when the Guomindang Nationalist Government was making its most strenuous efforts to rescind foreign consular courts in China, the *China Weekly Review* reported that the Municipal Council of the International Settlement had coincidentally launched a drive against gambling in the foreign quarters of Shanghai. Raids staged by the Shanghai foreign police on gambling dens popularly known as "wheels" resulted in the arrest of some three hundred people, both foreign and Chinese. the *China Weekly Review* listed the wildly varying legal consequences of the very same crime for defendants of different nationalities:

> The Chinese, of course, got the worst of it, because this type of gambling is clearly illegal under Chinese law and the Chinese were immediately arraigned in their Provisional Court where some 160 defendants received sentences ranging from 50 days' imprisonment to fines ranging from $200 to $450, the total amount of the fines collected approximating $30,000. Of the foreigners who were caught in consequence of the raids, those of British nationality, whose cases have been disposed of up to the present, were simply bound over not to frequent such gambling institutions in the future. In order to convict them it was necessary for the local British Court to dig up an old law passed in the time Henry VIII (time of the discovery of America). Those of Spanish nationality who were caught in the raids, were brought up in the local Spanish Consular Court and since this form of gambling apparently is not illegal under Spanish law, they were simply cautioned and released. One Portuguese who was arrested is said to have been fined $50 and one Japanese has had his case remanded for future hearing in the Japanese Consular Court. . . . Two unfortunate Russians, who have lost their extraterritorial rights [as a result of the 1924 treaty between China

and the U.S.S.R.], were arraigned in the local Chinese Provisional Court and received sentences of 50 days in jail, plus a fine of $200.[1]

This incident well illustrates the conflicting jurisdictions and sovereignty and the concomitant inequalities and failures in the justice system suffered by all nationalities under extraterritoriality (extrality or consular jurisdiction) in China. The story also reveals the paradox of equality and inequality which has been an ongoing feature of China's multifaceted encounter with the West since the mid-nineteenth century.

This chapter explores aspects of the paradox of equality and inequality from the perspective of the dissemination of international law in China. The paradox has three levels of meaning. First, the principle of extraterritoriality (or the practice of capitulations) was inserted into the Unequal Treaties which foreign countries imposed on China in the name of "justice and equality" in the aftermath of the Opium Wars (1840–1842, 1856–1860). However, as the above story illustrates, the actual legal consequences for different nationalities under extrality were all too unequal. Second, although sovereign nations are equal in principle, in reality they are politically and economically unequal. Third, from the mid-nineteenth century through the twentieth century, the Chinese made considerable efforts to conform to international law in the hope of achieving an equal status in the world of power politics.

As China's first experience of international law, the Unequal Treaties were long a source of antagonism, working as a reminder of the mistreatment that was suffered on a large scale over many decades and that made the Chinese particularly sensitive to issues of sovereignty. It was to take many decades before the Chinese experience of international law could be transformed into a positive one. The modern literature on the subject either emphasizes China's passivity in the face of the "universalization" of international law, or stresses language and translation as a tool of transmitting international legal theories in the nineteenth century.[2] In his carefully researched book, *China's Entrance into the Family of Nations: The Diplomatic Phase, 1858–1880,* Immanuel Hsü raises a question about the "national humiliations" suffered by China (often equated with the Unequal Treaties) that has continued to loom large in the Chinese consciousness: "Why, after the introduction of international law into China, did she [China] fail to use it as an instrument to assert her sovereignty and recover her lost rights?"[3] Moving away from such questions, however, I focus instead on the positive role played by the Chinese in the spread and development of international law. I also aim to extend the study of international law in China to the twentieth century, an undeservedly neglected topic in the field. Finally, I argue that the flow of legal information in the case of China was to a great extent determined by the Chinese historical and cultural experience with the Unequal Treaties.

Through an examination of the almost contemporary Chinese publications on imposed and unequal treaties, on the one hand, and public international law, on the other, I attempt to show that the interpretation of international law can take place only on the terms presented by a given nation's own culture and history. China's strong interest in topics such as the Unequal Treaties, national humiliations, and the indigenization of international law indicate that China today still believes it has a wrong to rectify, a bitter reminder of the nation's weakness and vulnerability to outside forces in the past. In the meantime, the numerous Chinese publications dealing with these topics and the evolution of international law itself point to both the challenges posed and the contributions made by Chinese to the theory and practice of international law.

To many Chinese, modern Chinese history has been naturally equated with the history of the Unequal Treaties. The realities of the Unequal Treaties have long framed the general reception and broader praxis of public international law in China. The transplantation of international law to Chinese soil can be divided into three phases. The first, which began in the nineteenth century and ended in 1912, marked the introduction of international law into China; the Chinese were forced to grapple with the paradox of the legal equality of sovereign nations guaranteed by international law and the inequality resulting from the Unequal Treaties. The second phase lasted from 1912 to 1949, when the Republic of China grafted international law onto the Chinese legal system as part of the search for solutions to the issue of inequality. During this period, international law was indigenized and struck firm roots in China. The final phase occurred in the latter half of the twentieth century, a period when China developed an original and innovative set of rhetorical formulas with which to interpret world events. The People's Republic of China made full polemical use of the concept of the Unequal Treaties, turning international law into an instrument of struggle against imperialism, colonialism and hegemonism in the dynamics of international bargaining. In addition, to Chinese, the true "internationalization" of international law demanded that it transcend its Christian European origins and expand to accommodate non-Western cultures.

THE BEGINNINGS OF INTERNATIONAL LAW IN CHINA AND THE UNEQUAL TREATIES

In this section, I argue that of all the factors relevant to the origins and development of international law in China, the issue of the Unequal Treaties has had by far the strongest impact on its transmission, appropriation, and indigenization in modern China. When international law was first applied in China, the Chinese were perplexed by the paradox of the principle of equality between sovereign states and the unequal nature of the treaties imposed on China by the West.

In 1840, Qing Imperial Commissioner Lin Zexü was in Guangzhou to crack down on opium consumption and the opium trade. Through the efforts of his interpreters Yuan Dehui and Peter Parker, an American medical missionary, Lin became acquainted with Le droit des gens, the seminal work of the Swiss jurist Emmerich de Vattel (1714–1767).[4] The Chinese translation made by Parker and Yuan, however, was heavily glossed and scarcely intelligible to Lin. There is evidence that Lin was influenced by Vattel's work, translated as Geguo lüli [The laws and regulations of all nations], which was also excerpted in Wei Yuan's Haiguo tuzhi [An illustrated gazetteer of maritime countries]. For instance, in a letter to Queen Victoria in 1839, Lin protested, "To clearly summarize legal penalties as an aid to instruction has been a valid principle in all ages. Suppose a man of another country comes to England to trade, he still has to obey the En-glish laws; how much more should he obey in China the laws of the Celestial Dynasty?"[5]

In 1864, under the auspices of the Tsungli Yamen, three hundred copies of the Chinese translation of Henry Wheaton's Elements of International Law by William A. P. Martin (an American missionary, sinologist, and interpreter to William B. Reed, American minister to China) were distributed to Chinese officials.[6] Martin's work was well received among leading ministers of the Qing Tsungli Yamen, especially Wenxiang and Prince Gong. "International law," now always translated as guojifa,[7] was rendered by Martin as wanguo gongfa.[8]

In 1877, Martin, with Wang Fengzao, and others, cotranslated Theodore Dwight Woosley's Introduction to the Study of International Law into Chinese, titled Gongfa bianlan. Then, three years later, the Chinese version of the French translation of the German jurist's, Johann Caspar Bluntschli's Le droit international codifié, cotranslated by Martin and Lian Fang, and others, was published under the title Gongfa huitong.[9] Obviously, effort was made to translate international law into Chinese in the decade after its first introduction, from foreigners taking the lead in translation to Sino-foreign collaboration. Reversing their initial passive role, the Chinese increasingly got involved and eventually took over the process of transplanting international law in China.

At the time of its introduction into China, a number of officials immediately recognized international law as an important mechanism of conflict resolution. The reformist official Xue Fucheng wrote with implicit trust: "Nations, whether large or small, strong or weak, are in every way dependent upon international law to balance their differences and to alleviate potential conflicts. As far as weak and small nations are concerned, they must rely on international law for their survival."[10] However, in their encounter with the West in the late nineteenth century, the Chinese had to face up to the paradox that, while international law employed a formal concept of national sovereignty that made all nations equal, it could not guarantee that such equality would be respected or enforced in practice. Chinese were quick to learn that formal judicial equality between sovereign states was not to be confused with political equality. Thus while international law was universally regarded as reasonable and instrumental, it provided no remedy for political and economic inequality. This dilemma was only too well recognized by officials such as the reformist Zheng Guanying: "Although international law applies to all, it has not, by any means, always been observed. [My speculation is] that international law can govern the relationships between equally powerful states. However, if there is no equality of national power, then public international law will not necessarily work."[11] Or, in the words of a Qing diplomat, "International law is . . . reasonable but unreliable. If it is a case of right without might, then right will not prevail."[12]

Chinese officials also recognized that the *spirit* of international law was in conflict with the ways in which European powers—claiming the *name* of international law—had acted in their relations with China. In this connection, the Unequal Treaties are particularly important. On the issue of tariff rates, Guo Songtao, China's first minister to Britain and France (1876–1878), commented on the inequalities created by the series of treaties concluded between the Qing and various foreign countries. Compared with the uniform 5 percent ad valorem tariff charged on all foreign merchandise imported into China, he noted that countries such as En-gland, France, and the U.S. levied much higher taxes (set at differential rates) on imported commodities. On some items, the tariff rate was as high as 100 percent.[13] The Qing diplomat, Zeng Jize, minister to Britain, France, and Russia (1878–1885), was later to express the same concerns. Drawing a clear line between diplomatic immunity and nondiplomatic privilege, Zeng commented that, in accordance with Western practice, all diplomatic personnel enjoyed special diplomatic immunity. However, "foreign citizens with no diplomatic status are not supposed to be exempted from the jurisdiction of local authorities and laws."[14] Hence, in Zeng's opinion, international law consisted of "empty principles" (*xüli*):

> As far as public international law is concerned, weak nations make use of it for self-protection, while strong nations, nonetheless, often violate it. . . . As to its workings among states, both far and near, they do not necessarily comply with international law. Today, Western nations tend to regulate others by means of public international law; tomorrow, whenever they see opportunities to exploit our China, they will explain away theories of public international law in order to make their case. Their arguments [for requests] will come like swarms of bees so that the situation [China's dealings with foreigners] will resemble a flight of steps overgrown with brambles.[15]

There was another view of the nature of international law. As one author pointed out in *Waijiaobao* in 1901, international law was just an instrument that required good skills to make it work better:

> Those compatriots who have commented on international law often hold international law accountable for its inefficacy in regulating encounters between strong and weak nations. . . . [In my view,] the function of international law is the same as that of warships and fortresses. If one is not adept at operating

warships and defending fortresses and as a consequence suffers defeat at the hands of one's enemies, how come is it the fault of warships and fortresses [i.e., Can one really blame the warships and fortresses]?[16]

Historically, the Unequal Treaties were China's first exposure to international law, an experience that confounded the Chinese because of the very different implications it held for strong and weak nations. This was the difficult situation which confronted them in seeking to implement international law for themselves.

Studies of international law began to take shape at the turn of the nineteenth and twentieth centuries, as an integral part of Chinese efforts to pursue wealth, strength, and Western learning. In 1896, two translated works on international law were published—one was John Fryer and Wang Zhensheng's translated work *Gongfa zonglun*, the other was the Chinese version of Sir Robert Phillimore's (1810–1885) *Commentaries upon International Law*, *Geguo jiaoshe gongfa lun*, translated by John Fryer and Yü Shijue.[17] What was interesting from the late nineteenth century onward was that the Chinese seemed independently to take more initiatives to translate or initiate research about international law. In 1898 there was a loose study group, *Gongfa xuehui*, in existence from April to September 1898 in Changsha of Hunan Province. The bylaws of this study group indicate that topics—such as international law, the treaties between China and foreign countries in connection with their biggest problems, small blemishes, issues to be added to negotiations with foreigners and issues to be negotiated for changes—were highlighted for study and discussion.[18] Meanwhile, some young Chinese intellectuals compiled translated works in Chinese on international law, and some translated Japanese books on international law into Chinese. Such examples were Tang Caichang's (1867–1900) *Gongfa tongyi* in 1897 and Cai Er's (1882–1916) *Guoji gongfa zhi* in 1902.[19]

Besides wealth, strength, and Western learning, studying international law also served other political purposes. For instance, Hu Hanmin, one of the Tongmenghui's[20] leading polemicists, also disseminated knowledge of international law in order to arouse anti-Manchu sentiments among the Han Chinese. To justify the efforts made by the United League to topple the Manchu Qing government, Hu, in his treatise *Paiwai yü guojifa* published in *Minbao* from 1906 to 1907, singled out the treaties as well as the Qing government's legal mistakes as essential factors that gave rise to xenophobic feelings among the Chinese.[21]

FINDING A BASIS FOR THE APPLICATION OF INTERNATIONAL LAW IN CHINA (1912–1949)

In the Republic of China (1912–1949), the study of international law went hand in hand with the search for legal grounds on which to revoke the Unequal Treaties. The tensions between formal sovereign equality and actual political and economic inequality, which had been given scant attention within the traditional framework of international law, were extensively discussed by a variety of political and social agents in China. Furthermore, the perceived inadequacies of international law inspired scholarly interest in the subject, stimulating a body of literature on the Unequal Treaties and imperialist aggression in China. Third, Chinese research on international law corresponded with the flourishing printing business in the studies of international law as well as the Unequal Treaties. Finally, the indigenization of international law in China was characterized by the invocation of existing legal theories and practices in calling for changes to the status quo.

In the 1910s, Chinese knowledge of international law was rudimentary and one of the main channels of dissemination was through legal works in Japanese. Translated publications of significance included an edited volume by Jin Baokang, *Pingshi guojifa* (1907), and a translation of the Japanese text *Pingshi guoji gongfa* (1911) by Chen Shixia, as well as *Guojifa yaolun* by Shen Yüshan (1914).[22] Evidence also confirms that at the Beiyang Fazheng Zhuanmen Xuexiao at Tianjin[23] adopted works in Japanese as textbooks for students to study international law. One of the founders and early leaders of the Chinese Communist Party, Li Dazhao (1888–1927), studied law there.[24] In 1909–1910, as a third year student of the Preparatory School, Li spent considerable time studying his textbook in Japanese on the general theories of law, one chapter of which is about public and private international law.[25] A few years later while studying at Waseda University in Tokyo, Li, together with his classmate and friend Zhang Runzhi, translated Imai Yoshiyuki's *Zhongguo guojifa lun* with a focus on foreign extraterritoriality in China.[26]

Li Dazhao's translated book of *Zhongguo guojifa lun* provides us with a window through which four characteristics of the propagation of international law in China in the 1910s can be discerned: First, the Chinese should firmly believe in the authority of international law as the basis of international covenants. Second, the power of international law and national strength should be based upon the equality of international status. Third, changes to or elimination of international compacts by invoking the power of law should be in the hands of the Chinese. Fourth, Li Dazhao felt embarrassed by the fact that foreign legal scholars, such as Imai Yoshiyuki, took the lead in research about international law and international relations related to China, whereas the Chinese intellectuals, absorbed by the politics of saving China, had found little time to devote to academic research.

The political instability of the 1920s did little to dampen Chinese enthusiasm for public international law, and the publication of both translations of original legal scholarship and Chinese indigenous writings flourished in this period. Observations that can be made about promotion of international law in the 1920s China are, first, international law emerged as a mature field of study and as a formal academic discipline. Many of the Chinese publications on international law in this period were university textbooks, which was an obvious advance on the situation in the 1910s when Chinese textbooks were lacking.[27] A greater number of translations appeared, including the translation of Lassa Oppenheim's (1858–1919) classic *The Future of International Law* by Chen Zongxi.[28] Second, we see a group of European trained Chinese international lawyers devoting their entire life to the study and dissemination of international law in China. These people—Zhou Gengsheng, Zhou Wei, Wang Tieya, Chen Tiqiang, and Zhou Ziya, and so forth—were critical figures assuming the role of teachers of international law in twentieth-century China.[29] Third, instead of simply reproducing what points made by Western jurists, the specialized monographs in Chinese on international law displayed a greater grip by the Chinese on the whole nature and development of the subject. For example, in lucid language, Zhou Gengsheng in *Guojifa dagang* stated with precision what contemporary international law courses should cover: the nature, subjects, sources, basic rights, and jurisdictions of nation states, treaties, international negotiations, diplomatic representation, resolutions to international disputes, and the nature of international organizations. With regard to equality and inequality between nation states, Zhou made it clear that national equality refers to legal equity in spite of the fact that the fact that nation states are politically unequal. Political inequality cannot eliminate legal equality. In his summary of the differences among naturalists, Grotians and positivists, Zhou apparently agreed that positivism was the main direction in which international law evolved.[30] *Xin guoji gongfa* by Zhou Wei, in a different style from Zhou Gengsheng's *Guojifa dagang*, engages in the discussion about the rubrics of international law with more emotions by introducing examples specific to China throughout the two volumes.

Several other legal and historical works on international law and the Unequal Treaties also received attention. The nature of capitulations (extraterritorial rights) in connection with the Unequal Treaties, for example, was thoroughly discussed in Liu Shih Shun's *Extraterritoriality: Its Rise and Its Decline*.[31] In his comprehensive legal study of the Unequal Treaties, Tseng Yu-hao, then President of the High Court of Justice for Anhui Province, devoted the first chapter to the issue of capitulations and the Unequal Treaties.[32]

In the history of international law, the terms extraterritoriality, extrality, and capitulations refer to the diplomatic immunities secured where one state permitted another to exercise the latter's jurisdiction over its own nationals within the former's boundaries. Today such a privilege is granted only to certain diplomatic agents exempt from both criminal and civil charges in the countries where they are accredited, as stipulated in the Convention on Diplomatic Relations signed in Vienna in 1961.[33]

Both Liu and Tseng argued that the historical practice of capitulations originated in the inadequacy of local laws reflecting ancient familial and agricultural practices to embrace the complex business activities undertaken by foreign merchants. Thus, in the ninth century BC, Memphis and other Egyptian cities allowed Phoenician and Greek merchants to be subject to their own laws. Similar treatment was given to Phoenicians in Greece, to non-Roman citizens in the Roman Empire in the third century BC, as well as to certain citizens of Italian city-states in Antioch and Jerusalem in 1098 and 1123. Both Byzantine emperors and the Ottoman sultans followed such practices to avoid administrative and legal burdens. In 1535, the Franco-Ottoman Treaty was signed between Francis I of France and Süleyman I of Turkey granting the French consuls jurisprudence over the criminal and civil affairs of French nationals in Turkey. Medieval Europe witnessed the establishment of permanent consulates by merchants of a particular city in other cities of the same country or in foreign countries; they settled business disputes and exercised jurisdiction over merchants sharing their nationality.[34] Liu and Tseng argued that these examples were more a matter of convenience or the gratuitous granting of territorial powers than the surrender of sovereignty.

In the mid-nineteenth century, the modern conception of the sovereign nation state, one of the basic concepts of international law, took shape in Europe. This concept emphasized reciprocity and equality among independent nation states, as embodied in the Peace of Westphalia in 1648. Liu and Tseng pointed out that the modern notion of sovereign supremacy and exclusiveness inevitably came into conflict with the precedents for extraterritoriality reviewed above. In the 1606 treaty between England and France, the 1787 treaty between France and Russia, the 1788 treaty between France and the U.S., and a series of treaties concluded between Portugal (1696), France (1701), England (1713), and Spain, reciprocal extraterritoriality was accorded.[35] While Europeans and Americans attempted to discontinue the ancient and medieval practice of capitulations among themselves, they happily imposed extrality on Turkey, China, Japan, and Siam—but with no corresponding rights given to nationals of those countries residing in Europe and the U.S. Extraterritoriality was brought to an end in Japan in 1899, in Turkey in 1923 (by the Treaty of Lausanne), and in China in 1943.

The work of the American historian Eileen Scully has added nuances to the picture of extraterritoriality in China. She challenges the common assumption that Western governments, consulate personnel, and their colonial nationals, as a monolithic unit, worked together harmoniously under the protection of extraterritoriality. "Far from being a blunt instrument imposed on a passive, victimized indigenous society by singled-minded imperialists, extrality was more in fact a complex balancing act in which metropolitan governments, colonial sojourners, indigenous elites, and opportunists of all nationalities battled for advantage."[36] Nonetheless, for Liu and Tseng such subtleties were neither an historical nor a legal concern. On the contrary, what interested Chinese jurists the most was the legal validity of the Unequal Treaties.

In his work, Tseng recognized the conceptual vagueness of unilateral treaties and unequal treaties in international law and identified the Unequal Treaties with "those conventions and agreements concluded in the Orient with Christian powers when the idea of territorial sovereignty was not seriously defended."[37] Referring to China's Unequal Treaties as "decaying institutions," Tseng noted that the growing attention given to the topic had broadened research in the field of international law in the 1920s. He quoted the comments made by Raymond L. Buell at the 1927 meeting of the American Society of International Law: "There is a group of treaties which I imagine may be called unequal. You have treaties granting extraterritorial rights, of which the Chinese treaties are an example."[38] At the same time, Tseng drew attention to similar concerns about this contradiction in the world of politics, such as the Porter Resolution of January 1927 by the U.S. Sixty-first Congress.[39]

The subject of a change of conditions relative to the termination of a treaty was given detailed attention in Tseng's book, which contended that the doctrine of *rebus sic stantibus* (conditions which warrant that the conclusions of a contract no longer exists) must be applied in the case of China, and thus would provide the necessary legal grounds for China to nullify certain treaties and to relieve itself of certain treaty obligations, including the Twenty-one Demands of 1915 signed with Japan.[40] Such examples illustrate the close connection of academic studies of the Unequal Treaties and international law in the Chinese context.

In the 1930s, the Chinese study of international law and the transplantation of the theory of the subject came to maturity. This had involved a dual process—the translation of Western theory and original Chinese research into international law. In 1934, the first Chinese translation of Oppenheim's *International Law: A Treatise* became available and has been the most popular and most frequently reprinted international law treatise in China.[41] Influential indigenous Chinese writings included Tseng Yu-hao's compilation *Guoji gongfa li'an*, Zhou Gengsheng's *Xiandai guojifa wention*, and Liu Daren's and Yuan Guoqin's *Guojifa fada shi*.[42] Approaching international law from a historical perspective, Liu Daren and Yuan Guoqin undertook a thorough examination of its definition, structure, nature, historical evolution, objects and subjects, neutrality, and regulations—as well as the international diplomatic organizations and procedures that have arisen from it, and the solutions it offers for international disputes.

The proliferation of Chinese literature on the Unequal Treaties is characteristic of the spread of international law in China; to a great extent it overlaps with publications on "national shame" (*guochi wenxue*) and the literature on imperialist aggression against China.[43] In the words of Chen Tiqiang, "the only field in which Chinese international lawyers made intensive study was the question of unequal treaties and special rights of foreign powers in China."[44] These two subdisciplines of the history of modern China developed in the latter half of the 1920s, and became perennial topics of discussion for many different interest-groups in the twentieth century. Nearly one hundred entries can be found under the heading of *diguo zhuyi qinhuashi* in *Minguo shiqi Zongshumu* [A comprehensive bibliography of the Republican period].[45] From its first appearance in 1925 to 1930, Wang Jingwei's *Diguo zhuyi qinlue Zhongguo de qüshi he bianqian lun* [Characteristics and evolution of the imperialist penetration of China] was reprinted eleven times.[46] The publication of more than a dozen books whose titles contain the phrase *bupingdeng tiaoyue* underlines the point that the literature of the Unequal Treaties was flourishing by the mid-1920s.[47] Jin Baokang divided the Unequal Treaties into three categories—those treaties that should be terminated without consent; those that should be abrogated with bilateral agreement; and those that should be terminated unilaterally.[48] Qiu Zuming offered a solid study of the Unequal Treaty system examining its origins, earlier critiques, and strategies for revision.[49] He singled out the Treaty of Nanjing, Tianjin, the Boxer Protocol, and the Twenty-one Demands as the most "damaging to the existence of the nation."[50] Drawing on international legal theory, Qiu itemized those national rights lost through the negotiation of foreign treaties. Qiu thus argued that China's sovereignty and independence were contingent on the Unequal Treaties, and the chief task of China's diplomacy was to fight for national rights. With respect to international law, Qiu held that "public law can be used for constructing arguments but cannot be relied upon. . . . Since it has been the case, ever since antiquity, that diplomacy is backed up by military power."[51]

Zhang Tinghao's *Bupingdeng tiaoyue de yanjiu* drew on the Leninist notions of imperialism and colonialism to interpret the phenomenon of the Unequal Treaties as an extension of developments in domestic capitalism.[52] In consequence, Zhang wrote, "As a hunk of fat meat in Asia, China naturally fell prey to European and American imperialism. For the imperialists, the Unequal Treaties entailed rights for them to enjoy, whereas for us they meant obligations to be fulfilled."[53] In this connection, Zhang characterized public international law as "an instrument for imperialists to deceive weak and small nations in protection of their illegal rights."[54] A sample of the Unequal Treaties literature of the later 1920s thus illustrates the interest the subject evoked among scholars, jurists, government officials, and writers of all political inclinations.[55]

The Chinese perception was that public international law primarily served the purposes of assisting Western expansionism. Their unease about the principle of sovereign equality and the extent to which it negated differences in power were evident in Chinese pronouncements on the function of international law in world politics. As we have seen, the principle of equality was not honored in most treaties signed between China and foreign countries. To what extent, then, could sovereign equality be applied to China? Disparities in national power were a perennial issue in the dissemination of international law in China, as well as in China's struggle with the Unequal Treaties.

As a result, the diffusion of international law cannot be simply understood as a matter of spreading the word of law in the sense of a mere transfer, but it also involves the assimilation of the appropriate legal framework and legal language into the indigenous culture of the host nation at a particular historical moment. One example can be given here. Historically, international law was composed of two parts, public and private.[56] Today, international law, also known as public international law or the law of nations, refers to standards of conduct and rules that apply between sovereign states. This is distinct from private international law, which deals with the conflict of laws, that is, legal problems arising from the multiplicity of legal systems obtaining in different states.[57] For Chinese in the first half of the twentieth century, private international law was of little interest since it had no relevance to the questions thrown up by their immediate historical context.

INDIGENIZING (*BENTUHUA*) INTERNATIONAL LAW IN THE CHINESE CONTEXT: THE SECOND HALF OF THE TWENTIETH CENTURY

Over the last half century, the People's Republic of China (P.R.C., 1949–present) has developed set formulas and a systematic rhetorical vocabulary for interpreting world events. Here I argue that it uses this rhetoric to define its position on a variety of issues, to invoke public international law to serve its own purposes, and to modify internationally accepted interpretations of domestic and international events with which it does not agree.

In 1971, at the height of modern China's isolation from the outside world, Jerome Alan Cohen prophetically observed,

> It would be surprising if the PRC did not make some distinctive impact upon international law in view of its Marxist-Leninist-Maoist ideology of struggle against imperialism; the fierce nationalism that derives from China's bitter heritage of foreign exploitation; the totalitarian order, "socialist transformation" of the economy, and Cultural Revolution that have been instituted internally; the continuing civil war with the Nationalist forces; and the PRC's long-standing exclusion from many international organizations and bilateral diplomatic relationships.[58]

Though Cohen's remarks were hardly propitious under the particular circumstances of the Cold War, they challenged the conventional (and still prevailing) wisdom that emphasizes the passivity of China in its entry into the family of nations, the collapse of its traditional tributary system, and its forced compliance with international norms.[59]

The great encounter between China and Europe between 1500 and 1800 made a significant impact on both sides. Yet it was in the period after the 1840s, with the new external threat posed by the West from the sea and the ongoing contest for legitimacy between rival governments (most notably the first Republic's warlord government in Beijing versus the Guomindang (GMD) government in Canton; the GMD's Nanjing government versus the CCP; and the GMD government in Taiwan versus the P.R.C.), that China and the world were confronted with a multitude of fascinating and challenging legal problems.[60]

We can distinguish four separate facets of the adaptation of international law to the Chinese context. First, China managed to resolve the paradox of sovereign equality and political and economic inequality that classical theories of international law had not been designed to deal with. Working in the positivist mode pioneered by Oppenheim, Chinese international lawyers treat major inequalities between powers as political rather than legal issues. They have staunchly defended the principles of sovereignty and legal equality as the basis for the regulation of state-to-state conduct, advocating enhanced opportunities for small or weak states to influence legal development and to "pursue agendas that are not simply those of the powerful."[61] However, China's most prominent jurist, Wang Tieya, stressed that such arguments must not be equated with the doctrine of absolute or unrestricted sovereignty—under which nation states enjoy freedom to act at will, perhaps leading to the emergence of a single "superpower" or even "world government"—which would only lead to anarchy. This is the kind of situation which P.R. China has perceived as paving the way for past imperialist expansionism and aggression.[62] The Chinese argument is that

> the principle of equality does not mean that states are all equal in fact. The fact that states are different in size and population—large or small—and in terms of power—strong or weak—cannot be ignored. However, this actual inequality should not be a reason for the denial of the legal equality of states as the basis of interstate relations and a fundamental principle of international law.[63]

Wang viewed this underpinning legal equality as "a safeguard" for the small and the weak "against encroachments on their rights by larger and stronger powers."[64] Chinese international lawyers also argue that the limited enforceability of international law should be regarded as a potential strength rather than a deficiency. The source of authority in international law lies in "equitable coordination" among sovereign states in the international legal order rather than in the ability of any one state or grouping of states to act as the world's policeman.[65]

The second way in which international law has been adapted to the Chinese context results from globalization and multinationalism. These ubiquitous features of the contemporary world have confirmed Chinese jurists in opposing the radical change in the modern conception of national sovereignty proposed in some recent work in international law. Their objection derives from China's "bitter experience" of the Unequal Treaties in the past, as well as from the conviction that the doctrine of sovereignty is "the only foundation upon which international relations and international law can be established and developed."[66]

The history of international law demonstrates broad support for national sovereignty as "territorial supremacy" and for sovereign equality as a fundamental principle of an international legal system.[67] Nonetheless, there was no consensus on its theoretical basis, and "unease about it persisted in practice."[68] Among international law theorists, three positions predominate with regard to the paradox of equality and inequality. Benedict Kingsbury summarizes them as follows:

> Vattel's naturalistic approach, with its remarkable analogy between equality of individuals and equality of states, has remained influential. . . . It persists in assertions that the exclusion of individuals from democratic participation in local and national government is the same injustice as exclusion of large third world states from permanent membership in the Security Council. . . . The positivist alternative, well represented by Oppenheim, sees equality as a logical corollary of sovereignty. A third explanation, reciprocity, is preferred by structural realists in international relations (for whom particular configurations of power among states will largely determine the patterns of inter-states interactions), as reciprocity potentially accounts for the otherwise puzzling acceptance by states of formal equality despite disparities of power.[69]

Chinese international lawyers have been more at ease with positivists (Oppenheim) than naturalists (Grotius, Pufendorf, and Vattel), a stance clearly related to China's experience with the Unequal Treaties.[70] Provoked by the discrepancy between the principles of international law that Western nations preached and what they actually practiced, Chinese viewed the transplantation of international law to their country as a bitter and humiliating experience involving the cynical separation of theory and practice.[71] Nonetheless, despite the fact that international affairs were often not conducted in accordance with the principle of equality between sovereign states, Chinese international lawyers accepted the practical value of international law in providing the legal framework for a coherent world order.

As a third major point of distinction, Chinese discourse on international law displays a universalist rhetoric that demands that the subject be sufficiently elastic to adapt itself to a constantly changing world environment. From time to time, this universalist rhetoric appears self-contradictory. On the one hand, Chinese scholars stress that international law dealt initially with only a few European states. Developments since World War II, however, have created a legal system that applies to all nations universally. On the other hand, Chinese legal scholars argue that, given China's size and importance, "the extent to which contemporary international law can really be said to be universal in character depends largely on China's attitudes towards international law."[72]

Fourth, having accepted the efficacy of international law, China has exerted considerable pressure on traditional international legal doctrine. As a result of their violent history, the Chinese came to believe that public international law could be an effective instrument of struggle against imperialism, colonialism and hegemonism.[73] In nearly all the textbooks on international law published in the P.R.C., a prominent place is given to the Five Principles of Peaceful Co-existence as leading principles of international law.[74] The Five Principles were first formulated and proclaimed as the basis of international relations in a treaty known as the Agreement between the Republic of India and the People's Republic of China on the Trade and Intercourse between the Tibet Region of China and India signed on April 29, 1954. This agreement was later reconfirmed in several international documents, including the Ten Principles adopted at the Bandung Conference in 1955, and the Charter of Economic Rights and Duties of States approved by the UN General Assembly on December 12, 1974.[75] The five principles are: mutual respect for each other's territorial integrity and sovereignty; mutual nonaggression; mutual noninterference in each other's international affairs; equality and mutual benefit; and peaceful coexistence.

China's reading of international law and the Unequal Treaties has been seminal in shaping both academic perspectives on the subject and its stance on foreign relations, resulting in an emphasis on incorporating international law into research on modern China's foreign relations. An important example is Cheng Daode's *Jindai Zhongguo waijiao yü guojifa*, which examines such issues as foreign extrality in China, the concession system, tariffs, and the Treaty of Friendship and Alliance between China and the U.S.S.R. of 1945.[76]

CONCLUSION

The issue of legal equality versus political and economic inequality engages with a broad range of debate in China on the meaning of modernity (expressed in the desire for international standards) and nationalism (molding and reconstructing national identity through the story of the Unequal Treaties and national humiliations), whether in the age of imperialism, the period of nationalist movements, or the postimperialist period.

The conclusion that emerges from a study of the dissemination of international law in China and its links with the story of the Unequal Treaties is that the tangled web of connections between two significant collective impulses—the desire to conform with international standards and the concomitant molding and reconstructing of cultural, ethnic, and historical memories—should not be overlooked as a factor in the development of Chinese nationalism in the twentieth century.

The paradox of equality and inequality enters into the discussion of Chinese nationalism on two levels. First, there is the narrative of the past that constitutes cultural and historical memories. The working of memory in popular consciousness, as Paul A. Cohen remarks, is primarily about defining identity and "framing the past interpretively" in such a way that it ultimately makes the past square with a preferred present.[77] In the case of China, memories of the Unequal Treaties and the one-sided application of international law reinforce a deep sense of injustice, or fear of injustice in a world of power politics, that is central to modern Chinese identity. This fear, bordering on paranoia, is well illustrated in the following two examples.

At the end of eight months of negotiations over the sixteen-article MacKay Treaty of 1902, as detailed in chapter 1, China's chief negotiator Zhang Zhidong commented that, for fear of losing more *zhuquan* (sovereignty), *zhiquan* (rights related to extraterritoriality), *caiquan* (rights related to finance), and *liquan* (interests), the Chinese "had met [with the British] more than 60 times, and bargained over and over again about every single detail of each treaty clause till their tongues and lips were parched."[78] My second example is taken from a series of seminars on international law run by the CCP Central Committee in 1996. On December 9, 1996, at the end of one of the seminars, then Chinese President Jiang Zemin warned the participants that, owing to their lack of knowledge of international law, some local and departmental cadres were severely disadvantaged in their work. Therefore, Jiang urged, "our leaders and cadres, especially those of high rank, ought to take note of international law and enhance their skills in applying it. . . . We must be adept at using international law as 'a weapon' to defend the interests of our state and maintain national pride."[79] Jiang's talk was later characterized by Wang Tieya as a "second spring" in twenty years of international law in China (the "first spring" being the launching of reform in China in 1978).[80] In addition to the element of anxiety, these examples also illustrate China's search for a balance between the acceptance of international legal standards (by reasoning things out, *shuoli*) and vigilance over any verbal or actual provocation that might pose a threat to its sovereignty.

The second level at which the paradox works in the context of nationalism is seen in the formulation of a distinctive language of controversy and polemic used to communicate China's interpretation of current events to the wider world. On March 21, 2003, on the eve of the U.S. attack on Iraq, Chinese jurists met and agreed that the impending war had no legal basis and was in violation of both international law and the United Nations Charter. The president of the Chinese Association of International Law, Wang Hongli, commented, "The American war on Iraq is the result of the bad reasoning of 'One Powerism' and unilateralism. Subjecting international law to 'the law of the fist' will surely bring about a catastrophe for humanity."[81]

This line of argument resonates with what China defines as the true "internationalization" of international law after WWII. For China, the fundamental changes in international relations that characterized the postwar period included the abandonment of the principles and rules that justified imperialism and colonialism and their replacement by the principles of self-determination and sovereign equality among all nations.[82] Disputing the existence of what some commentators have called "a crisis" of international law as a result of the "disappearance" of "cultural unity," Wang Tieya described the task of international lawyers as "taking account of [the] different histories and cultures of various countries" and seeking principles of law and justice which are common to all.[83] What this means for China is that any application of international law in matters where China is concerned must take into consideration its historical situation as well as its national culture.

NOTES

1. "Gambling and the Extraterritorial Question," *China Weekly Review* (June 29, 1929): 186–88.

2. Examples are as follows: Hsü, *China's Entrance*; Chao-chieh Li, "International Law in China: Legal Aspect of the Chinese Perspective of World Order" (Ph.D. dissertation, University of Toronto, 1996); Lydia H. Liu, *Tokens of Exchange: The Problem of translation in Global Circulations*; Lydia H. Liu, *Translingual Practice*; Yongjin Zhang, *China in the International System, 1918–1920: The Middle Kingdom at the Periphery* (New York: St. Martin's Press, 1991).

3. Hsü, *China's Entrance*, 121.

4. Emmerich de Vattel, *The Law of Nations, or Principles of the Law of Nature Applied to the Conduct and Affairs of Nations and Sovereigns*, translated from French, 2 vols. (London: Printed for J. Newbury and J. Coote, 1760); Tian Tao, "Ding Weiliang yü *Wanguo gongfa*" [William Martin and the public laws of the ten thousand nations], *Shehui kexue yanjiu* 5 (1999): 107–12.

5. Teng and Fairbank, *China's Response to the West*, 26–27.

6. Henry Wheaton, *Elements of International Law: With a Sketch of the History of the Science* (Philadelphia: Carey, Lea & Blanchard, 1836). Chinese translation: *Wanguo gongfa*, trans. Ding Weiliang (Chongshi guan, 1864; Taibei: Zhongguo guojifa xuehui, 1998).

7. *Guojifa* is a term first adopted by Mitsukuri Rinsho in 1873, according to Immanuel Hsü.

8. "The public laws of the ten thousand nations." Hsü, *China's Entrance*, 129.

9. Chen Shicai, "Bismarck and the Introduction of International Law into China," *Chinese Social and Political Science Review* 15 (1931–1932): 98–101; Chen Shicai, *Guoji faxue* [International law] (Taibei: Jinghua yinshuguan, 1954), 1:5.

10. Xue Fucheng, *Chouyang chuyi* [A brief discussion of tactics for dealing with foreign countries] (Shenyang: Liaoning renmin chubanshe, 1994), 156–57. Xue Fucheng was considered to favor the adoption of international law in China. Liu Baogang, "Lun wanqing shidafu gongfa guannian de yanbian" [Changing perceptions of public international law among the late Qing literati], *Zhejiang xuekan* 3 (1999): 152–56.

11. Zheng Guanying, *Shengshi weiyan* [Warnings to a prosperous age] and *Gongfa* [Public international law], in *Zheng Guanying ji*, ed. Xia Dongyuan, vol. 1.

12. Cui Guoyin (1831–1909), *Chushi Meiribi riji* [Diary of my mission to the U.S., Japan, and Peru], vol. 2 (Shanghai: Shanghai guji chubanshe, 1995), journal entry for April 12, 1891.

13. Zhong Shuhe et al., *Guo Songtao Lundun yü Bali riji*, 706–7. Also see chapter 1.

14. Yang X., et al., *Zeng Jize chushi Yingfa riji*, 164–65. Also see chapter 1.

15. Zeng Jize, *Zeng Jize yiji* [The posthumous works of Zeng Jize] (Changsha: Yuelu shushe, 1983), 181–82.

16. "Lun gongfa yü qiangquan zhi guanxi" [On the relations between international law and power], *Waijiaobao*, issue 1, "Gonglun" (1901). See *Waijiaobao huibian*, 1:1–3.

17. Fu Lanya (John Fryer) and Wang Zhensheng, trans., *Gongfa zonglun* [General introduction to public laws] (n.p.: Hongwen shujü, 1896); Fu Lanya (John Fryer) and Yü Shijue, trans., *Geguo jiaoshe gongfa lun* [On public laws of all nations] (n.p.: Hongwen shujü, 1896).

18. Duanmu Zheng, "Zhongguo diyige guojifa xueshu tuanti" [The first Chinese scholarly organization of international law], *Zhongguo guojifa niankan* [Chinese yearbook of international law] (Beijing: Falü chubanshe, 1998), 105–11.

19. Duanmu, "Zhongguo diyige guojifa xueshu tuanti," *Zhongguo guojifa niankan*, 105–11.

20. Its English translation is the United League, the forerunner of the Guomindang founded in 1905 in Japan by Sun Yat-sen.

21. Hu Hanmin, "Paiwai yü guojifa" [Xenophobia and international law], *Minbao*, nos., 4, 6, 8, 9, 10, and 13. Reprinted in 3 vols. (Beijing: Kexue chubanshe, 1957).

22. Jin Baokang, ed., *Pingshi guojifa* [International law in peacetime] (Shanghai: Bingwushe, 1907); Dan Tao, trans., *Guojigongfa tigang* [An outline of public international law] (Shanghai: Changming gongsi, 1910); Nakamura Shingon, *Pingshi guojigongfa* [Public international law in peacetime], trans. Chen Shixia (Shanghai: Shangwu yinshuguan, 1911); Riben pu wenxuehui, comp., *Guoji gongfa gongji sifa wenti yijie* [Explaining public international law and private international law], trans. Gonghe fazheng xuehui bianjibu (Shanghai: Gonghe fazheng xuehui, 1913); Edon Genroku, *Guojifa yaolun* [Essential international law], trans. Shen Yüshan (Zhenjiang: Qinrun shushe, 1914).

23. The Beiyang School of Law and Government.

24. Li's pursuit of law has normally not been taken notice of by scholars because of his active part in leading the Communist movement in China. Boorman, *Biographical Dictionary*, 2:329–33.

25. Li Daozhao, *Li Daozhao quanji* [The complete collection of Li Dazhao's works] (Shi Jiazhuang: Hebei jiaoyü chubanshe, 1999), 1:1–161.

26. Imai Yoshiyuki (1878–1951), a graduate in law from the Tokyo Imperial University, taught at the Beiyang University of Law and Politics in Tianjin from 1908 to 1913. Li D., *Li Daozhao quanji*, 2:1–296; Imai Yoshiyuki, *Zhongguo guojifa lun* [On Chinese international law], trans. Li Dazhao and Zhang Runzhi (Tokyo: Jian xingshe, 1915). See also Li D., *Li Daozhao quanji*, 2:1–293; Han Depei, Luo Chuxiang, and Che Ying, "Li Daozhao de guojifa sixiang" [The international legal thought of Li Dazhao], *Wuhan daoxue xuebao* 243, no. 4 (1999): 3–6.

27. For example, Ning Xiewan, *Wanguo gongfa* [The public international law of the ten thousand nations] (Changsha: Hunansheng lifazheng zhuanmen xuexiao, 1919); Ning Xiewan, *Xianxing guojifa* [Introduction to international law] (Beijing: Beijing zhengfa daxue, 1923).

28. Chen Zongxi, *Guojifa zhi jianglai* [The future of international law] (Shanghai: Taidong tushujü, 1928).

29. Zhou Gengsheng, *Lingshi caipanquan wenti* [The question of extraterritoriality] (Shanghai: Shangwu yinshuguan, 1923); Zhou Gengsheng, *Guojifa dagang* [An outline of international law] (Shanghai: Shangwu yinshuguan, 1929, 1935, 1941, 1989); Cen Dezhang, trans., *Guoji fadian* [Code of international laws]; Hugo Grotius, *De Jure Belli ac Pacis* [On War and Peace], originally published in Latin in 1625, trans. into Chinese from the English translation (Shanghai: Shangwu yinshuguan, 1931); Zhou Wei, *Xin guoji gongfa* [New international public law], 2 vols. (Shanghai: Shangwu yinshuguan, 1930).

30. Zhou G., *Guojifa dagang*, 1935 ed., 20–25. For more on the different schools of international law, see next section of the chapter.

31. Shih Shun Liu, *Extraterritoriality: Its Rise and Its Decline* (New York: Columbia University, 1925).

32. Tseng, *The Termination of Unequal Treaties*.

33. "Extraterritoriality," *Encyclopedia Britainnica* 2003, Encyclopedia Britannica Premium Service, http://www.britannica.com/ed/article?eu=3405804 (accessed April 4, 2003). The first le-

gal expression of this doctrine was formulated by Pierre Ayrault (1536–1601), and later adopted by Hugo Grotius (1583–1645) and Samuel von Puffendorf (1623–1694). "Extraterritoriality" was introduced as a legal term by Georg Friedrich von Martens (1756–1821) in 1788.

34. George W. Keeton, *The Development of Extraterritoriality in China*, 1969 ed., 2 vols. (New York: Howard Fertig, 1928), 2:155–63.

35. Shih Shun Liu, *Extraterritoriality*, 35–43.

36. Scully, *Bargaining with the State*, 9.

37. Tseng, *The Termination of Unequal Treaties*, 12, 17.

38. Tseng, *The Termination of Unequal Treaties*, 10.

39. The exercise in China of American extraterritorial rights as well as the established regime of customs duties was found to be inequitable and nonreciprocal in character. The Porter Resolution concluded that "the treaty relations between the two countries [China and the U.S.] shall be upon an equitable and reciprocal basis and will be such as will in no way offend the sovereign dignity of either of the parties or place obstacles in the way of realization by either of them of their several national aspirations or the maintenance by them of their several legitimate domestic policies." Tseng, *The Termination of Unequal Treaties*, 13; Revision of Treaties with China, House of Representatives, Report No. 1891, *Congressional Record* (February 21, 1927), 4347.

40. Tseng, *The Termination of Unequal Treaties*, 105–14. In international law, the doctrine of *rebus sic stantibus* is defined as "a name given to a tacit condition, said to attach to all treaties, that they shall cease to be obligatory so soon as the state of facts and conditions upon which they were founded has substantially changed." Lassa Oppenheim, *International Law: A Treatise*, 2 vols. (London: Longmans, Green and Co., 1912), 1:539.

41. Lassa Oppenheim and Ronald Roxburg, eds., *Ao Benhai guojifa* [original English title *International Law: A Treatise*], trans. Cen Dezhang (Shanghai: Shangwu yinshuguan, 1934).

42. Zeng Youhao, *Guoji gongfa li'an* [Cases in public international law] (Shanghai: Shanghai faxue shujü, 1934); Zhou Gengsheng, *Xiandai guojifa wenti* [Questions of modern international law] (Shanghai: Shangwu yinshuguan, 1931); Liu Daren and Yuan Guoqin, *Guojifa fada shi* [The development of international law] (Shanghai: Shangwu yinshuguan, 1937).

43. Paul A. Cohen has called for attention to be paid to the rich *Guochi* literature in China. See his "Remembering and Forgetting National Humiliation in Twentieth-Century China."

44. Chen Tiqiang, "The People's Republic of China and Public International Law," *Dalhousie Law Journal* 8, no. 1 (1984): 8.

45. Beijing tushuguan, ed., *Minguo shiqi zongshumu* [A comprehensive bibliography of the Republican period] (Beijing: Shumu wenxian chubanshe,1985).

46. Wang Jingwei, *Diguo zhuyi qinlue zhongguo de qüshi he bianqian lun* [Characteristics and evolution of the imperialist penetration of China] (n.p.: Guomin gemingjun zong silingbu, 1925).

47. Beijing tushuguan, *Minguo shiqi zongshumu*, "zhengzhi."

48. Jin Baokang, *Jiejue bupingdeng tiaoyue de buzhou* [Steps toward solving the Unequal Treaties] (n.p.: Beijing, Huabei, Pingmin, Chaoyang, Zhongguo minguo wu sili daxue, 1925).

49. Qiu Zuming, *Zhongwai dingyue shiquan lun* [On lost rights in the negotiation of treaties between China and foreign countries] (Shanghai: Shangwu yinshuguan, 1926).

50. Qiu, *Zhongwai dingyue shiquan lun*, 3.

51. Qiu, *Zhongwai dingyue shiquan lun*, 51.

52. Zhang Tinghao, *Bupingdeng tiaoyue de yanjiu* [A study of the Unequal Treaties] (Shanghai: Guanghua shujü, 1926).

53. Zhang, *Bupingdeng tiaoyue de yanjiu*, 3.

54. Zhang, *Bupingdeng tiaoyue de yanjiu*, 143.

55. Waijiaobu tiayue weiyuanhui, ed., *Bupingdeng tiaoyue biao* [Charting the Unequal Treaties] (Beijing: Waijiaobu, 1929); Zhou Gensheng, *Bupingdeng tiaoyue shijiang* [Ten lectures on the Unequal Treaties] (Shanghai: Taipingyang shudian,1928); Guomingdang Shanghai tebieshi dangwu zhidao weiyuanhui xuanchuanbu, *Bupingdeng tiaoyue yanjiuji* [Studies on the Unequal Treaties] (Shanghai: Mingguo ribao, 1929); Wang Tieya, *Xinyue yanjiu* [A study of the new treaty

of 1943] (Chongqing: Qingnian chubanshe, 1943). See also the CCP publication *Zhongmei Zhongying qianding xinyue: bainian zhiku yidan feichu* [The signing of the new Sino-U.S. and Sino-British treaties: Smashing the shackles of a hundred years] (n.p.: Huabei xinhua shudian, 1943).

56. This view became standard after the term "private international law" was coined in 1841 by the German jurist Schaffner. "Conflict of Laws," *Encyclopedia Britannica* 2004, Encyclopedia Britannica Premium Service, http://www.britannica.com/eb/article?eu=117329 (accessed February 20, 2004).

57. The study of the "conflict of laws" (private international law), an expression first used in 1653 by the Dutch jurist Christian Rodernburg (1618–1668), coincided with the beginnings of modern public international law. The doctrines of modern international law were first developed by the Anglo-Dutch School, especially Alberico Gentili (1552–1608) and Hugo Grotius (1583–1645). "International Law," *Encyclopedia Britannica* 2004, Encyclopedia Britannica Premium Service, http://www.britannica.com/eb/article?eu=109303 (accessed February 20, 2004).

58. Jerome Alan Cohen, "Introduction," in *China's Practice of International Law: Some Case Studies*, ed. Jerome Alan Cohen (Cambridge, Mass.: Harvard University Press, 1972).

59. Hsü, *China's Entrance*; Y. Zhang, *China in the International System*.

60. David Mungello characterizes the three centuries of encounter between China and the West as a reciprocal process of acceptance and rejection, at different times and in different ways. David E. Mungello, *The Great Encounter of China and the West, 1500–1800* (Lanham, Md.: Rowman & Littlefield Publishers, 1999).

61. Benedict Kingsbury, "Sovereignty and Inequality," *European Journal of International Law* 9 (1998): 621; Ronald St. John Macdonald, ed., *Essays in Honour of Wang Tieya* (Boston: M. Nijhoff Publishers, 1994).

62. Deng Zhenglai, ed., *Wang Tieya wenxuan* [Selected works of Wang Tieya] (Beijing: Zhongguo zhengfa daxue chubanshe, 1993), 355–58; Zeng Lingliang, "Ping Liang Xi zhubian zhi Guojifa" [A review of Liang Xi's *Guojifa*], *Faxue pinglun* 3 (1994): 85–88.

63. Deng, *Wang Tieya Wenxuan*, 363.

64. Deng, *Wang Tieya Wenxuan*, 363.

65. Jiang Guoqing, "Lun guojifa yü guoji tiaoyue" [On international law and international treaties], *Zhenli de zhuiqiu* 9 (2000): 33–37.

66. Shaoquan Leng, "Chinese Law," in *Sovereignty within the Law*, ed. Arthur Larsen, C. Wilfred Jenks, et al. (Dobbs Ferry, N.Y.: Oceana Publications, 1965), 260–61.

67. Lassa Oppenheim, *International Law: A Treatise*, 2 vols. (London: Longmans, Green, and Co., 1905–1906), 1:171.

68. Kingsbury, "Sovereignty and Inequality," 603.

69. Kingsbury, "Sovereignty and Inequality," 603–4.

70. Important naturalist writers agreed that national and international laws derived "not from any deliberate human choice or decision, but from principles of justice which had a universal and eternal validity and which could be discovered by pure reason; law was to be found, not made." Malanczuk, *Akehurst's Modern Introduction*, 15–17. By the nineteenth century, the theory of the law of nature was challenged by positivism, which argued that law was largely positive and man-made. In other words, positivism held that law and justice were not the same thing, and international law was credited through states' behavior and practice. Concerning treaties, positivists normally "assert legal rules can be found by consulting provisions of treaties that have entered into force. Among these scholars, there seems to be a great deal of sanctity accorded to the written text." Ku and Diehl, *International Law*, 25.

71. He Qinhua, "Luelun mingguo shiqi Zhongguo yizhi guojifa de lilun yü shijian" [Short studies on the Chinese transplantation of international legal theories and practices during the Republican period], *Fashang yanjiu* 84, no. 4 (2001): 136–144.

72. Zhaojie Li, "Teaching, Research and the Dissemination of International Law in China: The Contribution of Wang Tieya," *The Canadian Yearbook of International Law* 31 (1993).

73. A good example is Chen Tiqiang's *Guojifa lunwenji* [A collection of papers related to international law] (Beijing: Falü chubanshe, 1985).

74. Liang Xi, ed., *Guojifa* [International law], reprint ed. (Wuhan: Wuhan daxue chubanshe, 1993, 2000); Wang Tieya, ed., *Guojifa* [International law] (Beijing: Falü chubanshe, 1981); Wang Tieya, ed., *Guojifa yinlun* [A primer of international law] (Beijing: Beijing daxue chubanshe, 1998).

75. Chen T., "The People's Republic of China and Public International Law." In this article, Chen details the origins, development and significance of the Five Principles from the perspective of the P.R. China. See also "Bandung Conference," Encyclopedia Britannica. 2004, Encyclopedia Britannica Premium Service, http://www.britannica.com/eb/article?eu=12297 (accessed March 23, 2004).

76. Cheng Daode, ed., *Jindai zhongguo waijiao yü guojifa* [Modern Chinese foreign relations and international law] (Beijing: Xiandai chubanshe, 1993).

77. Paul A. Cohen, "Introduction: Politics, Myth, and the Real Past," *Twentieth-Century China* 26, no. 2 (2001): 1–15.

78. Wang Yanwei, comp., *Qingji waijiao shiliao* 3, no. 162:2602.

79. "Zhonggong zhongyang jüxing guojifa zhishi jiangzuo" [International law seminars held by the CCP Central Committee], *Renmin ribao*, no. A (December 10, 1996).

80. Wan Xia, "Huigu yü zhanwang: gaige kaifang er'shi nian guojifa zai Zhongguo de fazhan" [Looking forward and backward: The development of international law in China in the twenty years since China's opening-up], *Waijiao xuebao* 2 (1999): 62–66; "Beijing daxue guojifa yanjiusuo xuexi Jiang Zemin zhuxi jianghua zuotanhui" [The forum held by the Institute of International Law at Beijing University on President Jiang's Speech], *Zhongguo guojifa niankan* (1996): 450.

81. "Quantoufa buneng gaoyü guojifa" [The law of the fist cannot supersede international law], *Renmin ribao*, no. F (March 22, 2003).

82. "Quantoufa buneng gaoyü guojifa."

83. Tieya Wang, "International Law in China: Historical and Contemporary Perspectives," *Hague Academy of International Law, Recueil des cours* 221, no. 2 (1990): 356.

Conclusion: Defining and Redefining the Past

The founding principles of the Western states are trade and contact, two elements as inseparable as longitude and latitude. Signing treaties by putting ideas on paper is like forming alliances during the Spring and Autumn period: compliance smoothes things out, whereas disobedience makes things tortuous. This determines peace and war, in which both sides have a high stake. This has been the rule since China commenced contact [with the Western countries].

Li Hongzhang in 1886[1]

Because rights of consular jurisdiction are embedded in the treaties, the treaties must be modified before such rights are dissolved. . . . There is no way that treaty revision can become a reality without first completing the codification of laws; there is no hope for the removal of the consular jurisdiction rights, nor for the reinstatement of our national sovereignty, until the treaties are revised.

Yang Tingdong in 1909[2]

The relatively favorable outcome of the diplomatic overtures to Britain on this occasion is attributable to the fact that foreign countries are all aware that the Nationalist Government is the government of the party. Standing behind the Nationalist Government is the great and strong Nationalist Party, which represents the popular nationalist movement. . . . We, the people, must devote ourselves to consolidating the party's foundation before the complete abolition of the Unequal Treaties can be realized in the not-too-distant future.

Chen Youren in 1926[3]

This book began with a discussion of some core texts in which the moral, legal, and rhetorical implications of the Unequal Treaties in China were embedded. The evolving Chinese understandings of and approaches to the Unequal Treaties are illustrated in the three quotations given above

—compliance; the search for legal means of revising or even nullifying the treaties; and party leadership, that is, political power through mobilization, as the ultimate path to treaty abolition. These diverse responses have shaped not only the diplomatic character of modern Chinese nationalism, but also its legal, political, and cultural consequences. Central to Chinese nationalism are the notions of sovereignty, independence, national unity, and power. The analysis undertaken here of the changing implications of the Unequal Treaties, both in the past and present, shows how the protracted conflict over the treaties shaped the Chinese nation's collective perception of its past, and illustrates the different ways in which Chinese history since the mid-nineteenth century has been understood and presented.

In conclusion, I want to look briefly at some further issues that arise out of China's incessant attempts to define and redefine its place in the world through this repeated reinterpretation of the Unequal Treaties.

First, the political character of the controversy over the treaties should alert one to the danger of reinterpreting the past to suit immediate political exigencies. Historian Mao Haijian notes that "[passing judgments] of 'good' and 'bad' has been the traditional rule in Chinese historiography. Although it attaches itself to historical sources, it sets its eyes on the present."[4] The conscious pursuit of the meaning of the past from within one's own perspective can have its own legitimacy, as Paul Cohen demonstrates in his examination of the Boxer Movement as event, experience, and myth.[5] However, the fact that it is possible to understand and interpret historical events in different ways and from different perspectives does not mean that one can or should dispense with the distinction between fictional and historical narrative—the latter being defined by a set of constraints aimed at maximizing its truthfulness. The danger inherent in reinterpreting the past to suit present political agendas lies in the temptation to ignore these constraints. In her article "Memory and Commemoration: The Chinese Search for a Livable Past," Vera Schwarcz expresses concern about "slanted" historical accounts of the May Fourth Movement in which the patriotism of the student participants is emphasized at the expense of their democratic aspirations.[6] What worried Schwarcz was exactly that the historical facts of the case were not merely interpreted but were deliberately altered.

The ultimate outcome of such an attitude receives its classic fictional treatment in George Orwell's *Nineteen Eighty-Four*, where the past is constantly recreated in the minutest detail to fit with present reality as it is conceived by the party:

> The Party said that Oceania had never been in alliance with Eurasia. He, Winston Smith, knew that Oceania had been in alliance with Eurasia as short a time as four years ago. But where did that knowledge exist? Only in his own consciousness, which in any case must soon be annihilated. And if all others accepted the lie which the Party imposed—if all records told the same tale—then

the lie passed into history and became truth. "Who controls the past," ran the Party slogan, "controls the future: who controls the present controls the past." And yet the past, though of its nature alterable, never had been altered. Whatever was true now was true from everlasting to everlasting. It was quite simple. All that was needed was an unending series of victories over your own memory. "Reality control," they called it: in Newspeak, "doublethink."[7]

The danger of this reinscription of history is not merely that it produces false accounts of the past but that it has a certain subversive logic that ultimately undermines the distinction between fictional and historical narratives.[8]

My second point is that, although the debates over the Unequal Treaties and the authentic leadership of Chinese nationalism are likely to persist in the future, there is some evidence that a changed political atmosphere would at the very least alter the parameters within which this contestation process takes place.[9] For instance, in reevaluating the 1946 Treaty of Friendship, Commerce, and Navigation between China and the U.S., some scholars apply a new category of "favorable" and "unfavorable" treaties transcending the constraints of the "unequal/equal" paradigm.[10] A more sober, balanced and sympathetic approach—involving stepping into the shoes of the historical actors involved—has slowly evolved in academic discussion of the treaties among historians in China and Taiwan, in step with changing relations across the straits.[11] This shift of discourse on the Unequal Treaties has accompanied a reevaluation in Chinese historiography of controversial figures such as Zeng Guofang, Li Hongzhang, and Wang Jingwei.[12]

In mainland China, in spring 2003, intense debate over Li Hongzhang (1823–1901), the Qing statesman responsible for signing a significant number of unequal treaties, was triggered by the fifty-nine-episode television series *Zouxiang gonghe* (Towards the People's Republic) which portrays Li as a tragic hero who—though not lacking in diplomatic skill—in the historical circumstances in which he found himself, had no choice but to put his signature to over thirty treaties.[13] This reversal of the dominant verdict in the People's Republic of China on Li as a "traitor to the nation" (*maiguo zei*) has been endorsed by distinguished historians such as Wong Fei and Lei Yi, who considered the portrait of Li presented in the series as "by and large close to historical reality."[14] These historians argue that it would be inappropriate to assess Li's action from a contemporary perspective; Li's situation gave him no choice but to concede to foreign demands, and it is therefore improper to label him as a traitor. One scholar argues that "scientifically to assess the gains and losses of Li Hongzhang's diplomatic activities is not merely to clarify the historical responsibilities Li ought to have assumed, but also more importantly to demonstrate what historical lessons we should learn."[15]

In recent years, there have been renewed and vigorous efforts to tap into nationalistic sentiment in order to construct an uncontroversial and widely accepted account of Chinese history transcending political, social, and economic differences.[16] Websites have appeared focusing on Chinese history and the Unequal Treaties, among them *Xuezhu Zhonghua* (Build China with blood),[17] *Renminwang* (The People's net),[18] *Minzuhun* (The national spirit),[19] and *Zhongqing wangzhang* (The web of China's youth).[20] These "web memorials" (*Wangshang jinianguan*), which contain a wealth of patriotic educational materials, are sponsored by such organizations as the Chinese Communist Youth League, the Institute of Modern History of the Chinese Academy of Social Sciences, and the Chinese Adolescence Social Services Center. The sponsors of the website *Xuezhu Zhonghua* indicate that its sources are drawn from seventy-two publications, including newspapers and serious academic works on modern China.[21] The preface to the section on the Unequal Treaties states that it aims to "provide the general public with some basic ideas about some influential unequal treaties, in order to prevent people from forgetting the motherland's humiliating modern history, to maintain patriotic traditions, and to continue the struggle for the great revival of the Chinese nation."[22]

These interactive websites allow readers to enter their responses in a visitors' book. After browsing the website Opium War Memorial (*Yapian Zhanzheng Jinianguan*), one reader with the pseudonym *Huainian Yingxiong* ("In memory of heroes") asked, "Is 'the Macau Lin Zexü Museum' (*bowuguan*) a typo? Isn't it 'the Macau Lin Zexü Memorial' (*jinianguan*)? Hope you can verify this. Don't hurt the people's feelings."[23] Here, a web error in mistaking the Macau Lin Zexü Memorial as the Macau Lin Zexü Museum easily set off nationalistic protests. Obviously, such a typo, in the eyes of this reader, was insulting to mainland Chinese, who perceive Lin Zexü—the Qing imperial commissioner, the drug "Tsar" of China, in charge of cracking down on foreign opium smuggling in the 1830s—a national hero. Another example also demonstrates the Chinese nationalistic sensitivity: Responding to the Manchurian Incident Memorial site, one reader, Gong Chaodong, wrote, "From now on, I am determined not to buy any merchandise produced by little Japan, and not to patronize shops owned by little Japan. We must resist buying Japanese products and bankrupt little Japan's economy. (Of course, it's alright to hold onto Japanese products purchased before. Don't waste things.)"[24]

In sum, these official and semiofficial websites represent an attempt to create a collective memory of the Chinese past. Central to their presentation of Chinese history is the triple theme of China's past humiliations, its rise to greatness, and the party's role in the success of China.[25] Again we can see the polemical discourse of the Unequal Treaties being extended into the present. It remains a discourse with an emotional appeal aimed at establishing the legitimacy and patriotic credentials of the CCP. It reflects the CCP's practical concern with how to perpetuate its leadership and unify the Chinese nation under its auspices. The discourse of the Unequal Treaties, therefore, constitutes a Chinese way of defining and redefining the past.

NOTES

1. Li Hongzhang, "Tongshang yuezhang leizuan xü" [Preface to the directory of commercial treaties and agreements], in *Tongshang yuezhang leizuan* [The directory of commercial treaties and agreements] (Tianjin: Tianjin guanshujü, 1886) (punctuation added by the present author). Li Hongzhang (1823–1901) was a leading Qing statesman and diplomat. Because of his position as the governor of the paramount provinces Jiangsu-Zhejiang, Hunan-Hubei, and Zhili since the 1860s, as one of the two imperial commerce commissioner (see chapter 2), and as grand secretary of the Grand Council, he was responsible for signing a series of treaties with foreign countries—including the Chefoo Agreement (1876), the Treaty of Shimonoseki (1895), and the Boxer Protocol (1901)—which have been considered harmful to China. See Chen X., et al., *Zhongguo jindaishi cidian*, 322–23; Michael Dillon, ed., *China: A Cultural and Historical Dictionary* (Richmond, U.K.: Curzon Press, 1998), 186–87.

2. Yang Tingdong, "Lun gaizheng tiaoyue yü bianding falü you lianjie zhi guanxi" [On the connection between treaty revision and legal codification], *Waijiaobao*, "Lunshuo," issue 254 (September 18, 1909). See also *Waijiaobao huibian*, 2:533–37. Yang Tingdong (1878–1950) studied at Waseda University in Japan. After the outbreak of the 1911 Revolution, he served as parliamentary member of the Nanjing provisional government and the Beijing government. Chen Yütang, *Zhongguo jindai renwu minghao da cidian* [Dictionary of the names and aliases of Chinese in modern times] (Hangzhou: Zhejiang guji chubanshe, 1993), 266. The birth and death years of Yang, indefinite in Chen's dictionary, are my inference.

3. The original remarks by Chen Youren are in Gao Chengyuan, ed., *Geming waijiao wenxian (Guangzhou Wuhan shiqi)* [Sources on revolutionary diplomacy (Guangzhou and Wuhan period)], 1930 reprint (Guangzhou: Shenzhou guoguang she, 1927), 161. Chen Youren (1878–1944, also known as Eugene Ch'en), was a publicist, lawyer, editor, and diplomat. While in London, he became associated with Sun Yat-sen, the founder of the Guomindang. In 1919, Chen attended the Paris Peace Conference as a member of the Southern group representing the GMD Guangzhou government in the Chinese delegation. Chen was also known for his radical anti-imperialist policy while he was in charge of foreign affairs in the GMD government in Wuhan and Nanjing in 1926–1927 and 1932. Boorman, *Biographical Dictionary*, 1:180–83.

4. Mao H.,*Tianchao de bengkui*, 20.

5. P. Cohen, *History in Three Keys*.

6. Vera Schwarcz, "Memory and Commemoration: The Chinese Search for a Livable Past," in *Popular Protest and Political Culture in Modern China*, ed. Jeffery N. Wasserstrom and Elizabeth J. Perry (Boulder, Colo.: Westview Press, 1989, 1994).

7. George Orwell, *Nineteen Eighty-Four* (London: Secker & Warburg, 1949; London: Penguin Books, 2003), chapter 3.

8. "What frightens Winston Smith is that Big Brother's attitude to history has a certain logic which subverts the very distinction between fiction and historical truth. . . . Big Brother's reconstruction of the past is pragmatically true in that it serves well the purpose of confirming his own authority, foresight, and wisdom. And if we use this subverted notion of truth we can also say that Big Brother's reconstruction of the past is an imaginative truth, an account of how the past ought to have been, constructed by the human mind, by help of imagination and intelligence." See Lamarque and Olsen, *Truth, Fiction, and Literature*, 303.

9. I am grateful to Paul A. Cohen for this point.

10. See chapter 4.

11. A similar view is expressed in Tang Ch'i-hua's assessment of research on Republican diplomacy. "'Beiyang waijiao' yanjiu pingjie" [Evaluating research on Beiyang Diplomacy], *Lishi yanjiu* 287, no. 1 (2004): 99–113.

12. This kind of shift in the perspective of mainland Chinese historiography has also been noted by some other scholars. Yingjie Guo and Baogang He, "Reimagining the Chinese Nation: The 'Zeng

Guofan' Phenomenon," *Modern China* 25, no. 2 (1999): 142–70; Ke-wen Wang, "Irreversible Verdict? Historical Assessments of Wang Jingwei in the People's Republic and Taiwan," *Twentieth-Century China* 28, no. 1 (2002): 57–81.

13. This debate was widely covered in Chinese newspapers and news websites in spring 2003.

14. Wang Jian, "*Zouxiang gonghe* shifou meihua Li Hongzhang yin zhengyi" [The controversy over the alleged exoneration of Li Hongzhang in *Towards the People's Republic*], *Beijing yüle xinbao* (April 29, 2003); *Lingdao kexue*, no. 13 (2003): 15; Wang Jian, "Yueyan yuehuo, yuezheng yuelie, *Zouxiang gonghe* yinfa yinping zhendang" [The longer it screens, the more popular it becomes; the more the debates, the fiercer they get: The uproar caused by *Towards the People's Republic*], *Shenzhen wanbao* (May 16, 2003). For alternative opinions, see Zhang Wei, "Zhiyi *Zouxiang gonghe*" [Questioning *Towards the People's Republic*], *Dianying*, no. 7 (2003): 4–6; Li Wenhai, "*Zouxiang gonghe* gei renmen tigong le shengmoyang de 'xin de lishi guandian'" [What kind of "new historical perspective" does *Towards the People's Republic* offer people?]; Zhang Haipeng, "Shi yibu lishi zhenglunjü, er bushi lishi zhengjü: guanyü lishijü *Zouxiang gonghe* de lingxing ganxiang" [A historical political drama, but not an orthodox historical drama: Some loose thoughts on *Towards the People's Republic*], *Gaoxiao lilun zhanxian*, no. 6 (2003).

15. Ouyang Yuefeng, "Yetan lishi renwu pingjia de xiangguang lilun wenti: yi Li Hongzhang de waijiao huodong weili" [Theoretical issues relating to the judgment of historical figures: A case study of the diplomatic activities of Li Hongzhang], *Shixue lilun yanjiu*, no. 3 (2003): 130–40.

16. Bruce Dickson remarks on the apparent shift in the political priorities of the CCP expressed in the way in which the fourth generation of the CCP leadership emphasizes that it represents the "fundamental interests of the vast majority of the people." Bruce J. Dickson, "Beijing's Ambivalent Reformers," *Current History* 103, no. 674 (2004): 249–55. Differentiating official nationalism from popular nationalism, Zheng Yongnian contends that, in understanding Chinese nationalism, domestic factors, such as problems arising out of the post-Mao reforms, must be taken into account. Yongnian Zheng, *Discovering Chinese Nationalism: Modernization, Identity, and International Relations* (Cambridge: Cambridge University Press, 1999).

17. http://www.china1840–1949.net.cn (accessed September 23, 2004).

18. http://www.people.com.cn (accessed September 23, 2004).

19. http://www.chinaspirit.net.cn (accessed September 23, 2004).

20. http://www.cynet.com (accessed September 23, 2004).

21. http://www.china1840–1949.net.cn (accessed September 23, 2004). Click on *Ziliao laiyuan* (sources of information).

22. http://www.china1840–1949.net.cn (accessed September 23, 2004). Click on *Bupingdeng tiaoyue* (The Unequal Treaties).

23. http://www.china1840–1949.net.cn (accessed September 20, 2004). Click on *Liuyan ban* (The visitors' book).

24. http://www.china1840–1949.net.cn (accessed September 20, 2004).

25. Suisheng Zhao, "Chinese Intellectuals' Quest for National Greatness and Nationalistic Writings in the 1990s," *The China Quarterly* 152 (1997): 725–45.

Glossary

bainian guochi 百年國恥

Beijing zhengfu 北京政府

beipan zhongguo geming 背叛中國革命

Beiyang zhengfu 北洋政府

Bentuhua 本土化

Bowuguan 博物館

buduideng zhi tiaoyue 不對等之條約

bugong 不公

buli 不利

bupindeng tiaoyue 不平等條約

bupingdeng tiaoyue xue 不平等條約學

bupingdeng zhi tiaoyue 不平等之條約

caiquan 財權

changguan 常關

chu 處

chuchang shui 出廠稅

chumai minzu liyi 出賣民族利益

congjia zhibai chouwu 從價值百抽五

daili 代理

dan 擔

ding zeli 定則例

e'wai quanli 額外權利

feichu bupingdeng tiao-
  yue 廢除不平等條約

feiyue yundong 廢約運動

gaiding tongshang tiao-
  yue 改定通商條約

gaiyue 改約

gaizheng tiaoyue 改正条約

gongfa xuehui 公法学会

gongping 公平

Gu Weijun yanjiu re
  顧維鈞研究熱

guaiwu 怪物

guochi 國恥

guochi jinianri 國恥紀念日

guochi wenxue 國恥文學

guojifa 國際法

hanjian 漢奸

hanjian maiguozei 漢奸賣國賊

Huiban Dachen 會辦大臣

Humen tiaoyue 虎門條約

Humenzai 虎門寨

hushenfu 護身符

jiaoban 剿辦

Jiaoshe Shi 交涉使

Jiaoshe Shu 交涉署

Jiaoshe Si 交涉司

141

jiasuo 枷鎖
jimi 羈縻
jin 斤
jinianguan 紀念館
Jinshen Lu 縉紳錄
Jiuyue 舊約
junfa zhuyi 軍閥主義
junzi wu waijiao 君子无外交
liang 兩
liangong 聯共
lika 厘卡
liquan 利权
maiguo zei 賣國賊
maishen qi 賣身契
Makai tiaoyue 馬凱條約
mei baijin er lian wu qian
　每百斤二兩五錢
miezhong dahuo 滅種大禍
minzu bailei 民族敗類
Minzuhun 民族魂
Nanbeiyang Tongshang Dachen
　南北洋通商大臣
neidi 内地
neigang 内港
nuli shenfen 奴隸身份
pianmian zuihuiguo daiyü 片面最惠
　国待遇
pingdeng xinyue 平等新約
qian 錢
qianxian ren 牽纖人
qichi daru 奇恥大辱
qieshi zhibai chouwu 切實值百抽五
qüxiao bupingdeng tiaoyue
　取消不平等条约
qüxiao qiman tiaoyue yundonghui
　取消期滿条约运动会
Renminwang 人民网
ronggong 容共
shengsi guantou 生死關頭
shibao 施報

shouyue 守約
shufu 束縛
shuoli 說理
si 司
Tepai Jiaoshe Zhuanyuan
　特派交涉專員
ting 廳
Tongwenguan 同文館
Tsungli Yamen 總理衙門
Waijiao Xi 外交系
Waijiaobu 外交部
Waiwubu 外務部
Wangshang jinianguan 網上紀念館
Wanguo gongfa 万国公法
wonu 倭奴
Wukou tongshang shanhou fu-
　zhan tiaokuan 五口通商善後附粘
　条款
Wukou tongshang zhangcheng:
　haiguan shuize
　五口通商章程: 海關稅則
xianlie zhishi 先烈志士
xilü 西律
xin jiyuan 新紀元
xuechi 雪恥
xüli 虛理
Xuezhu Zhonghua 血鑄中華
yanhe gangkou 沿河港口
Yapian Zhanzheng Jinianguan
　鸦片战争纪念馆
yiqie bupingdeng tiaoyue
　一切不平等條約
yiti junzhan 一體均沾
youli 有利
yühu moupi 與虎謀皮
Zhangjing 章京
zhaoyue 照約
zhengquan 政權
zhiquan 治權
zhiwai faquan 治外法權

zhongliu dizhu 中流砥柱
Zhongqing wangzhang 中青網站
zhuquan 主權
ziding guanshui 自定關稅
Zongli Dachen 總理大臣
Zongli Geguo Shiwu Yamen
　總理各國事務衙門
Zongli Qinwang 總理親王
Zongshu 總署
zougou 走狗
Zouxiang gonghe 走向共和
zuihuiguo tiaokuan 最惠國條款
zujie 租界

Selected Bibliography

American Society of International Law, ed. *Proceedings of the American Society of International Law at Its Twenty-First Annual Meeting (April 28-30, 1927)*. Washington, D.C.: American Society of International Law, 1927.

Anderson, Benedict. *Imagined Communities: Reflections on the Origin and Spread of Nationalism*. 2nd ed. London: Verso, 1983, 1991.

Auslin, Michael R. *Negotiating with Imperialism: The Unequal Treaties and the Culture of Japanese Diplomacy*. Cambridge, Mass.: Harvard University Press, 2004.

"Bandung Conference." *Encyclopedia Britannica*. 2004. Encyclopedia Britannica Premium Service. http://www.britannica.com/eb/article?eu=12297 (accessed March 23, 2004).

Banno, Masakata. *China and the West: The Origins of the Tsungli Yamen*. Cambridge, Mass.: Harvard University Press, 1964.

Beijing tushuguan (北京圖書館), ed. *Minguo shiqi zongshumu* [《民國時期總書目》(1911-1949) A comprehensive bibliography of the Republican period]. Beijing: Shumu wenxian chubanshe, 1985.

Bodenhorn, Terry, ed. *Defining Modernity: Guomindang Rhetorics of a New China, 1920-1970*. Ann Arbor, Mich.: University of Michigan Press, 2003.

Bonsal, Stephen. *Suitors and Suppliants: The Little Nations at Versailles*. New York: Prentice-Hall, 1946.

Boorman, Howard L., ed. *Biographical Dictionary of Republican China*. 5 vols. New York: Columbia University Press, 1968.

Borg, Dorothy. *American Policy and the Chinese Revolution, 1925-1928*. New York: Macmillan, 1947.

Brunnert, H. S., and V. V. Hagelstrom. *Present-Day Political Organization of China*. Trans. A. Beltcheko and E. E. Morgan. Shanghai: Kelly and Walsh, 1912.

Buss, Claude A. "The Relationship of Tariff Autonomy to the Political Situation in China." Ph.D. dissertation, University of Pennsylvania, 1927.

———. *War and Diplomacy in Eastern Asia*. New York: Macmillan, 1941.

Chan, K. C. "The Abrogation of British Extraterritoriality in China 1942-43: A Study of Anglo-American-Chinese Relations." *Modern Asian Studies* 2, no. 2 (1977): 257-91.

Chang, Richard T. *The Justice of the Western Consular Courts in Nineteenth-Century Japan*. Westport, Conn.: Greenwood Press, 1984.

Chang, Yü-fa (張玉法 Zhang Yüfa). *Zhongguo xiandai shi* [《中國現代史》 Modern Chinese history]. 9th ed. Taibei: Donghua shujü, 1997.

Chen, Buxiu (陳不朽), and Lin Jian (林健), eds. *Zhongsu miyue* [《中蘇密約》 The secret agreement between the People's Republic of China and the Soviet Union]. Taibei: Taipingyang xinwenshe, 1950.

Ch'en, Jerome. "The Communist Movement 1927-1937." In *The Cambridge History of China*, edited by John K. Fairbank and Albert Feuerwerker, vol. 13, 168-229. Cambridge: Cambridge University Press, 1986.

———. *Yuan Shih-K'ai*. 2nd ed. Stanford, Calif.: Stanford University Press, 1972.

Chen, Jian. *Mao's China and the Cold War*. Chapel Hill, N.C.: University of North Carolina Press, 2001.

Chen, Shicai (陳世材). "Bismarck and the Introduction of International Law into China." *Chinese Social & Political Science Review* 15 (1931-1932): 98-101.

———. *Guoji faxue* [《國際法學》 International law]. Taibei: Jinghua yinshuguan, 1954.

Chen, Tiqiang (陳體強). *Guojifa lunwenji* [《國際法論文集》 A collection of papers related to international law]. Beijing: Falü chubanshe, 1985.

———. "The People's Republic of China and Public International Law." *Dalhousie Law Journal* 8, no. 1 (1984): 3-31.

———. *Zhongguo waijiao xingzheng* [《中國外交行政》 The Administration of Chinese Diplomacy]. Chongqing: Commercial Press, 1943.

Chen, Xiukui (陳秀夔), ed. *Zhongguo caizheng shi* [《中國財政史》 The economic history of China]. Taibei: Zhengzhong shujü, 1968.

Chen, Xülu (陳旭麓), et al., eds. *Zhongguo jindaishi cidian* [《中國近代史詞典》

Dictionary of modern Chinese history]. 4th reprint. Shanghai: Shanghai cishu chubanshe, 1984.

Chen, Yan (陳雁). *Yan Huiqing zhuan* [《顏惠慶傳》 Biography of Yan Huiqing]. Shijiazhuang: Hebei renmin chubanshe, 1999.

Chen, Yütang (陳玉堂). *Zhongguo jindai renwu minghao da cidian* [《中國近現代人物名號大辭典》 Dictionary of the names and aliases of Chinese in modern times]. Hangzhou: Zhejiang guji chubanshe, 1993.

Chen, Zongxi (陳宗熙). *Guojifa zhi jianglai* [《國際法之將來》 The future of international law]. Shanghai: Taidong tushujü, 1928.

Cheng, Daode (程道德), ed. *Jindai Zhongguo waijiao yü guojifa* [《近代中國外交與國際法》 Modern Chinese foreign relations and international law]. Beijing: Xiandai chubanshe, 1993.

Cheng, Daode, et al., eds. *Zhonghua minguo waijiaoshi ziliao xuanbian (1919-1931)* [《中華民國外交史資料選編》 Selected Diplomatic Sources on the Republic of China]. Beijing: Beijing daxue chubanshe, 1985.

Cheng, Taisheng (成台生). *Hu Hanmin de zhengzhi sixiang* [《胡漢民的政治思想》 The political thought of Hu Hanmin]. Taibei: Liming wenhua shiye gufen youxian gongsi, 1980.

Cheng, Weijia (程為嘉). "Feichu bupingdeng tiaoyue wenti" [廢除不平等條約問題 The question of the abolition of the Unequal Treaties]. *Dongfang zhazhi* [《東方雜誌》 The Eastern Miscellany] 23, no. 12 (December 25, 1926): 5-23.

Ch'i, Hsi-sheng. *Warlord Politics in China, 1916-1928.* Stanford, Calif.: Stanford University Press, 1976.

Chiang, Kai-shek (Jiang Jieshi). *China's Destiny.* Trans. Wang Chonghui. New York: MacMillan, 1947.

———. *Soviet Russia in China: A Summing-up at Seventy.* New York: Farrar, Straus & Cudahy, Inc., 1957.

China Weekly Review. Unknown author. "Gambling and the Extraterritorial Question." June 29, 1929, 186-87.

Chinese Inspectorate General of Customs. *Documents Illustrative of the Origin, Development, and Activities of the Chinese Customs Service.* 7 vols. Shanghai: Statistical Department of the Chinese Inspectorate General of Customs, 1937-1940.

Chinese Repository

Ch'ing Hua Ta Hsueh (Qinghua University). *Who's Who of American Returned Students.* Peking (Beijing): Tsing Hua College, 1917.

Chiu, Hungdah. "China's Struggle against the 'Unequal Treaties,' 1927-1946." In *Chinese Yearbook of International Law and Affairs*, 1-28. Baltimore, Md.: Occasional Paper/Reprints Series in Contemporary Asian

Studies, Inc., 1985.

―――. "Comparison of the Nationalist and Communist Chinese Views of Unequal Treaties." In *China's Practice of International Law: Some Case Studies*, edited by Jerome Alan Cohen, 239-67. Cambridge, Mass.: Harvard University Press, 1972.

Chow, Kai-wing, ed. *Constructing Nationhood in Modern East Asia*. Ann Arbor, Mich.: University of Michigan Press, 2001.

Clifford, Nicholas R. *Spoilt Children of Empire: Westerners in Shanghai and the Chinese Revolution of the 1920s*. Hanover, N.H.: Middlebury College Press, 1991.

Cohen, Jerome Alan. "Introduction." In *China's Practice of International Law: Some Case Studies*, edited by Jerome Alan Cohen. Cambridge, Mass.: Harvard University Press, 1972.

Cohen, Paul A. *History in Three Keys: The Boxers as Event, Experience, and Myth*. New York: Columbia University Press, 1997.

―――. "Introduction: Politics, Myth, and the Real Past." *Twentieth-Century China* 26, no. 2 (April 2001): 1-15.

―――. "Remembering and Forgetting National Humiliation in Twentieth-Century China." *Twentieth-Century China* 27, no. 2 (April 2002): 1-39.

―――. *China Unbound: Evolving Perspectives on the Chinese Past*. New York: RoutledgeCurzon, 2003.

Cohen, Warren I. *America's Response to China: A History of Sino-American Relations*. 4th ed. New York: Columbia University Press, 2000.

"Conflict of Laws." *Encyclopedia Britannica*. 2004. Encyclopedia Britannica Premium Service. http://www.britannica.com/eb/article?eu=117329 (accessed February 20, 2004).

Craft, Stephen G. *V. K. Wellington Koo and the Emergence of Modern China*. Lexington, Ky.: University Press of Kentucky, 2004.

Cui, Guoyin (崔國因). *Chushi Meiribi riji* [《出使美日秘日記》 Diary of my mission to the U.S., Japan, and Peru]. Reprint ed. Shanghai: Shanghai guji chubanshe, 1995.

Cui, Zhihai (崔志海). "Shilun 1903 nian Zhongmei Tongshang xingchuan xuding tiaoyue" [試論1903年中美《通商行船續訂條約》 On the revised Sino-U.S. Commercial and Navigational Treaty of 1903]. *Jindaishi yanjiu* 5 (2001): 144-76.

Dan, Tao (但燾), trans. *Guojigongfa tigang* [《國際公法提綱》 An outline of public international law]. Shanghai: Changming gongsi, 1910.

Deng, Zhenglai (鄧正來), ed. *Wang Tieya wenxuan* [《王鐵崖文選》 Selected works of Wang Tieya]. Beijing: Zhongguo zhengfa daxue chubanshe,

1993.

————, ed. *Wang Tieya xueshu wenhua suibi* [《王鐵崖學術文化隨筆》 Wang Tieya's academic and cultural essays]. Beijing: Zhongguo qingnian chubanshe, 1999.

Dickinson, Frederick R. *War and National Reinvention: Japan in the Great War, 1914-1919*. Cambridge, Mass.: Harvard University Press, 1999.

Dickson, Bruce J. "Beijing's Ambivalent Reformers." *Current History* 103, no. 674 (2004): 249-55.

Ding, Mingnan (丁名楠), et al., eds. *Diguo zhuyi qinhuashi* [《帝國主義侵華史》 History of imperialist aggression towards China]. 2 vols. Beijing: Renmin chubanshe, 1986.

Ding, Shouhe (丁守和), et al., eds. *Zhongguo jindai qimeng yundong sichao* [《中國近代啟蒙運動思潮》 Modern Chinese enlightenment thought]. 2 vols. Beijing: Shehui kexue wenxian chubanshe, 1999.

Duanmu, Zheng (端木正). "Zhongguo diyige guojifa xueshu tuanti" [中國第一個國際法學術團體—"公法學會" The first Chinese scholarly organization of international law]. *Zhongguo guojifa niankan* [《中國國際法年刊》 Chinese yearbook of international law]. Beijing: Falü chubanshe, 1998.

Duara, Prasenjit. *Rescuing History from the Nation: Questioning Narratives of Modern China*. Chicago, Ill.: University of Chicago Press, 1996.

Easton, Harry Tucker. *The History of a Banking House (Smith, Payne and Smiths)*. London: Blades, East & Blades, 1903.

Ebrey, Patricia Buckley. *The Cambridge Illustrated History of China*. Reprint ed. Cambridge: Cambridge University Press, 2003.

Edelman, Murray. *Politics as Symbolic Action*. New York: Academic Press, 1971.

————. *The Symbolic Use of Politics*. Urbana, Ill.: University of Illinois Press, 1964.

Elleman, Bruce A. "The End of Extraterritoriality in China: The Case of the Soviet Union, 1917-1960." *Republican China* 21, no. 2 (April 1996): 65-89.

————. *Wilson and China: A Revised History of the Shandong Question*. Armonk, N.Y.: M. E. Sharpe, 2002.

Endo, Genroku (遠藤源六). *Guojifa yaolun* [《國際法要論》 Essential international law]. Trans. Shen Yüshan (沈豫善). Zhenjiang: Qinrun shushe, 1914.

Esherick, Joseph. *The Origins of the Boxer Uprising*. Berkeley, Calif.: University of California Press, 1987.

Etō, Shinkichi. "China's International Relations 1911-1931." In *The Cambridge History of China*, edited by John K. Fairbank and Albert Feuerwerker, vol.13, part 2, 74-115. Cambridge: Cambridge University Press, 1986.

"Extraterritoriality." *Encyclopedia Britannica*. 2003. Encyclopedia Britannica Premium Service. http//www.britannica.com/eb/article?eu=34058 (accessed April 4, 2003).

Fairbank, John K. *Trade and Diplomacy on the China Coast: The Opening of the Treaty Ports, 1842-1854*. Stanford, Calif.: Stanford University Press, 1969.

———. "The Creation of the Treaty System." In *The Cambridge History of China*, edited by John K. Fairbank and Denis Twitchett, vol. 13. Cambridge: Cambridge University Press, 1978.

Fairbank, John K., and Merle Goldman. *China: A New History*. Enlarged ed. Cambridge, Mass.: Harvard University Press, 1999.

Fishel, Wesley R. *The End of Extraterritoriality in China*. Berkeley, Calif.: University of California Press, 1952.

Fitzgerald, John. *Awakening China: Politics, Culture, Class in the Nationalist Revolution*. Stanford, Calif.: Stanford University Press, 1996.

Fu, Lanya (傅蘭雅 John Fryer), and Wang Zhensheng (汪振聲), trans. *Gongfa zonglun* [《公法總論》 General introduction to public laws]. n.p.: Hongwen shujü, 1896.

Fu, Lanya (John Fryer), and Yü Shijue (俞世爵), trans. *Geguo jiaoshe gongfa lun* [《各國交涉公法論》 On public laws of all nations]. n.p.: Hongwen shujü, 1896.

Fudan daxue lishixi, ed. *Riben diguo zhuyi duiwai qinlue shiliao xuanbian, 1931-1945* [《日本帝國主義對外侵略史料選編》 Selected historical sources on the aggression of the Japanese imperialists]. Shanghai: Shanghai renmin chubanshe, 1975.

Fung, Edmund S. K. "The Chinese Nationalists and the Unequal Treaties 1924-1931." *Modern Asia Studies* 21, no. 4 (1987): 793-819.

Gamer, Robert E., ed. *Understanding Contemporary China*. 2nd ed. Boulder, Colo.: Lynne Rienner Publishers, 2003.

Gao, Chengyuan (高承員), ed. *Geming waijiao wenxian (Guangzhou Wuhan shiqi)* [《革命外交文獻 (廣州武漢時期)》 Sources on revolutionary diplomacy (Guangzhou and Wuhan period)]. 1930 reprint. Guangzhou: Shenzhou guoguang she, 1927.

Gao, Fang (高放). "Jinxiandai zhongguo bupingdeng tiaoyue de lailong qümai" [近現代中國不平等條約的來龍去脈 The origins and development of the Unequal Treaties in modern China]. *Nanjing shehui kexue*. 2 (1999): 18-28.

Geddes, Darryl. "Trustee Emeritus Sol Linowitz Given Top Civilian Honor." *Cornell Chronicle* 20, no. 18 (January 22, 1998).

Gilbert, Rodney. *The Unequal Treaties: China and the Foreigners*. London: John Murray, 1929.

Grotius, Hugo. *De Jure Belli Ac Pacis Libri Tres* [On the Law of War and Peace]. Trans. F. Kelsey. Washington, D.C.: Carnegie Endowment for International Peace, 1925.

———. *Guoji fadian* [《國際法典》 Code of international laws. Chinese translation of the English translation of Hugo Grotius 1625's *War and Peace*]. Trans. Cen Dezhang (岑德彰). Shanghai: Shangwu yinshuguan, 1931.

Guandong shehui kexueyuan, ed. *Sun Zhongshan quanji* [《孫中山全集》 Collected works of Sun Zhongshan]. Beijing: Zhonghua shujü, 1986.

Guangzhou minguo ribao [《廣州民國日報》 Guangzhou Republican Daily]

Guo, Jianlin (郭劍林), et al. "Beiyang zhengfu waijiao jindaihua luelun" [北洋政府外交近代化略論 A brief account of the modernization of the diplomatic corps under the Beiyang government]. *Xueshu yanjiu* 3 (1991): 73-77.

Guo, Yingjie, and Baogang He. "Reimagining the Chinese Nation: The 'Zeng Guofan' Phenomenon." *Modern China* 25, no. 2 (April 1999): 142-70.

Guomindang Shanghai tebieshi dangwu zhidao weiyuanhui xuanchuanbu (國民黨上海特別市黨務指導委員會宣傳部). *Bupingdeng tiaoyue yanjiujiu* [《不平等條約研究集》 Studies on the Unequal Treaties]. Shanghai: Minguo ribao, 1929.

Guoshiguan (國史館), ed. *Guoshi nizhuan* [《國史擬傳》 Biographies related to the history of the Republic of China], 3 vols. Taibei: Guoshiguan, 1988.

Guoshiguan gongzhi bianzuan weiyuanhui (國史館公職編纂委員會), ed. *Zhonghua minguoshi gongzhi zhi (chu gao)* [《中華民國史公職志, 初稿》 Record of public officials of the Republic of China]. 1st draft. Taibei: Guoshiguan, 1990.

Han, Depei (韓德培), Luo Chuxiang (羅楚湘), and Che Ying (車英). "Li Daozhao de guojifa sixiang" [李大釗的國際法思想 The international legal thought of Li Daozhao]. *Wuhan daoxue xuebao* 243, no. 4 (1999): 3-6.

Hao, Yen-p'ing, and Wang Erh-min. "Changing Chinese Views of Western Relations, 1840-1895." In *The Cambridge History of China*, edited by John K. Fairbank, et al., vol. 11, part 2, 142-201. Cambridge: Cambridge University Press, 1980.

Harrison, Henrietta. *Inventing the Nation: China*. London: Arnold, 2001.

———. *The Making of the Republican Citizen: Political Ceremonies and Symbols in China, 1911-1929*. Reprint ed. Oxford: Oxford University Press, 2002.

He, Qinhua (何勤華). "Luelun mingguo shiqi zhongguo yizhi guojifa de lilun yü shijian" [《略論民國時期中國移植國際法的理論與實踐》 Short studies on the Chinese transplantation of international legal theories and practices during the Republican period]. *Fashang yanjiu* [《法商研究》] 84, no. 4 (2001): 136-44.

Hertslet, Godfrey E. P., ed. *Hertslet's China Treaties*. 2 vols. London: Harrison and Sons, 1908.

Hevia, James L. *English Lessons: The Pedagogy of Imperialism in Nineteenth-Century China*. Durham, N.C.: Duke University Press, 2003.

Hobsbawm, Eric J. *Nations and Nationalism since 1780: Programme, Myth, Reality*. Cambridge: Cambridge University Press, 1991.

———, ed. *The Invention of Tradition*. Cambridge: Cambridge University Press, 1992.

Horowitz, Richard Steven. "Central Power and State Making: The Zongli Yamen and Self-Strengthening in China, 1860-1880." Ph.D. dissertation, Harvard University, 1998.

Howland, Douglas R. *Translating the West: Language and Political Reason in Nineteenth-Century Japan*. Honolulu, Hawaii: University of Hawaii Press, 2002.

Hsü, Immanuel C. Y. *China's Entrance into the Family of Nations: The Diplomatic Phase, 1858-1880*. Cambridge, Mass.: Harvard University, 1960.

———. *The Rise of Modern China*. 4th ed. Oxford: Oxford University Press, 1990.

Hu, Hanmin (胡漢民). "Paiwai yü guojifa" [排外與國際法 Xenophobia and international law]. *Minbao* [民報], nos. 4, 6, 8, 9, 10, and 13. Reprint ed. 3 vols. Beijing: Kexue chubanshe, 1957.

Hu, Sheng (胡繩). "Yi shi wei jian, ai wo zhonghua" [以史為鑒, 愛我中華 History as a mirror—love our Chinese nation]. *Renmin ribao*, August 29, 1991.

Huang, Jilian (黃紀蓮), ed. *Zhongri Er'shi'yi'tiao jiaoshe shiliao quanbian (1915-1923)* [《中日 "二十一條" 交涉史料全編》 The negotiations over the Sino-Japanese "Twenty-one Demands": Collected documents]. Hefei: Anhui daxue chubanshe, 2001.

Huang, Zunxian (黃遵憲). *Riben guozhi* [《日本國志》 National history of Japan]. Shanghai: Tushu jicheng yinshujü, 1898.

"Humiliation and Revival: From the Treaty of Nanking to the Japanese

Surrender." The National Palace Museum, the Ministry of Foreign Affairs, the Academia Historica, and the Government Information Office. http://www.npm.gov.tw/exhibition (accessed February 10, 2003).

Hunt, Michael H. *Frontier Defense and the Open Door: Manchuria in Chinese-American Relations, 1895-1911.* New Haven, Conn.: Yale University Press, 1973.

———. *The Genesis of Chinese Communist Foreign Policy.* New York: Columbia University Press, 1996.

Hutchinson, John. "Ethnicity and Modern Nations." *Ethnic & Racial Studies* 23, no. 4 (2000): 651-70.

Imai, Yoshiyuki (今井嘉幸). *Zhongguo guojifa lun* [《中國國際法論》On Chinese international law]. Trans. Li Dazhao (李大釗) and Zhang Runzhi (張潤之). Tokyo: Jian xingshe, 1915.

Inspector General of Customs. *Treaties, Conventions, etc., between China and Foreign States.* 2 vols. Shanghai: Statistical Department of the Inspectorate General of Customs, 1917.

"International Law." *Encyclopedia Britannica.* 2004. Encyclopedia Britannica Premium Service. http://www.britannica.com/eb/article?eu=1093 03 (accessed February 20, 2004).

Iriye, Akira. *After Imperialism: The Search for a New Order in the Far East, 1921-1931.* Reprint ed. Chicago, Ill.: Imprint Publications, 1990.

Israel, Jerry. "The Economic Dimension of Sino-American Relations (1931-1949): Profits and Predictability." In *Perspectives in American Diplomacy: Essays on Europe, Latin American, China, and the Cold War,* edited by Jules Davids. New York: Arno Press, 1976.

Janis, Mark W. *An Introduction to International Law.* 4th ed. New York: Aspen Publishers, 2003.

Jia, Botao (賈伯濤), ed. *Jiang Zhongzheng xiansheng yanshuo ji* [《蔣中正先生演說集》Collected speeches of Mr. Jiang Jieshi]. Shanghai: Shanghai sanmin chubanshe, 1925.

Jia, Zhen (賈楨), et al., eds. *Xianfeng chao chouban yiwu shimo* [《咸豐朝.籌辦夷務始末》A complete account of the management of barbarian affairs under the Xianfeng regime]. Beijing: Zhonghua shujü, 1979.

Jiang, Guoqing (江國青). "Lun guojifa yü guoji tiaoyue" [論國際法與國際條約 On international law and international treaties]. *Zhenli de zhuiqiu* [《真理的追求》] 9 (2000): 33-37.

Jiang, Jieshi (蔣介石 Chiang Kai-shek). *Zhongguo zhi mingyun* [《中國之命運》China's destiny]. Chongqing: Zhengzhong shujü, 1943.

————. "Zhongmei zhongying pingdeng xinyue gaocheng gao quanguo junmin shu" [中美中英平等新約告成告全國軍民書 A letter to all servicemen and the masses to mark the conclusion of the new equal treaties between China and the U.S., and between China and Britain]. January 12, 1943. In *Xian zongtong Jianggong sixiang yanlun zongji* [《先總統蔣公思想言論總集》 Collected thoughts and speeches of the late President Jiang], edited by Zhongguo Guomindang zhongyang weiyuanhui (中國國民黨中央委員會), vol. 32, 4-7. Taibei: Zhongguo Guomindang zhongyang weiyuanhui, 1984.

Jiang, Xianbin (蔣賢斌). "Shilun jindai de difang waijiao jiaoshe jiguan" [試論近代的地方外交交涉機關 A preliminary study of local diplomatic bodies in the modern era]. *Jiangxi shifan daxue xuebao* 33, no. 4 (November 2000): 52-56.

Jiang, Yongjing (蔣永敬). *Hu Hanmin xiansheng nianpu* [《胡漢民先生年譜》 A chronicle of the life of Mr. Hu Hanmin]. Taibei: Zhongguo Guomindang dangshi weiyuanhui, 1978.

Jiefang ribao [《解放日報》 Liberation daily]

Jin, Baokang (金保康). *Jiejue bupingdeng tiaoyue de buzhou* [《解決不平等條約的步驟》 Steps toward solving the Unequal Treaties]. n.p.: Beijing, Huabei, Pingmin, Chaoyang, Zhongguo minguo wu sili daxue, 1925.

————, ed. *Pingshi guojifa* [《平時國際法》 International law in peacetime]. Shanghai: Bingwushe, 1907.

Jin, Guangyao (金光耀), ed. *Beiyang shiqi de Zhongguo waijiao* [《北洋時期的中國外交》 The Chinese diplomacy in the Beiyang era]. Shanghai: Fudan daxue chubanshe, 2005.

————. *Gu Weijun zhuan* [《顧維鈞傳》 Biography of Wellington Koo]. Shijiazhuang: Hebei renmin chubanshe, 1999.

————, ed. *Gu Weijun yü Zhongguo waijiao* [《顧維鈞與中國外交》 Wellington Koo and Chinese Diplomacy]. Shanghai: Shanghai guji chubanshe, 2001.

————. "Waijiaoxi chutan" [外交系初探 A preliminary study of the Clique of Diplomacy]. Paper presented at the international conference "Beiyang shiqi de Zhongguo waijiao" [北洋時期的中國外交 Chinese diplomacy during the Beiyang period], Fudan University, Shanghai, China, August 27-28, 2004.

Johnson, Chalmers A. *Peasant Nationalism and Communist Power*. Stanford, Calif.: Stanford University Press, 1962.

Juewu (《覺悟》 Awakening)

Keeton, George W. *The Development of Extraterritoriality in China*. 1969 reprint ed. 2 vols. New York: Howard Fertig, 1928.

Kelsen, Hans. *Principles of International Law.* New York: Rinehart, 1952.

King, Wunsz, ed. *V. K. Wellington Koo's Foreign Policy: Some Selected Documents.* Arlington, Va.: University Publications of America, 1976.

Kingsbury, Benedict. "Sovereignty and Inequality." *European Journal of International Law* 9 (1998): 599-625.

Kirby, William. "The Internationalization of China: Foreign Relations at Home and Abroad in the Republican Era." In *Reappraising Republican China,* edited by Frederic Wakeman Jr. and Richard Louis Edmonds, 179-204. Oxford: Oxford University Press, 2000.

Koo, Wellington. *Gu Weijun huiyilu* [《顧維鈞回憶錄》 The Wellington Koo Memoirs]. 13 vols. Trans. Zhongguo shehui kexueyuan jindaishi yanjiusuo (中國社會科學院近代史研究所). Beijing: Zhonghua shujü, 1983.

———. "The Status of Aliens in China." Ph.D. dissertation, Columbia University, 1912.

———. "The Wellington Koo Memoir," microfilm, New York, Columbia University, 1978.

Ku, Charlotte, and Paul F. Diehl, eds. *International Law: Classic and Contemporary Readings.* 2nd ed. Boulder, Colo.: Lynne Rienner Publishers, 2003.

Kuang, Heping (匡和平). "Zhongguo gongchandang yü bupingdeng tiaoyue de feichu" [中國共產黨與不平等條約的廢除 The Chinese Communist Party and the nullification of the Unequal Treaties]. *Nankai xuebao* 4 (2001): 7-12.

Lai, Xinxia (來新夏), et al. *Beiyang junfa* [《北洋軍閥》 The Beiyang warlords]. Tianjin: Nankai daxue chubanshe, 2000.

Lamarque, Peter, and Stein Haugom Olsen. *Truth, Fiction, and Literature: A Philosophical Perspective.* Oxford: Clarendon Press, 1994.

Lee, En-han (李恩涵). *Beifa hou de "geming waijiao"* [《北伐後的"革命外交", 1925-1931》 Revolutionary diplomacy after Beifa]. Taibei: Institute of Modern History, Academia Sinica, 1993.

Leng, Shaoquan. "Chinese Law." In *Sovereignty within the Law,* edited by Arthur Larson and C. Wilfred Jenks, et al. Dobbs Ferry, NY: Oceana Publications, 1965.

Levi, Werner. *Modern China's Foreign Policy.* Minneapolis, Minn.: University of Minnesota Press, 1953.

Li, Chao-chieh. "International Law in China: Legal Aspect of the Chinese Perspective of World Order." Ph.D. dissertation, University of Toronto, 1996.

Li, Dazhao (李大釗). *Li Daozhao quanji* [《李大釗全集》 Complete collection of the works of Li Dazhao]. Shijiazhuang: Hebei jiaoyü chubanshe, 1999.

Li, Hongzhang (李鴻章). "Tongshang yuezhang leizuan xü" [通商約章類纂序 Preface to the directory of commercial treaties and agreements.] In *Tongshang yuezhang leizuan* [《通商約章類纂》 The directory of commercial treaties and agreements]. Tianjin: Tianjin guanshujü, 1886.

Li, Jianmin (李健民). *Wusha hou de fanying yundong* [《五卅慘案後的反英運動》 The Anti-British movement following the May Thirtieth Incident, 1925-1926]. Taibei: Institute of Modern History, Academia Sinica, 1986.

Li, Kan (李侃), et al., eds. *Zhongguo jindaishi* [《中國近代史》 Modern Chinese history]. 4th ed. of 1993, 24th reprint. Beijing: Zhonghua shujü, 2001.

Li, Shaosheng (李紹盛). *Huashengdun huiyi zhi Zhongguo wenti* [《華盛頓會議之中國問題》 The China question at the Washington Conference]. Taibei: Shuiniu chubanshe, 1973.

Li, Wenhai (李文海). "*Zouxiang gonghe* gei renmen tigong le shengmoyang de 'xin de lishi guandian'" [《走向共和》給人們提供了什麼樣的 "新的歷史觀點"？ What kind of "new historical perspective" does *Towards the People's Republic* offer people?]. *Gaoxiao lilun zhanxian* [高校理論戰線] no. 6 (2003).

Li, Wenhai (李文海), and Kuang Jixian (匡繼先), eds. *Jindai Zhongguo bupingdeng tiaoyue xieshi* [《近代中國不平等條約寫實》 True records of the unequal treaties in modern China]. Beijing: Zhongguo renmin chubanshe, 1997.

Li, Xingyuan (李星沅). *Li Xingyuan riji* [《李星沅日記》 Diary of Li Xingyuan]. Beijing: Zhonghua shujü, 1987.

Li, Yümin (李育民). *Jindai tiaoyue zhidu* [《近代的條約制度》 The modern treaty system]. Changsha: Hunan shifan dauxue chubanshe, 1995.

Li, Zhaojie. "Teaching, Research and the Dissemination of International Law in China: The Contribution of Wang Tieya." *The Canadian Yearbook of International Law* 31 (1993): 189-218.

Li, Zhixue (李志學). "Cong qüru tuoxie dao duli zizhu: Zhongsu youhao tongmeng tiaoyue yü Zhongsu youhao tongmeng huzhu tiaoyue bijiao yanjiu" [從屈辱妥協到獨立自主：《中蘇友好同盟條約》與《中蘇友好同盟互助條約》比較研究 From humiliating compromise to independence: A comparative study of the Treaty of Friendship and Alliance between the Republic of China and the U.S.S.R., and the Treaty of Friendship, Alliance, and Mutual Assistance between the People's Republic of China and the U.S.S.R.]. *Xuexi yü tansuo* 3 (2002): 126-130.

Liang, Xi (梁西), ed. *Guojifa* [《國際法》 International law]. Reprint 2000. Wuhan: Wuhan daxue chubanshe, 1993.

Lin, Quan (林泉), ed. *Kangzhan shiqi feichu bupingdeng tiaoyue shiliao* [《抗戰時期廢除不平等條約史料》 Sources on the relinquishment of the Unequal

Treaties during the War Resistance period]. Taibei: Zhengzhong shujü, 1984.

Liu, Alan P. L. *Mass Politics in the People's Republic of China: State and Society in Contemporary China*. Boulder, Colo.: Westview Press, 1996.

Liu, Baogang (劉保剛). "Lun wanqing shidafu gongfa guannian de yanbian" [論晚清士大夫公法觀念的演變 Changing perceptions of public international law among the late Qing literati]. *Zhejiang xuekan* 3 (1999): 152-56.

Liu, Daren (劉達人), and Yuan Guoqin (袁國欽). *Guojifa fada shi* [《國際法發達史》 The development of international law]. Shanghai: Shangwu yin shuguan, 1937.

Liu, Guoli, ed. *Chinese Foreign Policy in Transition*. New York: Aldine de Gruyter, 2004.

Liu, Huanceng (劉歡曾). "Wang Zhengting boshi bailing mingdan zhigan" [王正廷博士百齡冥誕誌感 Commemorative thoughts on Dr. Wang Zhengting's 100th birthday]. *Zhuanji wenxue* 42, no. 2 (1992): 10-20.

Liu, Li (劉莉). "Zhongsu youhao tongmeng tiaoyue de qianding jiqi dui guogong liangdang guanxi de yingxiang" [《中蘇友好同盟條約》的簽定及其對國共兩黨關係的影響 The signing of the Treaty of Friendship and Alliance between the Republic of China and the U.S.S.R. and its impact on the relationship between the CCP and the GMD]. *Shiji qiao* 4 (2000): 29-30.

Liu, Lydia H. *Translingual Practice: Literature, National Culture, and Translated Modernity—China, 1900-1937*. Stanford, Calif.: Stanford University Press, 1995.

———, ed. *Tokens of Exchange: The Problem of Translation in Global Circulations*. Durham, N.C.: Duke University Press, 1999.

Liu, Shaoqi (劉少奇). *Jianguo yilai Liu Shaoqi wengao* [《建國以來劉少奇文稿》 The Liu Shaoqi paper since the founding of the People's Republic of China]. Beijing: Zhongyang wenxian chubanshe, 1998.

Liu, Shih Shun. *Extraterritoriality: Its Rise and Its Decline*. New York: Columbia University Press, 1925.

Liu, Shoulin (劉壽林), et al., eds. *Minguo zhiguan nianbiao* [《民國職官年表》 Tables of Republican officials by year]. Beijing: Zhonghua shujü, 1995.

Liu, Xifa (劉喜發). "Zhongsu youhao tongmeng tiaoyue pingxi" [中蘇友好同盟條約評析 An analysis of the Treaty of Friendship and Alliance between the Republic of China and the U.S.S.R.]. *Shehui kexue zhanxian* 3 (1996): 210-16.

Lo, Hui-min, ed. *The Correspondence of G. E. Morrison: 1895-1920*. 2 vols. Cambridge: Cambridge University Press, 1976.

Lo, Kuang (羅光). *Lu Zhengxiang zhuan* [《陸征祥傳》 Biography of Lu Zheng-xiang]. Taibei: Commercial Press, 1926.

Lu, Fanzhi (魯凡之). *Cong Yapian zhanzheng dao feichu bupingdeng tiaoyue* [《從鴉片戰爭到廢除不平等條約》 From the Opium War to the abolition of the Unequal Treaties]. Hong Kong: Yüxiang wenhua fuwushe, 1998.

Luo, Yüdong (羅玉東). *Zhongguo lijinshi* [《中國厘金史》 The history of the Chinese *likin*]. 2 vols. Reprint ed. Taibei: Wenhai chubanshe, 1979.

Macdonald, Ronald St. John, ed. *Essays in Honour of Wang Tieya*. Boston, Mass.: M. Nijhoff Publishers, 1994.

MacMurray, John V. A., ed. *Treaties and Agreements with and Concerning China*. 2 vols. New York: Oxford University Press, 1921. Reprint ed. Honolulu, Hawaii: University of Hawaii Press, 2004.

Malanczuk, Peter. *Akehurst's Modern Introduction to International Law*. 7th ed. New York: Routledge, 1997.

Malawer, Stuart S. "A Letter from Stuart S. Malawer." *New York Times*, September 12, 1983.

Mao, Haijian (茅海建), *Tianchao de bengkui: Yapian zhanzheng zai yanjiu* [《天朝的崩潰:鴉片戰爭再研究》 The fall of the celestial kingdom: A re-examination of the Opium War]. Beijing: Sanlian shudian, 1995.

———. *Kuming tianzi* [《苦命天子》 Ill-fated son of heaven]. Shanghai: Shanghai renmin chubanshe, 1995.

———. *Jindai de chidu: Laingci Yapian Zhanzheng junshi yü waijiao* [《近代的尺度: 兩次鴉片戰爭軍事與外交》 A modern assessment: Military and diplomatic aspects of the two Opium Wars]. Shanghai: Sanlian shudian, 1998.

Mao, Zedong (毛澤東). *Mao Zedong ji* [《毛澤東集》 Collected works of Mao Zedong]. n.p.: Yishan tushu, 1976.

———. *Mao Zedong xuanji* [《毛澤東選集》 Selected works of Mao Zedong]. Beijing: Renmin chubanshe, 1952.

"May Thirteenth Incident." *Encyclopedia Britannica*. 2004. Encyclopedia Britannica Premium Service. http://www.britannica.com/eb/article?eu =52852 (accessed July 19, 2004).

Mayers, William Frederick, ed. *Treaties between the Empire of China and Foreign Powers, Together with the Regulations for the Conduct of Foreign Trade*. Shanghai: J. Broadhurst Tootal, *North China Herald* Office, 1877. Reprint ed. Taibei: Chengwen Pub. Co., 1966.

McCord, Edward. *The Power of the Gun: The Emergence of Modern Chinese Warlords*. Berkeley, Calif.: University of California Press, 1993.

———. "Warlordism at Bay: Civil Alternative to Military Rule in Early Republican China." *Republican China* 17, no. 1 (November 1991): 38-70.

Medeiros, Evan S., and M. Taylor Fravel. "China's New Diplomacy." In *Chinese Foreign Policy in Transition*, edited by Guoli Liu, 387-98. New York: Aldine de Gruyter, Inc., 2004.

Meng, S. M. *The Tsungli Yamen: Its Organization and Functions.* Cambridge, Mass.: Harvard University Press, 1970.

Minzuhun (民族魂 The national spirit). http://www.chinaspirit.net.cn (accessed September 23, 2004).

Morse, Hosea Ballou. *The International Relations of the Chinese Empire.* 3 vols. New York: Longmans, Green, and Co., 1918. Reprint ed. Honolulu, Hawaii: University of Hawaii Press, 2004.

———. *The Trade and Administration of the Chinese Empire*, Reprint ed. Taibei: Cheng-wen Pub. Co., 1966.

Mungello, David E. *The Great Encounter of China and the West, 1500-1800.* Lanham, Md.: Rowman & Littlefield Publishers, 1999.

Murase, Shinya. "The Most-Favored-Nation Treatment in Japan's Treaty Practice during the Period 1854-1905." *The American Journal of International Law* 70, no. 2 (1976): 273-97.

Nakajima, Mineo. "Foreign Relations: From the Korean War to the Bandung Line." In *The Cambridge History of China*, edited by Roderick MacFarquhar and John K. Fairbank, vol. 14, 259-89. Cambridge: Cambridge University Press, 1987.

Nakamura, Shingon (中村進午). *Pingshi guojigongfa* [《平時國際公法》 Public international law in peacetime]. Trans. Chen Shixia (陳時夏). Shanghai: Shangwu yinshuguan, 1911.

Nathan, Andrew. "A Constitutional Republic: The Peking Government, 1916-1928." In *The Cambridge History of China*, edited by John K. Fairbank, vol. 12, part 1. Cambridge: Cambridge University Press, 1983.

———. *Chinese Democracy: Peking Politics, 1918-1923.* New York: Alfred A. Knopf, 1985.

———. "Some Trends in the Historiography of Republican China." *Republican China* 17, no. 1 (November 1991): 117-32.

National Archives Microfilm Publications. "Records of the Department of State Relating to Internal Affairs of China, 1910-1929." "A Dispatch from the Commander of the Japanese Fleet," John K. Davis (American Vice-Consul in Chefoo) to J. V. A. MacMurray (the American Legation in China), September 7 and 16, 1914. No. 329, Roll 7.

Ning, Xiewan (甯協萬). *Wanguo gongfa* [《國際公法》 The public international law of the ten thousand nations]. Changsha: Hunansheng lifazheng zhuanmen xuexiao, 1919.

————. *Xianxing guojifa* [《先行國際法論》 Introduction to international law].
　Beijing: Beijing Zhengfa daxue, 1923.

Nish, I. H. "Japan Reverses the Unequal Treaties: The Anglo-Japanese Co-
　mmercial Treaties of 1894." *Journal of Oriental Studies* VXIII, no. 2
　(1975): 137-45.

North-China Daily News

North-China Herald

Nozari, Fariborz. *Unequal Treaties in International Law.* Stockholm: S-Byran
　Sundt & Co., 1971.

"Opium Wars." *The Columbia Encyclopedia.* 6th ed. New York: Columbia
　University Press, 2001-2004. http://www.bartleby.com/65/ (accessed
　July 30, 2004).

Oppenheim, Lassa. *International Law, A Treatise.* 2 vols., 7th ed. Ed. Hersch
　Lauterpacht. London: Longmans, 1948-1952.

————. *International Law: A Treatise.* 2 vols. London: Longmans, Green,
　and Co., 1905-1906, 1912.

————. *Ao Benhai guojifa* [《奧本海國際法》 Oppenheim's International Law.
　Based on Ronald Roxburg edited version]. Trans. Cen Dezhang (岑德
　彰). Shanghai: Shangwu yinshuguan, 1934.

Orlean, M. E. "The Sino-American Commercial Treaty of 1946." *The Far
　East Quarterly* 7, no. 4 (1948): 354-67.

Orwell, George. *Nineteen Eighty-Four.* London: Secker & Warburg, 1949.
　Reprint ed. London: Penguin Books, 2003.

Ouyang, Yuefeng (歐陽躍峰). "Yetan lishi renwu pingjia de xiangguang
　lilun wenti: yi Li Hongzhang de waijiao huodong weili" [也談歷史人物評
　價的相關理論問題: 以李鴻章的外交活動為例 Theoretical issues relating to the
　judgment of historical figures: A case study of the diplomatic activities
　of Li Hongzhang]. *Shixue lilun yanjiu* [史學理論研究], no. 3 (2003): 130-40.

Pelcovits, Nathan A. *Old China Hands and the Foreign Office.* New York:
　American Institute of Pacific Relations, 1948.

Peng, Ming (彭明). *Zhongsu renmin youyi jianshi* [《中蘇人民友誼簡史》 A brief
　history of the friendship of Sino-Soviet peoples]. Beijing: Zhongguo
　qingnian chubanshe, 1995.

Pepper, Suzanne. "The KMT-CCP Conflict 1945-1949." In *The Cambridge
　History of China: Republican China 1912-1949,* edited by John K. Fair-
　bank and Albert Feuerwerker, vol. 13, part 2, 723-88. Cambridge:
　Cambridge University Press, 1986.

Perez, Louis G. *Japan Comes of Age: Mutsu Munemitsu and the Revision of the
　Unequal Treaties.* Cranbury, N.J.: Associated University Press, 1999.

Pollard, Robert T. *China's Foreign Relations, 1917-1931.* New York: Macmillan, 1933.

Pufendorf, Samuel. *De Jure Naturae et Gentium* [On the law of nature and nations]. Trans. C. H. Oldfather and W. A. Oldfather from the 1688 ed. Washington, D.C.: Carnegie Endowment for International Peace, 1934.

Pye, Lucian. *Warlord Politics: Conflict and Coalition in the Modernization of Republican China*. New York: Praeger, 1971.

Qi, Sihe (齊思和), et al., eds. *Di erci Yapiang zhanzheng* [《第二次鴉片戰爭》 The second Opium War]. 6 vols. Shanghai: Shanghai renmin chubanshe, 1978-1979.

Qian, Shifu (錢實甫), ed. *Beiyang zhengfu zhiguan nianbiao* [《北洋政府職官年表》 Tables of officials in the Beiyang government by year]. Shanghai: Huadong shifandaxue chubanshe, 1991.

———. *Qingdai de waijiao jiguan* [《清代的外交機關》 The diplomatic establishment of the Qing dynasty]. Beijing: Sanlian shudian, 1959.

Qianfeng (《前鋒》 Vanguard)

Qin, Xiaoyi (秦孝儀), ed. *Guofu quanji* [《國父全集》 The complete works of the founding father]. Taibei: Jindai zhongguo chubanshe, 1989.

Qiu, Zuming (邱祖銘). *Zhongwai dingyue shiquan lun* [《中外訂約失權論》 On lost rights in the negotiation of treaties between China and foreign countries]. Shanghai: Shangwu yinshuguan, 1926.

Ren, Donglai (任東來). *Zhengchao buxiu de huoban: meiyuan yü Zhongmei kangri tongmeng* [《爭吵不休的夥伴：美援與中美抗日同盟》 Quarrelling partners: American aid and the Sino-American anti-Japan alliance]. Guilin: Guangxi shifan daxue chubanshe, 1995.

Renmin ribao [《人民日報》 The people's daily]

Renminwang (人民網 The people's net). http://www.people.com.cn (accessed September 23, 2004).

Reynold, Douglas R. *China, 1898-1912: The Xinzheng Revolution and Japan*. Cambridge, Mass.: Harvard University Press, 1993.

Riben pu wenxuehui (日本普文學會), comp. *Guoji gongfa gongji sifa wenti yijie* [《國際公法國際私法問題義解》 Explaining public international law and private international law]. Trans. Gonghe fazheng xuehui bianjibu (共和法政學會編輯部). Shanghai: Gonghe fazheng xuehui, 1913.

Sanlian shudian (三聯書店), ed. *Chen Duxiu wenzhang xuanbian* [《陳獨秀文章選編》 Selected essays of Chen Duxiu]. Beijing: Sanlian shudian, 1984.

Saodang bao [《掃蕩報》 Mopping-up newspaper]

Sasaki, Masaya (佐佐木正哉). *Ahen Sensō no kenkyū. Shiryō hen* [《鴉片戰爭の研究》（資料篇） A Study of the Opium War (Sources)]. Tokyo: Kindai Chūgoku Kenkyū linkai, 1964.

Schoenhals, Michael. *Doing Things with Words in Chinese Politics: Five Studies*. Berkeley, Calif.: University of California Press, 1992.

Schwarcz, Vera. "Memory and Commemoration: The Chinese Search for a Livable Past." In *Popular Protest & Political Culture in Modern China*, edited by Jeffery N. Wasserstrom and Elizabeth J. Perry, 170-83. Boulder, Colo.: Westview Press, 1989, 1994 reprint.

Scott, James Brown, ed. *Treaties and Agreements with and Concerning China, 1919-1929*. Washington, D.C.: Carnegie Endowment for International Peace, 1929.

Scully, Eileen P. *Bargaining with the State from Afar: American Citizenship in Treaty Port China, 1844-1942*. New York: Columbia University Press, 2001.

Selden, Mark. *China in Revolution: The Yenan Way Revisited*. Armonk, N.Y.: M. E. Sharpe, 1995.

Shang, Hai (尚海), et al., eds. *Minguoshi da cidian* [《民國史大辭典》 Dictionary of the history of the Republic of China]. Beijing: Zhongguo guangbo dianshi chubanshe, 1991.

Shao, Yi (邵羲). "Lun gaiding tongshang tiaoyue yü Zhongguo qiantu zhi guanxi" [論改訂通商條約與中國前途之關係 On the relations between revision of commercial treaties and the future of China]. *Waijiaobao* [外交報], Lunshuo [論說], issue 224 (October 19, 1908) (戊申九月 二十五日).

Shen, Tongsheng (沈桐生), comp. *Guangxü zhengyao* [《光緒政要》 Documents of the Guangxü regime]. Reprint ed. Taibei: Wenhai chubanshe, 1961.

Sheng, Xuanhuai (盛宣懷). *Yüzhai cungao* [《愚齋存稿》 Collected works of the folly study]. Reprint ed. Taibei: Chengwen chubanshe, 1966.

Shi, Jianguo (石建國). *Lu Zhengxiang zhuan* [《陸征祥傳》 Biography of Lu Zhenxiang]. Shijiazhuang: Hebei renmin chubanshe, 1999.

Shi, Yuanhua (石源華). *Zhonghua minguo waijiao shi* [《中華民國外交史》 The diplomacy of the Republic of China]. Shanghai: Shanghai renmin chubanshe, 1994.

———. *Zhuming waijiaojia Gu Weijun* [《著名外交家顧維鈞》 The distinguished diplomat Wellington Koo]. Shanghai: Shanghai shehui kexueyuan, 1989.

Siu, Kong-Sou (徐公肅), and Chiu Chin-Tsan (丘瑾璋). *Shanghai gonggong zujie zhidu* [《上海公共租界制度》 The status of the Shanghai International Settlement]. Nanjing: Guoli zhongyang yangjiuyuan, 1933.

Smith, Anthony D. *The Ethnic Origins of Nations*. Oxford: Blackwell, 1986.

———. "Theories of Nationalism: Alternative Models of Nation Formation." In *Asian Nationalism*, edited by Michael Leifer, 1-20. New York: Routledge, 2000.

————. *Nationalism*. Cambridge: Polity Press, 2001.

Smith, Stephen Anthony. *Like Cattle and Horses: Nationalism and Labor in Shanghai, 1895-1927*. Durham, N.C.: Duke University Press, 2002.

Spence, Jonathan. *The Search for Modern China*. 2nd ed. New York: W. W. Norton & Company, 1999.

Stephens, Thomas B. *Order and Discipline in China: The Shanghai Mixed Court, 1911-27*. Seattle, Wash.: University of Washington Press, 1992.

Strauss, Julia C. *Strong Institutions in Weak Polities: State Building in Republican China, 1927-1940*. Oxford: Clarendon Press, 1998.

Sun, Xiaolou (孫曉樓), and Zhao Yinian (趙頤年). *Lingshi caipanquan wenti* [《領事裁判權問題》 The question of extraterritoriality]. Shanghai: Shangwu yinshuguan, 1937.

Sze, Sao-ke Alfred. *Addresses by Sao-Ke Alfred Sze*. Baltimore, Md.: John Hopkins University Press, 1926.

Tang, Ch'i-hua (唐啟華). *Beijing zhengfu yü guoji lianmeng (1919-1928)* [《北京政府與國際聯盟》 The Beijing government and the League of Nations]. Taibei: Dongda tushu gongsi, 1998.

————. "'Beiyang waijiao' yanjiu pingjia" ["北洋外交"研究評介 The state of the field on the "Beiyang Diplomacy"]. *Lishi yanjiu* 287, no. 1 (2004): 99-113.

————. *Beiyang "xiuyue waijiao" lunwen xuanji* [《北洋"修約外交"論文選集》 Collected writings on the Beiyang Treaty Revision Diplomacy]. Taibei: Zhengzhi duxue lishixi, 2004.

Tao, Wenzhao (陶文釗). *Zhongmei guoxi shi, 1911-1950* [《中美關係史, 1911-1950》 History of Sino-American relations]. Chongqing: Chongqing chubanshe, 1993.

Teng, Ssu-yu, and John K. Fairbank. *China's Response to the West: A Documentary Survey, 1839-1923*. Cambridge, Mass.: Harvard University Press, 1954.

Tian, Tao (田濤). "Ding Weiliang yü *Wanguo gongfa*" [丁韙良與《萬國公法》 William Martin and the public laws of the ten thousand nations]. *Shehui kexue yanjiu* 5 (1999): 107-112.

Townsend, James R. "Chinese Nationalism." *The Australian Journal of Chinese Affairs*, no. 27 (January 1992): 97-130.

————. *Political Participation in Communist China*. Berkeley, Calif.: University of California Press, 1967.

Tsao, Ju-lin (曹汝霖). *Yisheng zhi huiyi* [《一生之回憶》 Memoirs of Cao Rulin]. Hong Kong: Chunqiu zazhishe, 1966.

Tseng, Yu-hao. *The Termination of Unequal Treaties in International Law: Studies in Comparative Law of Nations*. Shanghai: Commercial Press,

1931.

Tu, Heng-chih (杜蘅之). *Zhongwai tiaoyue guanxi zhi bianqian* [《中外條約關係之 變遷》 The evolutions of the Sino-foreign treaty relations]. Taibei: Zhonghua wenhua fuxing yundong tuixing weiyuanhui, 1981.

Tung, William L. *China and the Foreign Powers: The Impact and Reaction to Unequal Treaties*. Dobbs Ferry, N.Y.: Oceana Publications, 1970.

"The Twists of Destiny: A Special Exhibition of Historical Documents on Macau." The National Palace Museum, the Ministry of Foreign Affairs, the Academia Historica, and the Government Information Office. http://www.npm.gov.tw/exhibition/mac9912/ehtm/emac9912.htm (accessed February 28, 2004).

Ulyanovsky, R. A., ed. *The Comintern and the East: The Struggle for the Leninist Strategy and Tactics in National Liberation Movements*. Moscow: Progress Publishers, 1979.

U.S. Department of State. *Foreign Relations of the United States: Diplomatic Papers: The Conferences of Malta and Yalta, 1945*. Washington, D.C.: U.S. Government Printing Office, 1955.

Vattel, Emmerich de. *The Law of Nations, or Principles of the Law of Nature Applied to the Conduct and Affairs of Nations and Sovereigns*. Translated from French. 2 vols. London: Printed for J. Newbury and J. Coote, 1760; Washington, D.C.: Carnegie Endowment for International Peace, 1916.

"Vienna Convention on the Law of Treaties." http://www.un.org/law/ilc/ texts/treaties.htm (accessed September 29, 2004).

Wagner, Rudolf G. *The Contemporary Chinese Historical Drama: Four Studies*. Berkeley, Calif.: University of California Press, 1990.

Waijiao gongbao [《外交公報》 Diplomatic bulletin]

Waijiaobao [外交報 Diplomatic newspaper]. Editorial, "Lun Zhongying shangyue" [論中英商約 On the Sino-British commercial treaty]. Lunshuo [論說], issue 23 (1902) (n.d.).

———. Author unknown, "Lun gongfa yü qiangquan zhi guanxi" [論公法 與強權之關係 On the relations between international law and power]. Gonglun [公論], issue 1 (1901) (n.d.).

Waijiaobao huibian [《外交報彙編》 Collected documents of the *Waijiaobao*]. Reprint of the 1914 *Waijiaobao* collection issued 1901-1910. Taibei: Guangwen shujü, 1964.

Waijiaobu (外交部), comp. "Minjiao su'an jinke anzhao yuezhang banli wuyong lingding tiaowen zi" [民教訟案盡可按照約章辦理毋庸另訂條文咨 Correspondence regarding law suits involving Christians and non-Christians should follow existing treaties and agreements, with no need to sign a further agreement]. *Waijiao gongbao* [《外交公報》], no. 1 (1921).

———. "Huayang susong zai xianshu chushen buzhun lüshi chuting wei ke yi dailiren zige chuting daisu yang zhuanchi zunzhao banli ling" [華洋訴訟在縣署初審不准律師出庭惟可以代理人資格出庭代訴仰轉飭遵照辦理令 Order prohibiting foreign attorneys at the preliminary mixed trial in the county Bureau and permitting foreign agents in the mixed court]. *Waijiao gongbao*, no. 36 (1924).

———. "Yantai Jiaoshe Yuan chengqing heshi guanyü huayang susong yiwen sandian qing heding jian fuhan" [煙臺交涉員呈請核示關於華洋訴訟疑問三點請核定見復函 Inquiries from the Yantai Jiaoshe yuan: On the reply concerning the three questions about the mixed legal case]. *Waijiao gongbao*, no. 63 (1926).

———. *Waijiaobu tiaoyue yanjiuhui baogao* [《外交部條約研究會報告》 Reports of the Association for Treaty Studies of the Foreign Ministry]. Beijing: the Foreign Ministry, 1913.

———, trans. *Ya'er'da huiyi mimi wenjian: youguan zhongguo ji yuandong bufen* [《雅爾達會議秘密文件: 有關中國及遠東部分》 Secret documents of the Yalta Conference relating to China and the Far East]. Taibei: Lifayuan waijiao weiyuanhui, 1955.

———, ed. *Zhongwai tiaoyue jibian* [《中外條約輯編》 Treaties between the Republic of China and foreign states, 1927-1957]. Taibei: Commercial Press, 1958.

Waijiaobu tiayue weiyuanhui (外交部條約委員會), ed. *Bupingdeng tiaoyue biao* [《不平等條約表》 Charting the Unequal Treaties]. Beijing: Waijiaobu, 1929.

Waiyü jiaoxue yü yanjiu chubanshe (外語教學與研究出版社), ed. *Xiandai hanying cidian* [《現代漢英詞典》 A Modern Chinese-English Dictionary]. 5th reprint. Beijing: Waiyü jiaoxue yü yanjiu chubanshe, 1991.

Waldron, Arthur. *From War to Nationalism: China's Turning Point, 1924-1925*. Cambridge: Cambridge University Press, 1995.

Wallace, Rebecca M. M. *International Law*. 3rd ed. London: Sweet & Maxwell, 1997.

Wan, Xia (萬霞). "Huigu yü zhanwang: gaige kaifang er'shi nian guojifa zai zhongguo de fazhan" [回顧與展望: 改革開放20年國際法在中國的發展 Looking forward and backward: The development of international law in China in the 20 years since China's opening-up]. *Waijiao xuebao* [《外交學院學報》] 2 (1999): 62-66.

Wang, Cheng-t'ing (Wang Zhengting). "Looking Backward and Looking Forward." Manuscript held at the Sterling Memorial Library of Yale University.

Wang, Dong. "The Discourse of Unequal Treaties in Modern China." *Pacific Affairs* 76, no. 3 (November 2003): 399-425.

———. "Redeeming 'a Century of National Ignominy': Nationalism and Party Rivalry over the Unequal Treaties, 1928-1947." *Twentieth-Century China* 30, no. 2 (April 2005).

Wang, Ermin (王爾敏 Wang Erh-min), *Wanqing Shangyue waijiao* [《晚清商約外交》 The diplomacy of the commercial treaties between China and foreign powers during the late Ch'ing Period]. Hong Kong: Chinese University of Hong Kong Press, 1998.

Wang, Ermin (王爾敏), and Chen Shanwei (陳善偉), eds. *Qingmo yiding zhongwai shangyue jiaoshe: Sheng Xuanhuai wanglai handian gao* [《清末議定中外商約交涉：盛宣懷往來函電稿》 Documents relating to commercial treaty negotiation between China and the West in the late Qing: Correspondence and telegrams of Sheng Xuanhuai]. Hong Kong: Chinese University of Hong Kong Press, 1993.

Wang, Gungwu. *Anglo-Chinese Encounters since 1800: War, Trade, Science, and Governance.* Cambridge: Cambridge University Press, 2003.

Wang, Huilin (王檜林), and Zhu Hanguo (朱漢國), eds. *Zhongguo baokan cidian (1815-1949)* [《中國報刊詞典》 Dictionary of Chinese newspapers and periodicals]. Taiyuan: Shuhai chubanshe, 1992.

Wang, Jian (王健). "*Zouxiang gonghe* shifou meihua Li Hongzhang yin zhengyi" [《走向共和》是否美化李鴻章引爭議 The controversy over the alleged exoneration of Li Hongzhang in *Towards the People's Republic*]. *Beijing yüle xinbao* [北京娛樂信報] (April 29, 2003) and *Lingdao kexue* [領導科學], no. 13 (2003).

———. "Yueyan yuehuo, yuezheng yuelie, *Zouxiang gonghe* yinfa yinping zhendang" [越演越火越爭越烈走向共和引發銀屏震盪 The longer it screens, the more popular it becomes; the more the debates, the fiercer they get: The uproar caused by *Towards the People's Republic*]. *Shenzhen wanbao* [深圳晚報], May 16, 2003.

Wang, Jianlang (王建朗). *Kangzhan chuqi de yuandong guoji guanxi* [抗戰初期的遠東國際關係 The international relations of the Far East in the initial phase of the anti-Japanese War]. Taibei: Dongda tushu gongsi, 1996.

———. *Zhongguo feichu bupingdeng tiaoyue de licheng* [《中國廢除不平等條約的歷程》 The record of abolishing all unequal treaties in China. Original translation of the book title]. Nanchang: Jiangxi renmin chubanshe, 2000.

Wang, Jingwei (汪精衛). *Diguo zhuyi qinlue Zhongguo de qüshi he bianqian lun* [《帝國主義侵略中國的趨勢和變遷》 Characteristics and evolution of the imperialist penetration of China]. n.p.: Guomin gemingjun zong sil-ingbu, 1925.

Wang, Ke-wen. "Irreversible Verdict? Historical Assessments of Wang Jngwei in the People's Republic and Taiwan." *Twentieth-Century China* 28, no. 1 (November 2002): 57-81.

Wang, Qisheng (王奇生). "Cong 'ronggong' dao 'rongguo': 1924-1927 nian guogong dangji guanxi zai kaocha" [從'容共'到'容國': 1924-1927 年國共黨際關係再考察 From "Inclusion of the Communists" to "Inclusion of the Guomindang": Reexamining the 1924-1927 GMD-CCP relationship]. *Jindaishi yanjiu* 4 (2001): 37-85.

Wang, Shijie (王世傑). *Wang Shijie xiansheng lunzhu xuanji* [《王世傑先生論著選集》 Selected works of Mr. Wang Shijie]. Taibei: Yütai gongsi, 1980.

———. *Zhongguo bupingdeng tiaoyue zhi feichu* [《中國不平等條約之廢除》 The abolition of the Chinese Unequal Treaties]. Taibei: Jaing Zongtong dui Zhongguo ji shijie zhi gongxian congshu bianzuan weiyuanhui, 1967.

Wang, Shu-hwai (王樹槐). *Gengzi peikuan* [《庚子賠款》 The Boxer Indemnity]. Taibei: Institute of Modern History, Academia Sinica, 1974.

Wang, Tao (王韜). *Taoyuan wenlu waibian* [《弢園文錄外編》 Supplementary collection of the writings of Wang Tao]. Shanghai: unknown publisher, 1897.

Wang, Tieya (王鐵崖), ed. *Guojifa* [《國際法》 International law]. Beijing: Falü chubanshe, 1981.

———. *Guojifa yinlun* [《國際法引論》 A primer of international law]. Beijing: Beijing daxue chubanshe, 1998.

———. "International Law in China: Historical and Contemporary Per-spectives." *Hague Academy of International Law, Recueil des cours* 221, no. 2 (1990): 194-369.

———. *Xinyue yanjiu* [《新約研究》 A study of the new treaty of 1943]. Chongqing: Qingnian chubanshe, 1943.

———. *Zhongwai jiu yuezhang huibian, 1689-1949* [《中外舊約章彙編》 Compilation of former treaties and conventions between China and foreign countries, 1689-1949]. 3 vols. 2nd ed. Beijing: Sanlian shudian, 1982.

Wang, Yanwei (王彥威), comp. *Qingji waijiao shiliao* [《清季外交史料》 Diplomatic sources of the late Qing]. Beijing: Shumu wenxian chu-banshe, 1987.

Wang, Yongxiang (王永祥). *Ya'er'da miyue yü zhongsu risu guanxi* [《雅爾達秘約與中蘇門蘇關係》 The secret agreements of the Yalta Conference and

Sino-Soviet and Japanese-Soviet relations]. Taibei: Dongda tushu gongsi, 2003.

Wang, Zhen (王真). *Dongdang zhong de tongmeng: Kangzhan shiqi zhongsu guanxi* [《動盪中的同盟: 抗戰時期中蘇關係》 Allies in uncertainty: The Sino-Soviet relation in the Anti-Japanese War]. Guilin: Guangxi shida chubanshe, 1993.

Wang, Zhengting (王正廷 Wang Cheng-t'ing). *Guomin zhengfu jin sannian lai waijiao jingguo jiyao* [《國民政府近三年來外交經過紀要, 民國十五年-十八年》 A summary of the foreign relations of the Nationalist government for the past three years, 1926-1929]. Reprint ed. Taibei: Wenhai chubanshe, n.d.

Wang, Zurong (汪祖榮), and Li Ao (李敖). *Jiang Jieshi pingzhuan* [《蔣介石評傳》 Biography of Jiang Jieshi]. Beijing: Zhongguo youyi chuban gongsi, 2000.

Wanyan, Shaoyuan (完顏紹元). *Wang Zhengting zhuan* [《王正廷傳》 Biography of C. T. Wang]. Shijiazhuang: Hebei renmin chubanshe, 1999.

Wasserstrom, Jeffrey N., and Elizabeth J. Perry, eds. *Popular Protest and Political Culture in Modern China: Learning from 1989*. Boulder, Colo.: Westview Press, 1991.

Welch, Ian. "Gunboat Diplomacy in China (Response)." http://www.h-net.msu.edu/~asia (accessed January 15, 2005).

Wheaton, Henry. *Elements of International Law: With a Sketch of the History of the Science*. Philadelphia: Carey, Lea & Blanchard, 1836.

———. *Wanguo gongfa* [《萬國公法》 The public laws of the ten thousand nations]. Trans. Ding Weiliang (William Martin). Chongshi guan, 1864. Reprint ed. Taibei: Zhongguo guojifa xuehui, 1998.

Whiting, Allen S. *Soviet Policies in China, 1917-1924*. 2nd ed. New York: Columbia University Press, 1957.

Wilbur, C. Martin, and Julie Lien-ying How. *Missionaries of Revolution: Soviet Advisers and Nationalist China, 1920-1927*. Cambridge, Mass.: Harvard University Press, 1989.

Willoughby, Westel W. *China at the Conference: A Report*. Baltimore, Md.: Johns Hopkins University Press, 1922.

———. *The Fundamental Concepts of Public Law*. New York: Macmillan, 1924.

———. *Foreign Rights and Interests in China*. Baltimore, Md.: Johns Hopkins University Press, 1927.

Wood, Frances. *No Dogs and Not Many Chinese: Treaty Port Life in China, 1843-1943*. London: John Murray, 2000.

Woodhead, Henry George W. *The China Year Book*. Tientsin: Tientsin Press,

1912-1931.

Wou, Odoric Y. K. *Mobilizing the Masses: Building Revolution in Henan.* Stanford, Calif.: Stanford University Press, 1994.

Wright, Stanley F. *China's Struggle for Tariff Autonomy: 1843-1938.* Shanghai: Kelly & Walsh, 1938.

———. *Hart and the Chinese Customs.* Belfast: W. Mullan, 1950.

Wu, Canghai (吳滄海). *Shandong xuan'an jiejue zhi jingwei* [《山東懸案解決之經緯》 The entire of process concerning the resolution of the Shandong question]. Taibei: Taiwan Shangwu yinshuguan, 1987.

Wu, Chaoshu. *The Nationalist Program for China.* New Haven, Conn.: Yale University Press, 1929.

Wu, Chengzhang (吳成章). *Waijiaobu yange jilue* [《外交部沿革紀略》 The history of the Foreign Ministry]. 1913. Reprint ed. Taibei: Wenhai chubanshe, 1987.

Wu, Fuhuan (吳福環). *Qingji Zongli Yamen yanjiu* [《清季總理衙門研究》 A Study of the Tsungli Yamen]. Taibei: Wenjin chubanshe, 1995.

Wu, Lin-chun (吳翎君). "1946 nian Zhongmei shangyue de lishi yiyi" [1946年中美商約的歷史意義 The historical significance of the 1946 Sino-American Commercial Treaty]. *Guoli zhengzhi daxue lishi xuebao* [國立政治大學歷史學報] 21 (May 2004): 42-66.

Wu, Yang. "CCP Military Resistance during the Sino-Japanese War: The Case of Beiyue and Jidong." *Twentieth-Century China* 29, no. 1 (November 2003): 65-104.

Wu, Yügan (武堉幹). *Zhongguo guoji maoyishi* [《中國國際貿易史》 History of Chinese international trade]. Shanghai: Shangwu yinshuguan, 1928.

Xia, Dongyuan (夏東元), ed. *Zheng Guanying ji* [《鄭觀應集》 Collected writings of Zheng Guanyin]. Shanghai: Shanghai renmin chubanshe, 1982.

Xiandai yingyü zhuanxiu xuexiao (現代英語專修學校 The dean's office of the Modern English Training School), ed. *Zhongmei zhongying xinyue wenxian* [《中美中英新約文獻》中英文對照 Anglo-Chinese edition of the new Sino-British and Sino-American Treaties and other related materials]. Chongqing: Tiandi chubanshe, 1943.

Xiangdao zhoubao [《嚮導週報》 Guide weekly]

Xiao, Zhizhi (蕭致治). *Yapian zhanzheng yü jindai Zhongguo* [《鴉片戰爭與中國》 The Opium War and modern China]. Wuhan: Hubei jiaoyü chubanshe, 1999.

Xinchou geguo heyue [《辛醜各國和約》 The Boxer Protocol of 1901]. Deposited at the Harvard-Yenching Library of Harvard University. Beijing: Waiwubu, 1901.

Xing, Heng (星恒). "Suqi yanjiu bupingdeng tiaoyue" [速起研究不平等條約 Expedite research on the unequal treaties]. *Liuxue tekan* [流血特刊 Bleeding special issue], *Ziqiang* [《自強》 Self-strengthening], no. 2 (June 9, 1925): 174-75. In *Wusha tongshi* [《五卅痛史》 The bitter history of May Thirtieth], edited by *Shenbao* and Qinghua xueshenghui [*Shenbao* and Qinghua Student Association]. Reprint ed. Taibei: Wenhai chubanshe, 1966-1987.

Xü, Guoqi. "The Age of Innocence: The First World War and China's Quest for National Identity." Ph.D. dissertation, Harvard University, 1999.

Xue, Fucheng (薛福成). *Chouyang chuyi* [《籌洋芻議》 A brief discussion of tactics for dealing with foreign countries]. Shenyang: Liaoning renmin chubanshe, 1994.

Xue, Xiantian (薛銜天). *Zhongsu guojia guanxishi ziliao huibian (1945-1949)* [《中蘇國家關係史資料彙編》 Collection of documents on the Sino-Soviet relations]. Beijing: Shehui kexue wenxian chubanshe, 1996.

Xue, Yü (薛鈺). "Kangri minzu tongyi zhanxian yü di'er'ci guogong he-zuo" [抗日民族統一戰線與第二次國共合作 The Anti-Japanese National United Front and the CCP-GMD Second United Front]. In *Kangri zhanzhengshi yanjiu shuping* [《抗日戰爭史研究述評》 Review of research on the Anti-Japanese War], edited by Guo Dehong (郭德宏), 179-215. Beijing: Zhonggong dangshi chubanshe, 1995.

Xuezhu Zhonghua [血鑄中華 Build China with blood]. http://www.china 1840-1949.net.cn (accessed September 23, 2004).

Yang, Gongsu (楊公素). *Zhonghua minguo waijiao jianshi* [《中華民國外交簡史》 A brief diplomatic history of the Republic of China]. Beijing: Shangwu yinshuguan, 1997.

Yang, Kuisong (楊奎松). "Zhongsu guojia liyi yü minzu qinggan de zuichu pengzhuang: yi Zhongsu youhao tongmeng huzhu tiaoyue de qian-ding wei beijing" [中蘇國家利益與民族情感的最初碰撞: 以中蘇友好同盟互助條約的簽定為背景 The initial encounter of state interests and national senti-ment between China and the Soviet Union: The signing of the Sino-Soviet Treaty of Friendship, Alliance, and Mutual Assistance]. *Lishi yanjiu*, no. 6 (2001): 103-19.

Yang, Tingdong (楊廷棟). "Lun gaizheng tiaoyue yü bianding falü you lianjie zhi guanxi" [論改正條約與編訂法律有連結之關係 On the connection between treaty revision and legal codification]. *Waijiaobao* [外交報], Lunshuo [論說], issue 254 (September 18, 1909).

Yang, Xiangquan (楊向泉), et al., eds. *Zeng Jize chushi yingfa riji* [《曾紀澤出使 英法日記》 Zeng Jize's diary in England, France, and Russia]. Changsha:

Yuelu shushe, 1985.

Yao, Weiyuan (姚薇元). *Yapian Zhanzheng* [《鴉片戰爭》 The Opium War]. Wuhan: Hubei renmin chubanshe, 1983.

Yen, W. W. (Yan Huiqing). *East-West Kaleidoscope, 1877-1944: An Autobiography*. New York: St. John's University Press, 1974.

Yinzhu jü (印鑄局). *Zhiyuan lu* [《職員錄》 Personnel directory]. Beijing: Yinzhu jü, 1912-1924.

Zeng, Jize (曾紀澤). *Zeng Jize yiji* [《曾紀澤遺集》 The posthumous works of Zeng Jize]. Changsha: Yuelu shushe, 1983.

Zeng, Lingliang (曾令良). "Ping Liangxi zhubian zhi Guojifa" [評梁西主編之《國際法》 A review of Liang Xi's *Guojifa*]. *Faxue pinglun* 3 (1994): 85-88.

Zeng, Youhao (曾友豪 Yu-hao Tseng). *Guoji gongfa li'an* [《國際公法例案》 Cases in public international law]. Shanghai: Shanghai faxue shujü, 1934.

Zeng, Zhi (曾志). "Meiguo yü Nanjing zhengfu de guanshui zizhu" [美國與南京政府的關稅自主 The U.S. and the tariff autonomy of the Nanjing government]. In *Meiguo yü jinxiandai zhongguo* [《美國與近現代中國》 The U.S. and modern China]. Edited by Tao Wenzhao and Liang Biying (梁碧瑩), 243-61. Beijing: Zhongguo shehui kexue chubanshe, 1996.

Zhang, Haipeng (張海朋), et al., eds. *Guochi baitan* [《國恥百談》 One hundred essays on national humiliation]. Beijing: Zhonghua shujü, 2001.

———. "Shi yibu lishi zhenglunjü, er bushi lishi zhengjü: guanyü lishijü *Zouxiang gonghe* de lingxing ganxiang" [是一部歷史政論劇, 而不是歷史正劇: 關於歷史劇《走向共和》的零星感想 A historical political drama, but not an orthodox historical drama: Some loose thoughts on *Towards the People's Republic*]. *Gaoxiao lilun zhanxian* [高校理論戰線], no. 6 (2003).

Zhang, Jiuhuan (張九桓). "The Spirit of Sun Yat-sen through Twenty-first-century Eyes." http://www.chinaembassy.org.sg/chn/26595.html (accessed September 29, 2004).

Zhang, Liheng (張禮恒). *Wu Tingfang zhuan* [《伍廷芳傳》 Biography of Wu Tingfang]. Shijiazhuang: Hebei renmin chubanshe, 1999.

Zhang, Tinghao (張廷灝). *Bupingdeng tiaoyue de yanjiu* [《不平等條約的研究》 A study of the Unequal Treaties]. Shanghai: Guanghua shujü, 1926.

Zhang, Wei (張瑋). "Zhiyi *Zouxiang gonghe*" [質疑《走向共和》 Questioning *Towards the People's Republic*]. *Dianying* [電影], no. 7 (2003): 4-6.

Zhang, Xi (張喜). *Fuyi riji* [《撫夷日記》 Diary of negotiations with the barbarians]. Reprinted in *Yapian zhanzheng dang'an shiliao* [《鴉片戰爭檔案史料》 Archival sources on the Opium War]. Vol. 5. Shanghai: Shanghai renmin chubanshe, 1987.

———. *Fuyi riji.* Trans. Teng Ssu-yu. *Chang Hsi and the Treaty of Nanjing,*

1842. Chicago, Ill.: University of Chicago Press, 1944.

Zhang, Xianwen (張憲文), et al., eds. *Zhonghua minguo da cidian* [《中華民國大 詞典》 Dictionary of the Republic of China]. Nanjing: Jiangsu guji chu-banshe, 2001.

Zhang, Yongjin. *China in the International System, 1918-1920: The Middle Kingdom at the Periphery*. New York: St. Martin's Press, 1991.

Zhang, Zhenkun (張振鵾). "Zaishuo 'er'shi'yi tiao' bushi tiaoyue" [再說"二 十一條" 不是條約 One more time: Twenty-one Demands are not a treaty]. *Jindaishi yanjiu* 1 (2002): 238-52.

Zhao, Suisheng. "Chinese Intellectuals' Quest for National Greatness and Naitonalistic Writings in the 1990s." *The China Quarterly* 152 (1997): 725-45.

Zheng, Hesheng (鄭鶴聲), ed. *Jinshi zhongxi shiri duizhaobiao* [《近世中西史日 對照表》 Lunar and solar calendars in modern history: A comparative study]. Beijing: Zhonghua shujü, 1980.

Zheng, Yongnian. *Discovering Chinese Nationalism: Modernization, Identity, and International Relations*. Cambridge: Cambridge University Press, 1999.

Zheng, Zemin (鄭則民). "Guanyü bupingdeng tiaoyue de ruogan wenti: yü Zhang Zhenkun xiansheng shangque" [關於不平等條約的若干問題: 與張振鵾 先生商榷 Some questions on the Unequal Treaties: A Discussion with Mr. Zhang Zhenkun]. *Jindaishi yanjiu* 1 (2000): 215-37.

Zhong, Shuhe (鍾叔河), et al., eds. *Guo Songtao Lundun yü Bali riji* [《郭嵩燾倫 敦與巴黎日記》 Guo Songtao: The London and Paris diaries]. Changsha: Yuelu shushe, 1984.

Zhongguo di'er lishi dang'an'guan (中國第二歷史檔案館 No. 2 Chinese His-torical Archives). "Waijiaoguan lingshiguan kaoshi zenlu kaojuan ji guize" [外交官領事官考試甄錄考卷及規則 The diplomatic and consular examination papers and rules]. Year 1916, Archive No. 1039-218.

———. "Renyuan lülibiao" [人員履歷表 Personnel resume]. Archive No. 1039-222.

———. "Jiangsu jiaoshe gongshu zhiyuan lülibiao" [江蘇交涉公署職員履歷表 Resumes and positions in the Jiangsu Bureau of Negotiations]. Year 1920, Archive No. 1039-26.

———. "Jingjibu dui Zhongmei shangyue cao'an yijianshu" [經濟部對《中美 商約》草案意見書 Reaction of the Ministry of Economics to the draft of the Sino-American Commercial Treaty]. "Zhongmei shangyue tanpan guocheng wenjian" [《中美商約》談判過程文件 Documents on the negotiation of the Sino-American Commercial Treaty]. Guomin zhengfu wai-jiaobu dang'an [國民政府外交部檔案 The Foreign Ministry Archives of the Nationalist Government]. Archive No. 3034-18.

———. *Waijiaobu ji zhuwai shilingguan zhiyuan lu* [外交部駐外領使館職員錄 Personnel directory of the Foreign Ministry and overseas embassies and consulates]. Archive No. 1039-24.

Zhongguo di'er lishi dang'an'guan (中國第二歷史檔案館), ed. *Zhonghua mingguoshi dang'an ziliao huibian* [《中華民國史檔案資料彙編》 Collected archival sources for the history of the Republic of China]. Nanjing: Jiangsu guji chubanshe, 1979-2000.

Zhongguo diyi lishi dang'an'guan (中國第一歷史檔案館 No. 1 Chinese Historical Archives), ed. *Yapian zhanzheng dang'an shiliao* [《鴉片戰爭檔案史料》 Archival sources on the Opium War]. Tianjin: Tianjin guji chubanshe, 1992.

Zhongguo gongchandang (中国共产党 Chinese Communist Party). *Zhongmei Zhongying qianding xinyue: bainian zhiku yidan feichu* [《中英中美簽訂新約: 百年桎梏一旦廢除》 The signing of the new Sino-U.S. and Sino-British treaties: Smashing the shackles of a hundred years]. n.p.: Huabei xinhua shudian, 1943.

Zhongguo guojifa niankan (《中國國際法年刊》). "Beijing daxue guojifa yanjiusuo xuexi Jiang Zemin zhuxi jianghua zuotanhui" [北京大學國際法研究所學習江澤民主席講話座談會 The forum held by the Institute of International Law at Beijing University on President Jiang's Speech]. 1996.

Zhongguo Guomindang zhongyangweiyuanhui dangshi weiyuanhui (中國國民黨中央委員會黨史委員會). *Geming wenxian* [《革命文獻》 Revolutionary documents]. Taibei: Zhongguo Guomindang zhongyangwei- yuanhui dangshi weiyuanhui, 1978.

Zhongguo jindai jingjishi ziliao congkan bianji weiyuanhui (中國近代經濟史資叢刊編輯委員會), ed. *Xinchou heyue dingli yihou de shangyue tanpan* [《辛醜和約訂立以後的商約談判》 The commercial treaty negotiations in the aftermath of the Boxer Protocol of 1901]. Beijing: Zhonghua shujü, 1993.

Zhongguo qingnian (中國青年 Chinese Youth)

Zhongguo shehui kexueyuan (中國社會科學院), trans. *Gongchan guoji youguan zhongguo geming de wenxian, 1919-1928* [《共產國際有關中國革命的文獻, 1919-1928》 The Comintern documents on the Chinese revolution]. Beijing: Zhongguo shehuikexue chubanshe, 1980.

Zhongguo shehui kexueyuan (中國社會科學院), and Zhongguo gongchandang dangshi xuehui (中國共產黨黨史學會). "Zhongguo gongchandang ge shiqi dangyuan renshu tongji shuzi" [中國共產黨各時期黨員人數統計數字 Statistics of CCP membership at different periods]. In "Wei zhonghua

zhi jueqi: jinian zhongguo gongchandang chenli bashi zhounian" [為
中華之崛起: 紀念中國共產黨成立八十周年 For the rise of China: In memory of
the 80th anniversary of the CCP]. http://www.cass.net.cn/zhuanti (accessed October 20, 2004).

Zhonghua renmin gongheguo waijiaobu (中華人民共和國外交部), and
Zhonggong zhongyang wenxian yanjiushi (中共中央文獻研究室), eds.
Mao Zedong waijiao wenxuan [《毛澤東外交文選》 Selected works of Mao
Zedong]. Beijing: Zhongyang wenxian chubanshe, 1994.

Zhongqing wangzhang (中青網站 The web of China's youth). http:///www.cy
net.com (accessed September 23, 2004).

Zhongyang dang'an'guan (中央檔案館), ed. *Zhonggong zhongyang wenjian
xuanji* [《中共中央檔選集》 Selected documents of the Central Committee
of the Chinese Communist Party]. Beijing: Zhonggong zhongyang
dangxiao chubanshe, 1989-1992.

Zhongyang ribao [《中央日報》 Central daily]

Zhou, Gengsheng (周鯁生). *Lingshi caipanquan wenti* [《領事裁判權問題》 The
question of extraterritoriality]. Shanghai: Shangwu yinshuguan, 1923.

———. *Bupingdeng tiaoyue shijiang* [《不平等條約十講》 Ten lectures on the
Unequal Treaties]. Shanghai: Taipingyang shudian, 1928.

———. *Guojifa dagang* [《國際法大綱》 An outline of international law].
Reprinted in 1935, 1941, and 1989. Shanghai: Shangwu yinshuguan,
1929.

———. *Xiandai guojifa wenti* [《現代國際法問題》 Questions of modern international law]. Shanghai: Shangwu yinshuguan, 1931.

Zhou, Wei, *Xin guoji gongfa* [《新國際公法》 New international public law]. 2
vols. Shanghai: Shangwu yinshuguan, 1930.

Zhu, Huan (朱寰), and Wang Hengwei (王恒偉), eds. *Zhongguo duiwai
tiaoyue cidian*[《中國對外條約辭典》 Dictionary of treaties between China
and foreign countries]. Changchun: Jilin jiaoyü chubanshe, 1994.

Zhu, Shoupeng (朱壽朋), ed. *Guangxü chao donghualu* [《光緒朝東華錄》
Documents of the Guangxü regime]. Beijing: Zhonghua shujü, 1958.

Index

About the Author

Dong Wang was educated in China and the United States. She is currently Assistant Professor of History at Gordon College and Research Associate of the Fairbank Center for East Asian Research at Harvard University. At Gordon College, she also directs the East-West Institute of International Studies. She is the author of several articles on nationalism, intellectual currents, religions, international law, and treaties, published in English and Chinese journals/volumes, including *Pacific Affairs* and *Twentieth-Century China*.

Among her most recent essays are "Circulating American Higher Education: The Case of Lingnan University (1888–1951)," *Journal of American–East Asian Relations*, and "From Lingnan to Pomona: Charles K. Edmunds and His Chinese-American Career," in *Encounters on the Cultural Frontier: China's Christian Colleges, 1900–1950*, edited by Daniel Bays and Ellen Widmer. She is at present completing a book on the cultural encounters between the United States and China, focusing on Lingnan University.